STAYING SAFE ON OUR ROADS

STAYING SAFE
on our
ROADS

The Small Margin For Error

BRIAN DENTON

Staying Safe
PO Box 185
Prince Rupert, B.C.
V8J 3P4

Library and Archives Canada Cataloguing in Publication

Denton, Brian (Brian Lawrence), author
    Staying safe on our roads : the small margin for error / Brian Denton.

Includes bibliographical references.
ISBN 978-0-9949943-0-1 (paperback)

    1. Traffic safety—Canada. 2. Traffic safety—United States. I. Title.

HE5614.5.C2D45 2016   363.12'50971   C2015-908627-2

Edited by Lynne Graham
Design and layout by Vancouver Desktop Publishing Centre

DEDICATION

This book has been written in the hope of making
our world a better and safer place and, on this basis,
is dedicated to all of humanity.

CONTENTS

Acknowledgements / xvii
About the Author / xix
Introduction / xxi

Chapter 1: Statistics Tell an Alarming Story
1.0 Introduction / 1
1.1 Canadian Traffic Collision Statistics / 2
    1.1.1 Canadian Traffic Fatalities / 2
    1.1.2 Canadian Traffic Injuries / 4
1.2 United States Traffic Collision Statistics / 4
    1.2.1 U.S. Traffic Fatalities / 6
    1.2.2 U.S. Traffic Injuries / 7
1.3 Worldwide Traffic Collision Statistics / 7
1.4 Costs of Traffic Collisions / 10
    1.4.1 Canada / 10
    1.4.2 United States / 11
    1.4.3 Worldwide / 12
1.5 Chapter Summary: Statistics Tell an Alarming Story / 13

Chapter 2: The Use of Our Roads
2.0 Introduction / 15
2.1 Risks of Collisions and Crashes / 16
2.2 Terminology: Collisions and Crashes / 17
2.3 Road Injuries and Deaths: Unacceptable and Avoidable / 17
2.4 Our Roadway and Motor Vehicle Industries / 18
2.5 Road Safety / 19
2.6 What if Things Do Not Change? / 20
2.7 Complacency / 21
2.8 Life is Not a Rehearsal / 21

Chapter 3: Speed and Impacts in Collisions
3.0 Introduction / 23
3.1 The Limitations of the Human Body / 23

3.2 Speed, Distance and Time / 25

3.3 Impacts Resulting From Falls / 29

3.4 Chapter Summary: Speed and Impacts in Collisions / 31

Chapter 4: Road Design and Operation

4.0 Introduction / 33

4.1 Road Design and Intended Use / 33

4.2 Jurisdiction / 35

4.3 Geometric Design of Roads / 36

    4.3.1 Summary: Geometric Design of Roads / 39

4.4 Speed Limits / 40

    4.4.1 Statutory Speed Limits / 40

      4.4.1.1 Summary: Statutory Speed Limits / 42

    4.4.2 Posted Speed Limits / 43

      4.4.2.1 Summary: Posted Speed Limits / 46

4.5 Sight Distance and Stopping Sight Distance / 47

    4.5.1 Brake Reaction Time (Perception and Reaction Time) / 48

    4.5.2 Braking Distance / 49

4.6 Calculating Stopping Sight Distance / 49

    4.6.1 Calculating Brake Reaction Distance / 51

    4.6.2 Calculating Braking Distance / 52

    4.6.3 Summary: Calculating Stopping Sight Distance / 53

4.7 Traffic Control Devices / 54

4.8 Widths of Traffic Lanes / 56

    4.8.1 Summary: Widths of Traffic Lanes / 57

4.9 Shoulders / 57

    4.9.1 Shoulders: Widths / 58

    4.9.2 Shoulders: Cost and Space Constraints / 59

    4.9.3 Shoulders: City Streets / 60

    4.9.4 Shoulders: Guard Rails and Concrete Barriers / 60

    4.9.5 Shoulders: Bicycle Lanes / 61

    4.9.6 Summary: Shoulders / 62

4.10 Rumble Strips / 64

4.11 Roadside Hazards / 65

4.12 Chapter Summary: Road Design and Operation / 66

Chapter 5: Motor Vehicles

5.0 Introduction / 69

5.1 Passenger Vehicles / 69

    5.1.1 Passenger Vehicles: Dimensions / 69

    5.1.2 Passenger Vehicles: Weights / 71

    5.1.3 Summary: Passenger Vehicles / 72

5.2 Transport Trucks / 72

    5.2.1 Transport Trucks: Regulatory Authority / 72

    5.2.2 Transport Trucks: Dimensions, Weights and Number of Axles / 73

        5.2.2.1 Transport Trucks: Width / 75

        5.2.2.2 Transport Trucks: Height / 78

        5.2.2.3 Transport Trucks: Length and Weight /78

        5.2.2.4 Transport Trucks: Number of Axles / 78

5.3 Significance of Dimensions and Weights of Motor Vehicles / 80

    5.3.1 Significance of Overall Sizes and Weights of Motor Vehicles / 81

    5.3.2 Significance of Motor Vehicle Width / 82

        5.3.2.1 Motor Vehicles in Narrow Traffic Lanes / 84

        5.3.2.1a Passenger Vehicles / 84

        5.3.2.1b Transport Trucks / 84

        5.3.2.2 Motor Vehicles in Wider Traffic Lanes / 85

        5.3.2.2a Passenger Vehicles / 85

        5.3.2.2b Transport Trucks / 85

    5.3.3 Significance of Motor Vehicle Height / 86

        5.3.3.1 Water, Slush or Snow Thrown from Tires / 86

        5.3.3.2 Visibility / 87

        5.3.3.3 Height of Undercarriages (Chassis) of Transport Trucks / 87

        5.3.3.4 Center of Gravity and Rollover / 88

    5.3.4 Significance of Motor Vehicle Length / 89

5.4 Miscellaneous Motor-Vehicle-Related Hazards / 90

    5.4.1 Convertibles / 90

    5.4.2 Power / 90

    5.4.3 Speed / 91

5.4.4 The Deadly Comforts of Motor Vehicles / 91
5.4.5 Turbulence / 92
5.5 Chapter Summary: Motor Vehicles / 93

Chapter 6: Hazards of Winter Driving
6.0 Introduction / 95
6.1 Roadway Winter Maintenance / 96
6.2 British Columbia's Highway Maintenance Program:
Maintenance Agreements / 98
6.2.1 Privatizing Highway Maintenance / 98
6.2.2 Lump-Sum Contracts / 99
6.2.3 10-Year Agreements / 101
6.2.4 Ministry Responsibilities / 101
6.2.5 Summary: B.C.'s Highway Maintenance Agreements / 102
6.3 British Columbia's Highway Maintenance Program:
Maintenance Specifications / 103
6.3.1 Highway Classifications / 103
6.3.2 Maximum Allowable Accumulations of Snow / 104
6.3.3 Time to Remove Compacted Snow or Ice / 105
6.3.4 Removal of Snow and Ice from Shoulders / 107
6.3.5 Removal of Sight Distance Obstructions / 110
6.3.6 Application of Winter Abrasives / 111
6.3.7 Freezing Rain and Black Ice / 113
6.3.8 Rest Areas / 114
6.3.9 Travel Advisory Notices / 115
6.4 British Columbia's Highway Maintenance Program: Service
Areas / 115
6.5 Hazards of Winter Driving: Margin for Error / 116
6.6 Police Enforcement During Adverse Winter Conditions / 117
6.7 Chapter Summary: Hazards of Winter Driving / 118

Chapter 7: Contributing Factors of Collisions
7.0 Introduction / 121
7.1 Contributing Factors of Injury and Fatal Collisions / 121
7.1.1 Source of Reference / 122

7.1.2 Collection of Statistical Data / 123

7.2 Percentage of Collisions Involving Each Contributing Factor / 123

7.3 Contributing Factors Grouped According to Category / 124

7.4 Review and Analysis: Contributing Factors of Collisions / 125

7.4.1 The Most Significant Contributing Factors / 125

7.4.2 Human, Environmental and Vehicle Condition
    Contributing Factors / 131

7.4.2.1 Vehicle Condition Contributing Factors / 131

7.4.2.2 Environmental Contributing Factors / 131

7.4.2.2a Adverse Road Conditions / 132

7.4.2.2b Adverse Weather / 132

7.4.2.2c Adverse Driving Conditions / 133

7.4.2.3 Human Contributing Factors / 133

7.5 Chapter Summary: Contributing Factors of Collisions / 134

Chapter 8: Underlying Causes of Collisions

8.0 Introduction / 137

8.1 Underlying Hazards of our Streets and Highways / 138

8.1.1 City Streets / 138

8.1.2 Highways and Freeways / 140

8.1.3 Intersections / 142

8.1.4 Shoulders / 143

8.1.5 Bicycle Lanes / 144

8.1.6 Motor Vehicles / 144

8.1.7 Roadside Hazards / 145

8.1.8 Improperly Maintained Streets or Highways / 145

8.1.9 Summary: Underlying Hazards of our Streets and
    Highways / 146

8.2 The Hazards of Speed / 147

8.2.1 Hazards When Driving Within the Posted Speed Limits / 147

8.2.2 Hazards of Exceeding the Posted Speed Limits / 149

8.2.3 Hazards of Driving too Fast for Conditions / 153

8.2.3.1 What is a Safe Speed in Adverse Driving
    Conditions? / 154

8.2.3.2 Choosing a Safe Speed in Adverse Driving Conditions / 156

8.3 Abuse of Alcohol and Drugs / 158

8.3.1 Alcohol / 158

8.3.1.1 Statistics / 158

8.3.1.2 Costs of Alcohol Abuse / 159

8.3.1.3 Alcohol: The Bigger Picture / 159

8.3.2 Drugs / 161

8.4 Following too Closely / 161

8.5 Pedestrian Error/Confusion / 163

8.6 Miscellaneous Underlying Causes of Collisions / 165

8.6.1 Driver Inexperience / 165

8.6.2 The Elderly / 166

8.6.3 Herd Mentality / 166

8.6.4 Lacking Road Education / 167

8.6.5 Lacking Self-Discipline / 167

8.6.6 Poor Time Management / 168

8.6.7 Use of Electronic Devices / 168

8.6.8 Pets in Vehicles / 169

8.7 Reducing the Risks of Being Injured or Killed in Collisions / 169

8.7.1 Seat Belts / 170

8.7.2 Motorcycles / 171

8.7.3 Helmets / 171

8.8 Television Commercials / 172

8.9 Chapter Summary: Underlying Causes of Collisions / 172

8.10 Questions that Remain to be Answered / 173

Chapter 9: The Road Safety Revolution

9.0 Introduction / 175

9.1 A New Approach to Road Safety / 176

9.2 Sweden's Vision Zero Approach to Road Safety / 177

9.3 Australia's Safe System Approach to Road Safety / 180

9.4 Volvo's Vision 2020 / 183

9.5 Driverless Cars / 184

9.6 Chapter Summary: The Road Safety Revolution / 184

Chapter 10: Conclusions and Recommendations
10.0 Conclusions: Staying Safe on Our Roads / 187
10.1 Recommendations: Staying Safe on Our Roads / 190
10.2 Final Comments: Staying Safe on Our Roads / 195

References / 197

TABLES

Chapter 1: Statistics Tell an Alarming Story

Table 1.1: 2013 Canadian Traffic Collision Statistics / 2
Table 1.2: 2013 United States Traffic Crash Statistics / 5

Chapter 2: The Use of Our Roads

No Tables this chapter.

Chapter 3: Speed and Impacts in Collisions

Table 3.1: Conversion Factors / 27
Table 3.2 (a): Distance Travelled Per Hour or Per Second Metric Units / 28
Table 3.2 (b): Distance Travelled Per Hour or Per Second Imperial Units / 28
Table 3.3: Height of Fall to Reach Various Speeds /31

Chapter 4: Road Design and Operation

Table 4.1: Stopping Sight Distances on Level Roadways / 50

Chapter 5: Motor Vehicles

Table 5.1: Average Passenger Vehicle Dimensions / 70
Table 5.2: Weights of Mid-Sized Passenger Vehicles and Added Width With Rear View Mirrors / 71
Table 5.3: Average Dimensions and Weights of Passenger Vehicles / 72
Table 5.4: Dimensions and Weights: Straight Truck / 76
Table 5.5: Dimensions and Weights: Tractor Semitrailer /76
Table 5.6: Dimensions and Weights: B Train Double / 77
Table 5.7: Dimensions and Weights: LCV-Turnpike Double / 77
Table 5.8: Summary of Transport Truck Lengths, Weights and Number of Axles / 79
Table 5.9 (a): Summary of Motor Vehicle Dimensions and Weights Metric Units / 80

Table 5.9 (b): Summary of Motor Vehicle Dimensions and Weights Imperial Units / 81
Table 5.10: Widths of Motor Vehicles and Traffic Lanes / 83

Chapter 6: Hazards of Winter Driving
Table 6.1: Snowfalls: Maximum Allowable Accumulations / 104
Table 6.2: Removal of Compacted Snow or Ice, All Travelled Lanes / 106
Table 6.3: Removal of Snow and Ice From Shoulders / 107
Table 6.4: Removal of Sight Distance Obstructions / 110

Chapter 7: Contributing Factors of Collisions
Table 7.1: Contributing Factors of Injury and Fatal Collisions: Percent of Collisions Involving Each Factor / 126
Table 7.2: Human Contributing Factors and Their Frequency / 127
Table 7.3: Environmental Contributing Factors and Their Frequency / 128
Table 7.4: Vehicle Condition Contributing Factors and Their Frequency / 129
Table 7.5: Summary of Contributing Factor Categories / 129
Table 7.6: Most Frequently Reported Contributing Factors / 130

Chapter 8: Underlying Causes of Collisions
No Tables this chapter.

Chapter 9: The Road Safety Revolution
No Tables this chapter.

Chapter 10: Conclusions and Recommendations
No Tables this chapter.

ACKNOWLEDGEMENTS

It would not have been possible to write this book without the vast amount of information now available on the Internet and the information documented in books, manuals and similar publications. I wish to thank those individuals, associations, corporations, government agencies and others who have made the information available through these various means. I especially wish to thank the staff at the Prince Rupert Public Library for their assistance in obtaining many of the publications referenced throughout this book.

I wish to specifically acknowledge and thank each of the following, whose works have been cited in this book:

American Association of State Highway and Transportation Officials (AASHTO); Barron's Educational Series, Inc.; British Columbia Minister of Transportation; British Columbia Ministry of Transportation and Highways; British Columbia Ministry of Transportation and Infrastructure; British Columbia Motor Vehicle Branch; Bunt & Associates; California Department of Motor Vehicles; California Department of Transportation; Canadian Council of Ministers and Deputy Ministers Responsible for Transportation and Highway Safety; Canadian Council of Motor Transport Administrators (CCMTA); City of Vancouver, British Columbia; Delaware Department of Transportation; Eno Center for Transportation, Washington, DC; Ernst Donlemar; Anders Eugensson; European Union; Ford Motor Company; Government of Canada; Illinois Department of Transportation; Insurance Corporation of British Columbia (ICBC); Robert L. Lehrman; Library of Parliament, Canada; Minister of Public Works and Government Services, Canada; Minister of Transport, Canada; Ralph Nader; NAFTA Land Transportation Standards Subcommittee; National Committee on Terrorist Attacks Upon the United States; National Defence Canada; National Geographic Society; New South Wales Government Transport Roads & Traffic Authority; New York City DOT/ The City of New York; New York State Department of Transportation; New Zealand Government, Ministry of Transport, National Road Safety Committee; Ontario Ministry of Transportation; Province of British Columbia;

Joseph Schulman; State of California; State of Delaware; State of Illinois; Statistics Canada; Swedish Government and Swedish Industry; The Canadian Encyclopedia; The Canadian Parking Association; The Railway Association of Canada; The Washington Post; Traffic Injury Research Foundation of Canada; Trafikverket Swedish Transport Administration; Transportation Association of Canada (TAC); Transport Canada; Transport for New South Wales; U.S. Department of Transportation; (U.S.) Federal Highway Administration (FHWA); (U.S.) National Highway Traffic Safety Administration (NHTSA); Vagverket Swedish Road Administration; Volvo Car Corporation; Wade-Trim; World Health Organization (WHO).

I also wish to thank my friends King Lee who assisted with the initial chapters of this book and Doug Cooper who twice offered to review my entire manuscript. I am especially grateful for the assistance of those who helped to bring this book to life: Lynne Graham (www.words-at-work.ca) who worked tirelessly and professionally, using her many skills and her pleasing, accommodating manner to edit this work; Patty Osborne (Vancouver Desktop Publishing Centre www.self-publish.ca) who similarly applied her skills with the planning, layout, formatting and cover design; and Craig Shemilt (Printorium Bookworks www.islandblue.com) who provided the services of his fine company with the initial printing of this book.

In addition, I wish to express my gratitude for the services offered by IngramSpark and CreateSpace (Amazon). If it were not for the services offered by companies such as these, this book and many others would not be available to the public.

Finally, I thank my family: my sister Linda for always being available to discuss this project; my son Trevor for providing the initial incentive to write this book; my daughter Laura for assisting me with understanding the complexities of publishing; my wife Penny for tolerating my obsession with this work and the extent to which this project dominated our home and lives, for the many years required to research, write and bring this book to print.

ABOUT THE AUTHOR

Brian Denton was born in Vancouver, grew up in Penticton and graduated from the University of British Columbia in Mechanical Engineering in 1968. Now retired, Brian lives in Prince Rupert on the north coast of British Columbia.

At the age of 16, Brian rolled his car and was thrown from his vehicle, sustaining serious but not life impairing injuries. Thus, at a young age, Brian learned the harsh realities of driving, where an error can quickly result in irreversible and potentially devastating consequences. In the years since this incident, Brian has driven extensively, collision free.

Over the years, Brian has become increasingly aware of the numerous inherently hazardous features of our roads and motor vehicles, of the often reckless behaviours of drivers and pedestrians, and of the additional hazards that arise during adverse winter conditions. Now a parent and a grandparent, and never hesitant to address a problem, Brian has used his retirement time and his methodical, analytical training as a professional engineer to research and write this incredibly informative book. Brian's purpose with this book: to identify the many hazards on our roads and to inform the public, especially our youth, what we, as individuals, can do to reduce our risks of being involved in a traffic collision.

Introduction

The primary purpose of this book is to identify, as well as possible, the many hazards that exist on our streets, highways and freeways (our roads) and to come to an understanding of what we, as individuals, can do to reduce our risks of being involved in a traffic collision, whether we are a driver or a passenger of a motor vehicle, a pedestrian, a motorcyclist or a bicyclist.

Fundamental to this book is the belief that the public, especially our youth, are not properly informed of the extent of the hazards that exist on our roads, or of the hazards associated with the various classifications of motor vehicles. This lack of information leaves road users unable to properly defend themselves from hazards they do not properly understand.

Those who have no concern for road safety are living in denial. As we shall see in Chapter 1, statistics on the collisions, injuries and deaths occurring on the roads in Canada, the United States and worldwide indicate the majority of us will be affected, one way or another, by this carnage. One fundamental problem is that the carnage has been occurring for so long that many have come to believe that such death and destruction is a part of life, that it is inevitable and is simply the price we must pay for our standard of living and for our mobile lifestyles. In short, many have become complacent with the risks on the roads and accept, fatalistically, the carnage that continues to occur. By the conclusion of this book, readers should have little doubt that the extent of collisions, injuries and deaths occurring on our roads is unacceptable, unnecessary and does not need to continue.

As we shall see in the following chapters, road safety is dependent upon many factors, some of the most significant being: speed; road design, construction, operation and maintenance; the sizes and weights of various classifications of motor vehicles; adverse road and weather conditions; and the behaviour of people using our roads and motor vehicles. The hazards associated with each of these components of our road systems are often interrelated. As we shall soon come to understand, there is a very small margin for error on our roads, and at the speeds commonly driven there is little time or distance for anyone to correct for their errors, or for the errors made by others.

One aspect of our roads that warrants particular attention relates to the hazards arising during adverse conditions, especially during winter months. Rarely are such hazards properly identified or explained. As we shall see, during winter months, road safety depends largely upon three factors: the weather, including temperatures and precipitation; the standards to which our roads are maintained; and the behaviours of people who use our roads during adverse conditions. These considerations are reviewed and analyzed in Chapters 6, 7 and 8.

Complexities Of Road Safety

The brief comments above begin to illustrate some of the complexities of road safety. To put road safety into perspective, it is useful to be aware of the views of the World Health Organization (WHO), as stated in their 2004 *World Report on Road Traffic Injury Prevention*:

> *"Of all the systems that people have to deal with on a daily basis, road transport is the most complex and the most dangerous."*[1]

We can see from this statement that our concerns about the hazards on our roads are very real. None of us should be led to believe that we are over-reacting to our concerns, objections or fears about what is occurring on our streets, highways or freeways. We are addressing what the WHO believes to be the most complex and dangerous system that we have to deal with on a daily basis. This is not, therefore, a remote or insignificant topic.

On the basis of the WHO's statement, our analysis of the hazards on our roads should not be overly simple or brief, since we are not dealing with a simple subject. A central philosophy of this book is that you don't just tell someone, especially teenagers, they should not, for example, speed. Rather, you need to take the time to prove why it is unsafe to speed and to identify the risks involved. Once people understand such matters, their natural instincts should govern their conduct accordingly. In this book, we therefore take the time to thoroughly review and analyze each subject to ensure the reader fully understands the complexities of the topic.

The Revolution in Road Safety

Before we begin to examine our streets, highways, freeways and motor vehicles, it is important to be aware of what is taking place in other parts of the world with road safety. As we shall see in Chapter 9, the complacent, fatalistic attitude and acceptance of the status quo, which appears to dominate our thinking in Canada and the United States about road safety, is not universal.[2] The Netherlands, Sweden, Australia, New Zealand and the European Union have rejected such an attitude and are taking revolutionary steps to reduce the extent of deaths and serious injuries occurring on their roads.[3,4,5] Sweden, in particular, has adopted a "Vision Zero" approach to road safety, wherein an underlying principle is that "No loss of life is acceptable."[6]

The revolutionary developments in these various European countries, and in Australia and New Zealand, can give us strength in our convictions: all is not well, or right with road safety in Canada or the United States. We do not need to accept or tolerate the carnage occurring on our roads as inevitable events. Although we should all strive to have our own countries adopt road safety strategies similar to those in Europe, Australia and New Zealand, our immediate objective as individuals must be to learn how to reduce our risks, and the risks of our loved ones, of being involved in a collision.

Staying Safe on our Roads

The many messages between the covers of this book are intended, first and foremost, for people who wish to reduce their risks, or the risks of their loved ones, on the roads. This book is especially directed towards our youth and to parents and grandparents, to provide the means of ensuring our children and grandchildren are properly educated in road safety matters. Our goal is not so much to change the world, but rather to come to an understanding of the world that exists, so we can all understand what we need to do to reduce our risks while using our roads and motor vehicles.

The messages in this book are also intended for people who abuse the use of our streets, highways, freeways and motor vehicles, thereby threatening the safety and well-being of others. The book's messages are also directed towards other people: those responsible for the actions taken by our courts and police forces in safe-guarding the public's safety on the roads; those responsible for the design, construction, operation and maintenance of our roads; and the regulators and manufactures of motor vehicles. Everyone involved with our roadways, in any capacity, has responsibilities for road safety and everyone needs to be accountable for their actions.

Road Safety Educational Program

This book is also intended for educators and for those with responsibilities for road safety and road safety education. It will become apparent from the information identified in this book that the public is poorly informed of the extent of the hazards on our roads. Due to the complexities of our roads, the many hazards that exist, and the extent of the collisions, injuries and deaths occurring every year, a well-designed road safety education program is essential for the safety of our youth. Regardless of a country's road safety strategy, it is imperative for road users to understand the numerous hazards associated with our roads. The only way of accomplishing this is through a proper education program.

Let us now begin our review and analysis of the many, sometimes complex hazards on our roads, and in the process learn how we, as individuals, can reduce the risks of being involved in a traffic collision.

ONE

Statistics Tell an Alarming Story

1.0 Introduction

Motor vehicles have been in use for more than 100 years and during this time there have been major improvements in their design and manufacturing. Compared to modern vehicles, the Model T Ford looks and is primitive. It is likewise with our roads; there have been vast improvements to the roads in use today, compared to those designed and constructed even a short time ago. However, in spite of the extensive improvements to motor vehicles and roads, an astonishing number of collisions, injuries and deaths continue to occur each and every day throughout Canada, the United States (U.S.) and the world.

The extent of collisions indicates that some very serious problems continue to exist on our roads. What are the problems and why do so many collisions continue to occur? Is the death and destruction that continues to occur the best we can do as a society?

One of the first steps in solving any problem is to determine the extent of the problem. In this case, we need to review collision statistics to understand the magnitude of the problems. By knowing the extent of the collisions, injuries and deaths, we can all evaluate the risks that exist—to us, to our children and grandchildren, and to anyone using our roads in any capacity. Our goal is to thoroughly understand the many hazards and to come to an understanding of what we can do as individuals to reduce the risks of being involved in a traffic collision.

1.1 Canadian Traffic Collision Statistics

Transport Canada provides useful statistics on the traffic collisions, injuries and deaths occurring across our vast country. At time of writing, their latest collision statistical report is for 2013. Table 1.1 highlights some of the statistics in Transport Canada's report.

Table 1.1: 2013 Canadian Traffic Collision Statistics[1]

Canada's population, 2013[2]	35,154,300
Injuries (Total)*	165,306
Serious Injuries**	10,315
Fatalities	
Drivers	964
Passengers	348
Pedestrians	300
Bicyclists	62
Motorcyclists	198
Others	51
Total fatalities all road users	1,923

*Note: "Total Injuries" include all reported severities of injuries, ranging from minimal to serious.

**Note: "Serious Injuries" include persons admitted to hospital for treatment or observation.

(Sources: Canada's Population: Statistics Canada, CANSIM, table 051-0001; Collision Statistics: Adapted from Transport Canada Canadian Motor Vehicle Traffic Collision Statistics 2013. Collected in cooperation with the Canadian Council of Motor Transport Administrators. Page 3. http://www.tc.gc.ca/media/documents/roadsafety/cmvtcs2013_eng.pdf)

1.1.1 Canadian Traffic Fatalities

First, we all need to pause for a moment and pay our respects to the people killed in traffic related collisions in Canada. For those who lost their lives and for their families, friends and acquaintances, we can only wish that we could turn the clock back and reverse what occurred. We cannot, of course, but we can all learn how to reduce the chances of similar incidents claiming more victims.

To put into perspective the magnitude of the deaths occurring on Canadian roads—1,923 in 2013—let's make two comparisons:

- Consider the number of aircraft that would need to crash to equal the deaths on our roadways. Imagine a commercial aircraft carrying 100 passengers and crew. It would take 19 such aircraft crashing and killing all occupants to approximately equal the number of deaths that occurred on Canadian roads in 2013. However, unlike many aircraft collisions that result in mostly fatal injuries, in traffic collisions a high percentage of people suffer non-fatal injuries. Transport Canada's records for 2013 show that in addition to the deaths on Canadian roadways, 165,306 people were injured, of whom 10,315 suffered injuries serious enough to be admitted to hospital.

- Alternatively, compare deaths during Canada's military actions in Afghanistan to the carnage on our roads. Between 2002 and the end of 2009, a period of almost 8 years, 139 lives were lost serving Canada in an attempt to help the people of Afghanistan.[3] In this same 8-year-period, approximately 21,600 people died on Canadian roadways.[1] In addition, during this period, 1,600,000 people were injured in traffic collisions in Canada and close to 118,000 were admitted to hospitals.[1]

Transport Canada's publication *Road and Motor Vehicle Safety* includes the following statement:

"More people have died on Canada's roads in the last 50 years than the number of Canadians killed in two world wars."[4]

Most people would agree that wars are one of mankind's most ugly characteristics. However, more Canadians are being killed on our roads than have been killed in all of our wars combined. In reality, Canadians are in a war that has been going on for decades. Our war is not with an enemy from another country, but with an enemy within our own borders. Our war is with ourselves and it is taking place on our roads.

1.1.2 Canadian Traffic Injuries

Having reviewed the statistics in Table 1.1 on the number of deaths occurring on Canadian roads, we now turn our attention to the number of injuries and serious injuries. We begin by paying our respects to those who have been injured over the years on Canadian roads.

The extent of injuries occurring on Canadian roads can be better understood using a simple calculation. Based upon the 165,306 people injured on Canadian roads in 2013, if our children live to be 80 years old and both the population of Canada and the number of road injuries remain at 2013 levels, more than 13 million people would be injured on Canadian roads during our children's lifetimes. Of these 13 million people incurring injuries, more than 825,000 would sustain injuries serious enough to require hospitalization. Many of the serious injuries would be deforming, disfiguring and permanently disabling, with huge implications and hardships not only for those injured, but also for their families.

If there is anything we can do to make this world a safer place for our children, we have the responsibility to do so. These statistics show that traffic collisions are unquestionably a terrible threat to our children's well-being and will continue to be throughout their lives, unless changes are made. The people responsible for road safety and for road safety education need to take action to reduce the hazards that exist and to ensure our youth are properly educated in road safety matters. As individuals, we all need to ensure we understand the many hazards that exist on our roads and that we are using our roads and motor vehicles properly and safely. Each of us has the opportunity and responsibility to do so, starting today.

1.2 United States Traffic Collision Statistics

In the U.S., the National Highway Traffic Safety Administration (NHTSA) National Center for Statistics and Analysis produces an extensive annual report titled *Traffic Safety Facts*. Table 1.2 highlights some of the statistics in the 2013 report.[5]

We see from Table 1.2 that there were approximately 5,687,000 police-reported motor vehicle crashes in the U.S. in 2013, with 4,066,000 of these resulting in "Property Damage Only," 1,591,000 resulting in injuries and 30,057 resulting in fatalities. Can anyone deny this is an astonishing number of crashes to have occurred in only one year in the U.S.? Any crash, even a Property Damage Only crash, would be a serious event in the lives of those involved. It is also important to realize that for every crash that occurred there were likely several "near misses." Thus we further see the enormity of the problems on our roads.

Table 1.2: 2013 United States Traffic Crash Statistics[5]

United States' Resident Population, 2013	316,128,839
Police-Reported Motor Vehicle Traffic Crashes	
Fatal	30,057
Injury	1,591,000
Property Damage Only	4,066,000
Total	5,687,000

Traffic Crash Victims	Killed	Injured
Occupants	22,383	2,099,000
Drivers	16,472	1,450,000
Passengers	5,844	648,000
Unknown	67	<1,000
Motorcyclists	4,668	88,000
Non-occupants	5,668	125,000
Pedestrians	4,735	66,000
Pedalcyclists	743	48,000
Other/Unknown	190	11,000
Total	32,719	2,313,000

(Source: U.S. Department of Transportation, National Highway Traffic Safety Administration (NHTSA). Traffic Safety Facts 2013. A Compilation of Motor Vehicle Crash Data from the Fatality Analysis Reporting System and the General Estimates System. Page 2. https://www-nrd.nhtsa.dot.gov/Pubs/812139.pdf)

1.2.1 U.S. Traffic Fatalities

As Table 1.2 shows, 30,057 fatal crashes occurred on U.S. roads in 2013, resulting in 32,719 deaths. Again, we all need to pause to pay our respects to the unfortunate individuals involved and to their families and friends. To put the number of deaths occurring on U.S. roads into perspective, it is useful to make some analogies, as follows:

- We again use the aircraft crash analogy, but since the U.S. has a larger population than Canada, let us consider aircraft having 200 people on board rather than the 100 we considered for Canada.

  It would take approximately 164 aircraft each carrying 200 passengers and crew to crash and kill all occupants, in order to reach the 32,719 death toll on U.S. roads in 2013. This would be roughly equivalent to an aircraft crashing every two days in the U.S., all year long, with each crash killing all 200 occupants. Again, however, the problems on U.S. roads are much more serious, because in addition to these deaths are the many people injured in traffic crashes.

- Using a military analogy, between late 2001 and the end of 2009, a total of 5,297 U.S. service members lost their lives in "Operation Iraqi Freedom" and "Operation Enduring Freedom."[6] In the same period, approximately 328,000 people lost their lives in traffic crashes in the U.S. and about 21,000,000 people incurred injuries.[7]

- The terrible events that took place in the U.S. on September 11, 2001 claimed close to 3,000 lives.[8] The horror of these events will be imbedded in people's minds throughout the world for generations to come. Indeed, it is difficult to recall them without becoming deeply saddened for the innocent individuals who lost their lives and for their families and friends.

It is sobering to realize that *every year* in the U.S. there are more than 10 times as many lives lost in U.S. traffic crashes than were lost in the events of September 11, 2001. This alone should put into perspective the extent and horror of motor vehicle related crashes.

1.2.2 U.S. Traffic Injuries

We now focus our attention on the number of traffic crash injuries occurring in the U.S.

As Table 1.2 shows, 2,313,000 people were injured in 2013 in U.S. traffic crashes. These injuries occurred to drivers or passengers of motor vehicles, motorcyclists, pedestrians or others. We again need to pause and pay our respects to those who suffered injuries.

Viewed from another perspective, if an American child is to live to be 80 and the population and number of injuries remain at 2013 levels, close to 185 million people would be injured in traffic crashes in the U.S. during that child's lifetime.

The American Association of State Highway and Transportation Officials (ASSHTO) has some sobering words. Its *AASHTO Strategic Highway Safety Plan* states:

"One out of every 90 children born today will die violently in a motor vehicle crash. And 70 of every 100 will be injured in a highway crash at some point during their lives, many more than once."[9]

Clearly, in both the U.S. and Canada, a "war" is taking place and it is on the roadways, where the numbers of deaths and injuries are staggering.

1.3 Worldwide Traffic Collision Statistics

In order to better understand the numerous hazards to road users, it is valuable to understand the road systems in low- and middle-income countries. Such an understanding can be acquired from two reports produced by the World Health Organization (WHO). The first is the *World Report on Road Traffic Injury Prevention*,[10] published in 2004, and the second is the *Global Status Report on Road Safety: Time for Action*,[11] published in 2009. Both reports provide valuable information, discussion and statistics on worldwide road injuries and deaths, such as the following:

- *"In most low-income and middle-income countries the majority of road users are vulnerable road users—pedestrians, cyclists, and those using motorized two- or three-wheelers. These groups of road users do not have a protective "shell" around them and are therefore more at risk than those in vehicles."*[12]

- *"Vulnerable road users are at additional risk where their needs have not been taken into consideration during the planning of land use or road construction."*[12]

- *"In developing countries, roads often carry a wide range of users —from heavy good vehicles to bicycles and pedestrians without any separation. Among the pedestrians, the most vulnerable are children and older people. The motorized traffic on these roads is capable of high acceleration and speed, both key factors in the causes of road crash injury."*[13]

From these statements, we see the differences in the risks to people using the roads in low- and middle-income countries as opposed to high-income countries. It is not only the fact that so many people living in these countries do not have a "protective shell" around them when they are on the roads, but there is also often a lack of planning to protect them. All of this leads to the disastrous consequences the WHO *Global Status Report on Road Safety* reveals:

- *"More than 1.2 million people die on the world's roads every year, and as many as 50 million others are injured. Over 90% of the deaths occur in low-income and middle-income countries."*[14]

- *"Pedestrians, cyclists, and users of motorized two- or three-wheelers ("vulnerable road users") together account for approximately half of all road traffic deaths around the world."*[15]

- *"WHO predicts that road traffic injuries will rise to become the fifth leading cause of death by 2030."*[16] (Traffic injuries were ranked the ninth highest cause of death in 2004.[16])

We see, therefore, the problems in underdeveloped countries where vulnerable road users are exposed to injury or death because they lack "shells" to protect them in the event of a crash. We see also how important it is to properly plan road systems and to consider the safety of all users, particularly the most vulnerable. Those of us living in Canada and the U.S. can learn from this and understand the increased risks we will experience when travelling in low- and middle-income countries. Further, these statistics should warn us of the increased risks we have in our own countries whenever we are "vulnerable" road users.

It is difficult to comprehend that over 1.2 million people worldwide are killed annually in motor vehicle related crashes. It is also difficult to comprehend that there could be upwards of 50 million people injured on the world's roads each year. What is important to learn from this is that traffic crashes are one of the leading causes of death worldwide and that the WHO expects this situation will become even worse in the years to come.

It is valuable to compare the deaths occurring on the world's roadways with other worldly events:

- Airline crashes:
  1.2 million people being killed annually on the roadways equates to approximately 3,300 people killed every day worldwide. Let us consider aircraft large enough to carry 300 crew and passengers. It would take 11 such aircraft crashing every day and killing all occupants to equal the deaths occurring on the roadways worldwide. In addition to deaths, more than 140,000 people are injured every day on the roads worldwide. Many of those injured would be badly scarred, deformed and unable to carry on a normal life.

- Sinking of the *RMS Titanic*:
  The sinking of the *RMS Titanic* is considered to be one of the worst peacetime maritime disasters in history, resulting in approximately 1,500 deaths. It would take the equivalent of sinking two *RMS Titanics* every day to equal the roughly 3,300 deaths

that occur daily on the world's roadways. And even that does not account for the roughly 140,000 people who are injured each day on the world's streets, highways and freeways.

- September 11, 2001:
  It is sobering to realize that *every day* there are close to the same number of people killed in motor vehicle collisions across the world, as were killed in that terrible act of terrorism, which occurred on September 11, 2001 in the U.S.

1.4 Costs of Traffic Collisions

Another consideration of the collisions, injuries and deaths occurring on our roads is the cost resulting from this carnage. The following statistics are mind boggling and beg the question: Why do we tolerate such waste?

1.4.1 Canada

Transport Canada published a report in 2007 titled *Analysis and Estimation of the Social Cost of Motor Vehicle Collisions in Ontario.*[17] Although the title suggests it was only for Ontario, the report was based upon collision data and estimates for all of Canada in 2004.[18] In referring to this report in a separate bulletin, Transport Canada identifies that the estimated social costs of motor vehicle collisions are based upon the following "direct" and "indirect" costs:

- *"Direct costs relate to property damage, emergency response, hospital care, other medical care and insurance administration, out-of-pocket expenses by victims of motor vehicle collisions and traffic delays (lost time, extra fuel use, environmental pollution)."*[18]

- *"Indirect costs relate to human consequences of collisions, such as partial and total disability of victims, activity and workdays lost—as well as the pain and suffering of victims and their families."*[18]

Using these direct and indirect costs, Transport Canada determined the following cost estimates:

- In Canada: *"The 613,000 motor vehicle collisions occurring in Canadian jurisdictions in 2004 resulted in social costs of $63 billion."*[19]

- In Ontario: *"The average social cost of a fatal collision in 2004 was $15.7 million."*[20]

- In Ontario: *"The average social cost of an injury collision in 2004 was $82 thousand."*[20]

Every collision in Ontario in 2004 that resulted in a fatality was estimated to have had a social cost of $15.7 million. Every collision that resulted in an injury in Ontario in 2004 had an estimated social cost of $82 thousand. Stunning figures! Even worse, the 613,000 motor vehicle collisions that occurred in Canada in 2004 have been estimated to have resulted in social costs totaling $63 billion.

1.4.2 United States

The National Highway Traffic Safety Administration (NHTSA) published a report in May 2014 identifying the total estimated costs related to motor vehicle crashes that occurred in the U.S. in 2010, stating:

"When quality of life valuations are considered, the total value of societal harm from motor vehicle crashes in 2010 was $871 billion."[21]

The combined *social costs* and *societal harm* resulting from traffic collisions and crashes in Canada and the U.S., therefore, approaches $1 trillion per year. These costs are indeed staggering and are hard for most of us to comprehend. To appreciate their magnitude let us use the analogy of one dollar equating to one second of time. Here, a million dollars equates to a million seconds, or approximately 12 days. A billion dollars equates to a billion seconds, or approximately 32 years. A trillion dollars—the social costs and societal harm resulting from collisions and crashes occurring in Canada and the U.S. every year—equates to a trillion seconds, or approximately 32,000 years!

Thus we are able to appreciate the significance of the costs related to the collisions and crashes occurring in Canada and the U.S. annually. They are astronomical and shed further light on the magnitude of the problems on our roadways. It would be difficult for anyone presented with these cost estimates and statistics to argue that we do not have huge problems on our roads.

On the basis of costs alone, one should question why more is not being done to reduce the extent of collisions, injuries and deaths on our roads. Why are those responsible for road safety and road safety education in Canada and the U.S. not doing more to properly identify the hazards inherent in using roads and motor vehicles?

1.4.3 Worldwide

In the 2009 WHO report, *Global Status Report on Road Safety*, the costs of traffic crashes are well recognized:

- *"The road traffic injury epidemic also has considerable impact on the economies of many countries, particularly low-income and middle-income countries that are frequently struggling with other development needs."*[22]

- *"Beyond the enormous suffering they cause, road traffic crashes can drive a family into poverty as crash survivors and their families struggle to cope with the long-term consequences of the event, including the cost of medical care and rehabilitation and all too often funeral expenses and the loss of the family breadwinner."*[14]

- *"Road traffic injuries also place a huge strain on national health systems, many of which suffer from woefully inadequate levels of resources."*[14]

These statistics, estimates and statements show that the costs resulting from motor vehicle related collisions are as staggering as the numbers of collisions, injuries and deaths. What is occurring on roads worldwide should be unacceptable to everyone and should be receiving far greater attention than society is giving it.

1.5 Chapter Summary: Statistics Tell an Alarming Story

Reviewing collision statistics is not a pleasant exercise, but is a necessary undertaking in order to understand the extent of the problems that exist. As statistics show, there are monstrous problems, resulting in numerous collisions, injuries and deaths year after year throughout Canada, the U.S. and the world. The costs associated with these incidents provide further insight into the magnitude of the problems on our roads.

The purpose of this book is to identify the many problems with our roadways, the problems with the way we use them and, ultimately, the actions we can take to reduce our risks of being involved in a traffic collision. Fundamental to this book is the belief our safety demands that we have a proper understanding of the hazards that exist on our roads.

TWO

The Use of our Roads

2.0 Introduction

During our lives, the majority of us will spend a considerable amount of time on or beside the world's vast network of streets, highways or freeways. As children, we are pushed in a baby carriage along the sidewalks, or are put into a car seat and taken somewhere in an automobile. Later, we ride our tricycles and then our bicycles on the sidewalks and city streets. Many people in the western world get a driver's license as soon as they are eligible and join the millions of others who drive to and from school, work and holiday destinations. If we are not drivers, we are often passengers in motor vehicles. We ride in school and city buses and taxis. If we are not in a motor vehicle or riding a bicycle, we are often beside a street or highway as a pedestrian, getting to and from school, work, the grocery store, or simply exercising.

Not only do we use our roads for personal reasons, but we also use them to transport vast quantities of everything imaginable. The number of transport trucks on the roads, small and large, is ample evidence of this. These trucks can be a significant hazard to anyone using our roads, as will become apparent in our following chapters.

Motor vehicles of all types have transformed society. Who would have thought 100 years ago that motor vehicles would dominate our lives to the extent they do today? Who would have thought we would be travelling at 100 kilometers or 60 miles per hour in heavy rain or darkness, or on icy roadways with only centimeters, or inches, separating us from adjacent or oncoming vehicles? Who would have thought we would be travelling at the speeds we commonly drive with motorists frequently being under the influence of alcohol or drugs, using a cell phone or texting a message? Who would have thought when motor vehicles first rolled off the assembly lines that these machines would result in so much death and destruction?

We see that the varied use of our roads is fundamental to our way of life, both personally and collectively as a society. If our use of motor vehicles was suddenly to come to an end, our entire way of life as we know it today would change drastically, instantly. However, as important as our streets, highways, freeways and motor vehicles are to our mobility, we must not overlook or ignore the safety aspects of our road systems.

2.1 Risks of Collisions and Crashes

In the introduction to this book, we referred to a statement by the World Health Organization (WHO), which deserves repeating:

> *"Of all the systems that people have to deal with on a daily basis, road transport is the most complex and the most dangerous."*[1]

Another significant statement made by the WHO is:

> *"While the risk of a crash is relatively low for most individual journeys, people travel many times each day, every week and every year. The sum of these small risks is considerable."*[2]

These statements should alert us to the complexities and hazards on our roads. Although the hazards on any particular journey on any particular day may not be overly great, over time these journeys add up to make our risks "considerable." Therefore, we should never take our safety for granted. As we shall see in the following chapters, a great deal can go wrong on or near our roads at any time, and when something does go wrong, events usually happen very rapidly.

2.2 Terminology: Collisions and Crashes

Another significant statement made by the WHO in their 2004 *World Report on Road Traffic Injury Prevention* is:

> *"The term 'accident,' which is widely used, can give the impression, probably unintended, of inevitability and unpredictability—an event that cannot be managed. This document prefers to use the term 'crash' instead, to denote something that is an event, or series of events, amenable to rational analysis and remedial action."*[2]

The WHO, therefore, does not use the term "accident" but rather "crash" to describe incidents that result in injuries or deaths on the world's roadways. Most organizations worldwide agree with the WHO on this matter. In the U.S., the National Highway Traffic Safety Administration's (NHTSA) National Center for Statistics and Analysis also uses the term "crash" and not "accident."[3] In Canada, Transport Canada uses either the term "collision" or optionally "crash" for traffic incidents resulting in damages, injuries or deaths.[4] Accordingly, the terms "collision(s)" or "crash(es)" are used throughout this book, as opposed to "accident(s)."

2.3 Road Injuries and Deaths: Unacceptable and Avoidable

The 2004 *World Report on Road Traffic Injury and Prevention* makes yet another very important statement concerning the use of our roads:

> *"It is the contention of the report, first, that the level of road deaths and injuries is unacceptable, and second, that it is to a large extent avoidable."*[1]

As we proceed through this book, the validity of this statement will become increasingly apparent. The collision statistics we reviewed in Chapter 1 should convince everyone that the level of deaths and injuries occurring on our roads is unacceptable. The information in the following chapters should provide ample evidence that traffic collisions are, to a large extent, avoidable.

2.4 Our Roads and Motor Vehicle Industries

Our road and motor vehicle industries are massive and employ thousands of people. There are government transportation departments in every province in Canada and every state in the U.S. that establish specifications for road construction and maintenance. Then there are people who carry out this work according to the specifications and others who determine the operational aspects of our road systems. There are the police and courts that enforce the laws governing these operations. There are people who design, build, sell and maintain motor vehicles. There are those working for the petroleum industries who find the natural resource to run our vehicles, who process these resources in refineries, who distribute them using trucks, trains, deep-sea ships or pipelines, and there are those who sell these resources at the fueling stations.

There are also the skilled, dedicated people within the medical system who deal with victims of collisions and help mitigate the damages. Together with the marvelous equipment and facilities available, they are an essential component of our complex, sophisticated and hazardous road systems.

There are, therefore, a large number of people who are employed by or who profit from the vast road transport systems. Some could feel threatened by criticism of these systems and, as a result, could be strongly opposed to any suggested or planned changes. Since this book identifies many aspects of our road systems that need improvement, it should be no surprise if there is strong resistance from some groups to its contents. Whatever the resistance, it should not distract us from our attempt to understand the hazards on our roads and our attempt to reduce our risks of being involved in a traffic collision.

2.5 Road Safety

In their 2004 *World Report on Road Traffic Injury Prevention*, the WHO makes yet another significant statement that deserves our attention:

> *"This joint WHO/World Bank report on road traffic injury prevention is an important part of the response to the world's road safety crisis. It is directed at international, regional and national policy-makers, international agencies and key professionals in public health, transport, engineering, education and other sectors, and aims to stimulate action for road safety."*[5]

From this statement we see that the WHO considers there is a worldwide road safety crisis. This is undoubtedly based upon the number of collisions, injuries and deaths occurring worldwide, the costs associated with these incidents and the expectation that the situation on our roads will become worse in the years ahead. As we saw from the statistics in our previous chapter and as we are seeing from statements by the WHO, there are many serious problems on our roads that threaten everyone's well-being. There should be no denial that there is a worldwide road safety crisis.

Another noteworthy aspect of this WHO statement is the large number of groups to which their report is being directed, including: "international, regional and national policy-makers, international agencies and key professionals in public health, transport, engineering, education and other sectors."[5] The WHO is not directing their report to the general public, but rather to those organizations responsible for our roads and motor vehicles. As individuals, it leaves us totally dependent upon the actions that these agencies and professionals may or may not take to reduce the hazards on our roads.

The question we should ask ourselves is: Do we want our safety to be left in the hands of the agencies and government professionals who are presently responsible for road safety? We must remember that our streets, highways, freeways and motor vehicles are constructed, operated and maintained to enable people and goods to get from one location to another quickly, efficiently and safely. Safety, therefore, is but one of the objectives. We must also remember that transport trucks are designed to carry large, heavy loads and the faster they get to their destination, the greater the profit to those involved. We need to be constantly aware of the fact that the people controlling the use of our roads and motor vehicles have other priorities and considerations besides safety. It is, therefore, we, as individuals, who must make our own safety our primary consideration. Getting to our destination safely must be our primary objective.

Why should ensuring our own safety be our primary concern? Because it is we who will suffer the pain, disfigurement, trauma or possible permanent disability from collisions. It is we who risk losing our lives in a collision or suffering the loss of a child, spouse, parent, other family member or close friend. It is we who pay the insurance premiums to cover the costs resulting from the collisions. Ultimately, we are the ones who suffer the consequences of traffic collisions and we should, therefore, take a much more aggressive interest in our own safety and the safety of our loved ones.

2.6 What If Things Do Not Change?

We are beginning to see that changes need to be made, not only in the ways in which we use our roads, but also in the design, construction, operation and maintenance of our roads, as well as in the design and manufacturing of motor vehicles. There is a saying: *If things do not change they will remain as they are.* This saying may appear to be comical and, if so, it will be one of the few lighter subjects in this book. Unfortunately, most of our discussions will necessarily be serious, pertaining to traffic collisions, injuries and deaths where humor would be inappropriate.

Returning to the saying *If things do not change they will remain as they are,* there are several considerations that are worthy of our attention. One of the first considerations when evaluating any subject is: Do we wish things to remain as they are? If we are content with the way things are, we will not want anything to change. However, if we decide that something is unsatisfactory, we will want to improve the situation and will need to decide what changes we wish to make.

Thus it is with road safety. We need to start by deciding if we are satisfied with the risks that exist. If we are not, then we need to decide what we can do, as individuals, to improve our safety and that of our loved ones. This is when we quickly become immersed in the complexities of road safety. First, how do we know when our safety is being threatened? Second, what are the threats? Third, how do we reduce these threats in order to improve our safety?

The purpose of this book is to address these questions. We shall examine the various components of our road systems and identify the hazards associated with each. From the understanding we develop of the hazards, we shall come to understand the threats to our safety and what options we have to reduce our risks of being involved in a traffic collision.

By the conclusion of this book, readers will have a very good understanding of the changes we can make to reduce our risks on the roads. From there it becomes a matter of choices. We can continue our present ways, or we can make some necessary changes. One thing is guaranteed: if we don't make changes, our risks on the roads will remain as they are.

2.7 Complacency

As a note of caution, we need to recognize that we all use our streets, highways, freeways and motor vehicles so often throughout our lives that it is easy to become complacent with the way in which we use them. Our complacency can easily lead to carelessness and thoughtlessness. Unfortunately, it is easy to forget that one moment of carelessness, or one thoughtless action or error can result in such terrible consequences.

2.8 Life is Not a Rehearsal

As a final note in this chapter, consider the saying: *Life is not a rehearsal*. As well as we know, this is the case; life is not a rehearsal, but a non-reversible event, influenced greatly by the decisions we make. Traffic collisions are non-reversible events. Once a collision occurs, there is nothing anyone can do to turn the clock back and to start again. What has happened has happened. What is important is to prevent the collision from occurring, or if collisions cannot be prevented, then to reduce the extent of the harm that could result from the incident. The best way to avoid collisions, injuries or deaths on the roads is to understand the hazards and to take appropriate corrective actions.

Having reviewed some of the horrifying statistics on traffic collisions, injuries and deaths, and having reviewed statements and statistics from the WHO on the use of roads around the world, we shall now examine many of the hazards that exist on our roads. In reality, there is an evolutionary process that we as humans are going through with the use of our roads. This book is seen to be a part of that process.

THREE

Speed and Impacts in Collisions

3.0 Introduction

It is important for all road users to understand that the extent of injuries in collisions will be greatly influenced by the speed or speeds at the moment of impact. It is equally important to understand the need to be protected, as well as possible, from the impacts that occur in collisions. These considerations are amongst the most important aspects of road safety. It is necessary, therefore, that we develop a better understanding of the significance of speed and impacts to our safety. We begin by reviewing the ability of the human body to withstand impacts.

3.1 The Limitations of the Human Body

One of the most important considerations of speed is the body's limited ability to withstand impacts in a collision. The following statements provide an insight into this matter:

- *"Human limitations are an important basis upon which to design the road transport system. This must be done through taking into account biological tolerance against external violence—in other words what the human body can stand. In this regard, there are scientifically established limit values based on the design of modern vehicles and roads:*

- *Most people survive if they are hit by a car travelling at 30 km/h.*
- *Most people are killed if they are hit by a car travelling at 50 km/h.*
- *A safe car protects occupants at speeds of up to 65–70 km/h in a head-on collision and at speeds up to 45–50 km/h in a side impact collision, assuming of course that everyone is wearing a seat belt."*[1]

- *"The human body is vulnerable and unlikely to survive an uncushioned impact at a speed of more than 30 km/h. Even relatively low speeds can kill or seriously injure unless the vehicle and the road and roadside environment take account of the physical vulnerability of all road users."*[2]

We begin to see from these statements how vulnerable humans are to the speeds at which we commonly travel on our roads. Without protection, our bodies are only able to withstand impacts occurring at relatively low speeds. Pedestrians may survive being struck by a vehicle travelling at 30 km/h, but they are unlikely to survive if the vehicle is travelling at 50 km/h. Occupants of motor vehicles are unlikely to survive a collision over 30 km/h, unless they are cushioned from the impact by seat belts and/or airbags. Even with seat belts and airbags, vehicle occupants are unlikely to be adequately protected in head-on collisions exceeding approximately 70 km/h and side impact collisions exceeding approximately 50 km/h.

At the upper range of our speeds on highways and freeways, we have little chance of surviving many of the collisions that frequently occur. Even the collisions that commonly occur on city streets frequently result in serious injuries or fatalities. It is important for all road users to understand the body's limited ability to tolerate impacts.

We immediately see from this information the need to "buckle up" as soon as we step into a motor vehicle, to ensure we are cushioned from the moment the vehicle begins to move. We also see the increased dangers that vulnerable road users are exposed to—the motorcyclists, bicyclists and pedestrians who do not have a "protective shell" around them and do not have seats belts or air bags to protect them in the event of a collision. We can better understand the need for motorcyclists and bicyclists to wear helmets at all times, since this offers at least some protection to their heads. Traffic collisions at virtually any speed can be very serious and the higher our speed the more serious collisions potentially become.

Let us now examine another fundamental aspect of speed: the distance we travel per second at normal speeds.

3.2 Speed, Distance and Time

We generally think of the speed at which we are travelling in terms of kilometers or miles per hour. These are the units of measurement on the speedometers of motor vehicles and on the speed limit signs posted beside our roadways. They serve our purposes well for the way in which we generally use them. However, when it comes to understanding the complexities of collisions, they only tell part of the story.

When something goes wrong on the roads, collisions can take place very quickly. A car loses traction on an icy road surface, slides out of control and into the path of an oncoming vehicle; a pedestrian steps from behind a parked vehicle and into the path of an oncoming vehicle; a driver fails to stop at an intersection and collides with another vehicle (or vehicles) in the intersection. The period of time involved in these and most collisions is best measured in seconds, not the hours indicated on our speedometers or posted on speed limit signs. Similarly, the distances involved in these collisions are best measured in meters or feet, not in kilometers or miles. This means that to better understand collisions, we need to examine road speeds in terms of the *meters* or *feet* we are travelling *per second* at any particular moment.

Converting our speeds from kilometers per hour (or miles per hour) into meters per second (or feet per second) is relatively simple. Let's say we are travelling at 100 km/h. How many meters per second (m/s) are we travelling?

We know that 100 kilometers = 100,000 meters and 1 hour = 3,600 seconds

Therefore: 100 km/h = 100,000 m/h divided by 3,600 s/h
= 27.8 m/s

The same can be done to convert 60 mi./hr. into feet per second (ft./sec.):

There are 5,280 feet per mile.
Therefore: 60 mi./hr. x 5,280 ft./mi. divided by 3,600 sec./hr.
= 88.0 ft./sec.

An alternative to making "long-hand" calculations is to use conversion factors that have been determined to simplify the work. Some of the conversion factors that we shall use in this book are shown on Table 3.1. We see, for example, that to convert kilometers per hour into meters per second, we simply multiply the speed in kilometers per hour by the factor of 0.278 to get the equivalent speed in meters per second. In the above example, 100 km/h multiplied by 0.278 equals 27.8 m/s. Conversion factors are often rounded off, leading to small differences from the "long-hand" calculations, but these will be of little consequence to our reviews in this book.

Using the appropriate conversion factor in Table 3.1, we can calculate the distance travelled per second at various speeds. Tables 3.2 (a) and 3.2 (b) provide the distances travelled per second in metric and imperial units, respectively.

Table 3.1: Conversion Factors

To Convert	To	Multiply By
kilometers	meters	1000
meters	centimeters	100
meters	inches	39.37
meters	feet	3.281
kilometers	miles	0.621
kilometers per hour	meters per second	0.278
kilometers per hour	miles per hour	0.621
kilometers per hour	feet per second	0.911
meters per second	centimeters per second	100
meters per second	feet per second	3.281
kilograms	pounds	2.205
feet	meters	0.305
feet	inches	12
inches	meters	0.0254
miles	kilometers	1.609
miles	feet	5280
miles per hour	kilometers per hour	1.609
miles per hour	feet per second	1.467
miles per hour	meters per second	0.447
feet per second	inches per second	12
pounds	kilograms	0.454

Table 3.2 (a): Distance Travelled Per Hour or Per Second

Metric Units

Kilometers Per Hour	Meters Per second
5 km/h* (x 0.278) =	1.4 m/s
10	2.8
20	5.6
30	8.3
40	11.1
50 km/h	13.9 m/s
60	16.7
70	19.5
80	22.2
90	25.0
100 km/h	27.8 m/s
110	30.6
120	33.4
130	36.1

Approximate walking speed.

Table 3.2 (b): Distance Travelled Per Hour or Per Second*

Imperial Units

Miles Per Hour	Feet Per Second
3 mi./hr.* (x 1.467) =	4.4 ft./sec.
10	14.7
20	29.3
30 mi./hr.	44.0 ft./sec.
40	58.7
50	73.4
60 mi./hr.	88.0 ft./sec.
70	102.7
80	117.4

Approximate walking speed.

Let's reflect upon the figures in Tables 3.2 (a) and (b). It is normal to think of the speeds we travel on our roads in terms of kilometers per hour, or miles per hour. However, it is when we consider our speed in terms of meters or feet travelled per second that we realize just how fast we are travelling. It is one thing to know it will take an hour to drive to the cottage 50 kilometers away, but another to realize it will take possibly only a second or two to pass through an intersection. It is one thing to know we are driving within the posted speed limit of, say, 100 kilometers per hour, but another to realize that at this speed we are moving at 28 meters per second and that adjacent or approaching vehicles are often only a meter or less away. As we shall see in Chapter 5, the average passenger vehicle is approximately 5 meters long. When we are travelling at 100 kilometers per hour (27.8 m/s) it takes only one second to pass through the space occupied by five passenger vehicles, placed bumper to bumper. Imagine the impacts that result from collisions at such speeds!

Knowing the distance we travel every second at various highway speeds, helps us understand that there is very little room for error on our roads and there is very little time available to correct for any errors we, or others, may make. We shall examine this more closely in our following chapters.

3.3 Impacts Resulting From Falls

There's a saying: *It is not speed that kills, but rather the sudden stop.* This is true. We can fly in aircraft or drive in motor vehicles at relatively high speeds with no adverse consequences. The problems arise if the aircraft or motor vehicle in which we are travelling collides with something, causing us to come to an abrupt stop.

One of the problems with understanding the hazards associated with the speeds at which we travel is that many people have not experienced the impacts that occur in collisions. Since the relationship between speed and impact is so fundamentally important to our safety on the roads, let us not wait to actually experience a collision before we understand the impacts that occur.

One way to understand the impacts on our bodies that will result from collisions is to relate them to personal experiences we have had when we have slipped or tripped and fallen. Perhaps we have fallen from a stool or ladder, or know others who have. In such events, when we fall we strike the ground, which brings us to an abrupt stop. We know from these experiences we can easily be hurt in such falls. In fact, relatively minor falls injure many people quite seriously.

The impacts we experience in falls are similar to those we are likely to experience if we are involved in a collision on our roads. In a traffic collision, the greater our speed, the greater the impact will be as we come to an abrupt stop. In a fall, the greater the height we fall, the greater our speed will be and the greater the impact will be when we hit the ground. Therefore, if we know the speeds we attain in falls and compare them to the speeds we commonly travel on our streets, highways and freeways, it will help us to understand the impacts that will occur in traffic collisions.

When we fall gravity pulls us to the ground. The force of gravity causes us to accelerate and to reach higher speeds the further we fall. We can calculate the speed (velocity) we will reach in a fall from the equation H $= V^2/2a$, where H is the height of our fall, (measured in meters or feet), V is the velocity or speed we reach in the fall (measured in meters or feet per second) and "a" is the acceleration due to gravity, considered to be 9.8 meters per second squared or 32 feet per second squared.[3, 4]

Now let us assume that we slip or trip while walking and fall a distance of 1 meter, which is approximately the "center of gravity" for a larger person. Using this equation, we calculate that when we fall 1 meter in height, we will reach a velocity (speed) of approximately 4.5 meters per second, which converts to a speed of 16 kilometers per hour. When we are in a motor vehicle travelling at 16 kilometers an hour the impact in a collision will be similar to the impact we would experience if we slipped or tripped and fell to the ground. This explains why people are so often injured in routine falls, and also helps us to better understand the impacts we experience at relatively low speeds on city streets. The impacts in collisions, even at slow speeds, can be serious.

Next, let us determine the heights we would need to fall to reach the various speeds we travel on our roads. Using the equation we used earlier, we obtain the results shown in Table 3.3. As we can see, the heights we would need to fall to reach various road speeds are astounding. A person would need to fall 3.5 meters to reach a speed of 30 kilometers per hour; 9.9 meters to reach 50 kilometers per hour; 39.4 meters to reach 100 kilometers per hour and 56.7 meters to reach 120 kilometers per hour.

Table 3.3: Height of Fall to Reach Various Speeds*

Road Speed (V)	Height of Fall (H)
30 km/h (8.3 m/s)	3.5 meters
50 km/h (13.9 m/s)	9.9 meters
100 km/h (27.8 m/s)	39.4 meters
120 km/h (33.4 m/s)	56.9 meters
30 mi./hr. (44 ft./sec.)	30.3 feet
60 mi./hr. (88 ft./sec.)	121 feet

*$H = V^2/2a$, where H = Height of fall (m or ft.); V = Velocity (speed) squared (m/s or ft./sec.); a = acceleration due to gravity (9.8 m/s^2 or 32 $ft./sec.^2$)

Considering these heights (or distances) can help us understand the seriousness of the impacts that occur in traffic collisions. The impact in a collision when travelling between 100 to 120 kilometers an hour, would be similar to the impact we would experience if we fell from a height of 40 to 60 meters. It is little wonder why few people survive head-on collisions above approximately 70 kilometers an hour, even with the cushioning provided by seat belts and airbags. Even impacts occurring at slow speeds can be serious. The faster we travel, the more serious collisions become. This demonstrates the need to use seat belts at all times in motor vehicles and the increased hazards all road users face when motorists exceed the posted speed limits. Further, it reminds us of the need for motorcyclists and bicyclists to wear helmets.

3.4 Chapter Summery: Speed and Impacts in Collisions

Our purpose in this chapter has been to develop an appreciation of the seriousness of the impacts the will inevitable occur should we be in a collision.

We saw that the human body has a low tolerance for impacts, which helps us to understand the need for all road users to be cushioned as well as possible at all times, due to the possibility of being involved in a collision. The higher our rate of travel, the greater the impacts will be in a collision and the greater will be our risk of injury. Even with the cushioning offered by seat belts and airbags, vehicle occupants are unlikely to survive head-on collisions at the higher rates of speed we travel on our highways and freeways.

It is also useful to consider speed from the perspective of the distances travelled per second. These units of measurement help us understand why collisions occur so frequently and why the impacts in collisions can be so severe. They also highlight the small margin for error that exists on our roads, as well as the limited distance and time available to correct for any errors we or others may make.

Finally, to understand speed, it is helpful to understand the height we would need to fall to reach the various speeds we travel on our roads. We saw that we would need to fall a considerable height to reach those speeds (velocities), which helps us to appreciate the impacts that will occur in collisions.

In the following chapters we will use the information identified in this chapter to help us review and analyze the hazards on our roads. Let us now examine the hazards that arise from the design and operation of our roads.

FOUR

Road Design and Operation

4.0 Introduction

In this and our next two chapters we shall systematically review our roadways, motor vehicles and highway winter maintenance programs, so that we can come to an understanding of many of the hazards that are inherent to our road systems. The information we gather in these chapters will be essential to our understanding of why collisions occur and, ultimately, to our understanding of what we can do as individuals to reduce our risks of being involved in a traffic collision.

4.1 Road Design and Intended Use

Not all streets, highways and freeways have been designed and constructed in accordance with current policies and standards. Even road systems built only a few years ago may not meet current standards. Whenever we use roadways that are obviously older, we must keep in mind they may not be as wide, straight or smooth as modern roads.

Regardless of whether our streets, highways or freeways are old, recently rehabilitated or new, they have many features that greatly influence our safety. Let's examine some of these features, while keeping in mind the World Health Organization's statement: "Of all the systems that people have to deal with on a daily basis, road transport is the most complex and the most dangerous."[1]

Roads are structures that we have built to get ourselves and the materials we use from one place to another. As with any tools, appliances and facilities, roads must be used according to the principles upon which they were designed and according to the way they are intended to be used. For example:

- Household appliances such as stoves, ovens, washers and dryers, dishwashers, microwaves, etc. must be used properly to prevent damaging the appliance itself, or damaging the home or possibly injuring the user.

- Tools such as lawn mowers, weed eaters, hedge trimmers, chain saws etc. must also be used properly, especially to prevent injury to the user.

- Our homes must be used as intended and according to their design. If heaters, furnaces, fireplaces, water and electrical outlets are used inappropriately, they will not provide the safety, comfort or benefits required or intended.

- Firearms must also be used as intended and according to their design to prevent harm to users and, of course, to prevent unintended harm to others.

- Aircraft must be used according to the flight manuals for the particular aircraft, the limitations of the weather, the limitations imposed by traffic regulations, and the presence of other aircraft. Safety is always the top priority.

- Water craft, small or large, must be properly guided at appropriate speeds to avoid colliding with other vessels or submerged rocks, all while considering navigation aids, the size and depth of each vessel, the weather forecast, tides and currents, and other relevant matters.

As basic as these examples are, they illustrate the fundamental need to use the tools mankind has built properly and safely. It is, of course, no different with our roads. One of the most important considerations when using our roads is to know they have been designed and constructed for specific purposes. If we violate the principles for the intended use of our roadways, we invite potentially serious consequences.

4.2 Jurisdiction

One of the complexities of our roads is the issue of responsibility. Who is responsible for the design, construction, operation, ongoing maintenance and costs of our roads? As we shall see, every province and state throughout Canada and the U.S. is generally responsible for all aspects of the roadways within its jurisdiction.

The Illinois Department of Transportation defines jurisdiction as follows:

- *"Jurisdiction is the authority and obligation to administer, control, construct, maintain and operate a highway.*[2]

- *"When an agency has jurisdiction of a street or highway, that agency is responsible for the upkeep of that highway, including reconstruction, signing, maintenance, etc. All of these responsibilities remain with the agency until the jurisdiction is transferred to another highway authority."*[2]

In Canada, our roads may be federal, provincial, territorial or municipal responsibilities, as the following statements show:

- *"Highways are considered under the general class of 'Local Works and Undertakings' in* The Constitution Act, 1867 *and are the responsibility of the provinces and territories."*[3]

- *"Highways in Canada, including the Trans Canada Highway and the National Highway System, fall within provincial/territorial jurisdiction. The only exceptions are highways through national parks and a portion of the Alaska Highway, which are managed by Parks Canada and Public Works and Government Services Canada, respectively. Provincial/territorial governments are therefore responsible for the planning, design, construction, operation, maintenance and financing of highways within their jurisdiction."*[4]

- *"Street systems in cities, towns and villages are the responsibility of municipalities, though sometimes subsidized by the provinces."*[5]

The U.S. delegates the responsibilities for its roads as Canada does, according to the following statement by the U.S. Department of Transportation's Federal Highway Administration (FHWA):

"Most (97 percent) roads and streets in the United States are under the jurisdiction of State and local governments. The Federal jurisdiction is mainly limited to National Parks, National Forests, and other government-owned land."[6]

We see that throughout Canada and the U.S., each province and state is responsible for the roads within its jurisdiction, while most cities and towns are usually responsible for the streets within their municipalities. The federal governments in Canada and the U.S. have specific but limited responsibilities.

Each province, state and municipality will have different ways of fulfilling their responsibilities for the roads within their jurisdiction. This introduces complexities and potential hazards, especially as we travel outside our home territory on roads under the jurisdiction of another authority. We will explore this subject more thoroughly in Chapter 6 when we examine winter maintenance programs.

4.3 Geometric Design of Roads

Road design can be broken into two major categories: structural and geometric. The structural considerations relate to the strengths of materials such as wood, steel, concrete, asphalt, rock, gravel, sand, bricks and other materials required to properly support heavy vehicular traffic. Structural considerations also include the design of bridges, tunnels and overpasses spanning long distances and carrying massive loads.

The other main category of road design is referred to as geometric design. For our purposes, we can think of geometric design as the non-structural design aspects of a road. These include the widths of traffic lanes and shoulders, as well as the speed limits, bicycle lanes, pedestrian requirements, and the slopes, grades, curvatures and line painting of our roads. California's *Highway Design Manual* provides a simple definition of geometric design, as follows:

"Geometric Design. The arrangement of the visible elements of a road, such as alignment, grades, sight distances, widths, slopes, etc."[7]

Fortunately, in Canada and the U.S., we rarely need to be concerned with the structural aspects of our roads. However, the public does need to be constantly aware of the geometric design considerations. From the public's perspective, it is primarily the geometric design of our streets, highways and freeways that governs how they are to be properly and safely used. In the remainder of this chapter we shall, therefore, be focusing our attention on the geometric design considerations of our roadways.

Throughout Canada and the U.S., experts have established comprehensive guidelines, standards and manuals to assist and guide those responsible for the geometric designs of roads. Most of this information is based upon years of background and scientific knowledge, and has been compiled from a wide range of sources and professionals around the country, often incorporating the views of experts in other countries. This is well summarized in Delaware's *Road Design Manual*, as follows:

"The concept of design standards has evolved from extensive highway agency field-testing, research, mathematical modeling and the study and

documentation of many years of application and experience. The findings and conclusions are documented in many publications that serve as guides for highway designers."[8]

Two publications are particularly significant to those responsible for the geometric design of roads in Canada and the U.S., namely the *Geometric Design Guide for Canadian Roads*[9] and *A Policy on Geometric Design of Highways and Streets.*[10]

The *Geometric Design Guide for Canadian Roads* is produced by the Transportation Association of Canada (TAC) and is often referred to as the *TAC Guide*. The TAC describes their publication as follows:

> *"The* Geometric Design Guide for Canadian Roads *is the principal geometric design reference source in Canada and an essential document for any organization involved in road design and construction. Road authorities across Canada co-operated in the preparation of the Guide, while federal, provincial and territorial governments in Canada sponsored the project."*[11]

In the U.S., *A Policy on Geometric Design of Highways and Streets*, often referred to as the "Green Book" because of the colour of the book's cover, is produced by the American Association of State Highway and Transportation Officials (AASHTO). This publication is used to guide authorities with the design of streets and highways, similar to the use of the *TAC Guide* in Canada. The AASHTO describe their latest edition of the "Green Book" as follows:

> *"A Policy on Geometric Design of Highways and Streets, 6th Edition, 2011, commonly referred to as the 'Green Book,' contains the current design research and practices for highway and street geometric design. The document provides guidance to highway engineers and designers who strive to make unique design solutions that meet the needs of highway users while maintaining the integrity of the environment. It is also intended as a comprehensive reference manual to assist in administrative, planning, and educational efforts pertaining to design formulation."*[12]

Unfortunately, neither the *Geometric Design Guide for Canadian Roads* nor *A Policy on Geometric Design of Highways and Streets* is available on line, free of charge. However, copies of these publications may be purchased in PDF format or in hard cover. Alternatively, local libraries may have, or be able to obtain, copies for public viewing.

The guidelines provided in the TAC and AASHTO publications are used extensively in Canada and the U.S. by provinces, states and municipalities when designing streets and highways within their respective jurisdictions, as the following examples show:

- Province of British Columbia (B.C.): *BC Supplement to TAC Geometric Design Guide 2007 Edition:*

  "The latest edition of the Transportation Association of Canada's 'Geometric Design Guide for Canadian Roads' (or TAC Guide) is the principal source for basic design principles. The AASHTO publication 'A Policy on Geometric Design of Highways and Streets' is also recommended as a secondary reference."[13]

- State of California: *Highway Design Manual:*

  "The standards in this manual generally conform to the standards and policies set forth in the AASHTO publications, 'A Policy on Geometric Design of Highways and Streets.'"[14]

- City of Vancouver, B.C.:

  "The Transportation Association of Canada Geometric Design Guide is used as a basis for the City's Transportation Branch to design City roadways and intersections."[15]

4.3.1. Summary: Geometric Design of Roads

In this section, we saw that the streets and highways in Canada and the U.S. are by no means randomly designed. Rather, throughout the multitude of jurisdictions, road design is based upon similar geometric design standards.

4.4 Speed Limits

There is likely no subject of greater importance to our safety and proper use of the roads than speed limits. We therefore need to examine this subject carefully.

4.4.1. Statutory Speed Limits

There are two main classifications of speed limits, "posted speed limits" and "statutory speed limits." Posted speed limits are those indicated by signs placed beside our streets, highways and freeways, whereas statutory speed limits are those established by statute or legislation by the province, territory or state responsible for the roadway. Statutory speed limits generally apply to all areas within a province or state, unless indicated otherwise by a "posted" speed limit sign. In B.C., for example, the statutory speed limits throughout the province for areas within and outside of municipalities are set out in section 146 (1) of B.C.'s *Motor Vehicle Act* which reads as follows:

> *"Speed limits*
>
> *146 (1) Subject to this section, a person must not drive or operate a motor vehicle on a highway in a municipality or treaty lands at a greater rate of speed than 50 km/h, and a person must not drive or operate a motor vehicle on a highway outside a municipality at a greater rate of speed than 80 km/h."[16]*

Therefore, unless there is a sign indicating otherwise, the statutory speed limit within a municipality in British Columbia is 50 km/h and the speed limit for any area outside of a municipality is 80 km/h. Statutory speed limits may also apply to school zones and playgrounds, such as set out in section 147 of B.C.'s *Motor Vehicle Act*:

"Schools and playgrounds

147 (1) A person driving a vehicle on a regular school day and on a highway where signs are displayed stating a speed limit of 30 km/h, or on which the numerals '30' are prominently shown, must drive at a rate of speed not exceeding 30 km/h while approaching or passing the school building and school grounds to which the signs relate, between 8 a.m. and 5 p.m., or subject to subsection (1.1), between any extended times that are stated on the signs.

(1.1) Extended times under subsection (1) may not begin later than 8 a.m. or end earlier than 5 p.m.

(2) A person driving a vehicle on a highway must drive the vehicle at a rate of speed not exceeding 30 km/h when approaching or passing, between dawn and dusk, a public playground for children where signs are displayed stating a speed limit of 30 km/h, or on which the numerals '30' are prominently shown."[17]

Two statutes in the *California Vehicle Code* are of particular interest. The first is set out in section 22350, under the heading of "Basic Speed Law," and reads as follows:

"Basic Speed Law

22350. No person shall drive a vehicle upon a highway at a speed greater than is reasonable or prudent having due regard for weather, visibility, the traffic on, and the surface and width of, the highway, and in no event at a speed which endangers the safety of persons or property."[18]

California's *Basic Speed Law* establishes that it is the responsibility of the driver to proceed at a speed appropriate for the conditions. It is worth noting that this section of the *California Vehicle Code* makes specific reference to the need to drive "having due regard" for the weather, visibility, traffic, road surface and the width of the highway. When conditions are adverse, the speed limits may be inappropriate. This is a subject we will examine more thoroughly in coming chapters.

Section 22352 of the *California Vehicle Code* sets out the speed limits when traversing rail grade crossings, alleys and intersections of highways.[19] The intent of this section is stated in layman's terms in the *California Driver Handbook*, as follows:[20]

"Near Railroad Tracks
The speed limit is 15 mph within 100 feet of a railroad crossing where you cannot see the tracks for 400 feet in both directions. You may drive faster than 15 mph if the crossing is controlled by gates, a warning signal, or a flag man."[20]

"Blind Intersections
The speed limit for a blind intersection is 15 mph. An intersection is considered 'blind' if there are no stop signs at any corner and you cannot see for 100 feet in either direction during the last 100 feet before crossing. Trees, bushes, buildings, or parked cars at intersections can block your view to the side. If your view is blocked, edge forward slowly until you can see."[20]

"Alleys
The speed limit in any alley is 15 mph."[20]

This section of the *California Vehicle Code* is important to us for a number of reasons. First, it brings to our attention the need to exercise particular caution and judgment when driving. Second, it emphasizes the importance of reducing our speed in confined areas to allow more time for everyone involved to take corrective action, if necessary. Finally, it demonstrates that statutory speed limits are often specific to individual highway jurisdictions and that people not familiar with the area could become easily confused.

4.4.1.1 Summary: Statutory Speed Limits

For all sections of our streets and highways there is an intended speed. If there are no speed limit signs, then the speed limits are those established by statute, by the authority responsible for the speed limits for that street or highway. Statutory speed limits may exist for areas in- and outside of municipalities, for school zones and playgrounds and for railroad crossings, highway intersections and alleys, according to statutes and laws passed by the responsible highway authority. Statues such as the *Basic Speed Law* in California place the onus on drivers to reduce their speed in adverse conditions.

There is unquestionably the potential for people using our streets or highways to be unaware or uncertain of the statutory speed limits for the area. This applies especially to people travelling outside of their home province or state, or in foreign countries. Those not familiar with the statutory speed limits for the region in which they are travelling are a hazard to themselves and to others. *Knowing the speed limit is vital at all times, anywhere.*

Remember what we learned in Chapter 3, section 3.1 about the limitations of the human body to withstand impacts resulting from collisions? We learned that whereas most people survive if they are hit by a car travelling at 30 km/h, most people are killed if they are hit by a car travelling at 50 km/h. This supports the wisdom of reduced speed limits near school zones and playgrounds and the need for reduced speeds at blind intersections and in places such as alleys, where visibility is often limited. It is the responsibility of every driver to comply with reduced speed limits at all times for the safety of everyone involved.

4.4.2 Posted Speed Limits

Whereas statutory speed limits are often obscure because they are tucked away in Acts and Codes and other printed material, posted speed limits are conspicuously placed beside our streets and highways. We need to explore how the posted speed limits are determined.

Roads are designed to get people and goods from one point to another within a reasonable period of time. This requires that roads be designed to allow traffic to move at certain speeds. The design speed of the street, highway or freeway is, however, only one of many factors used to determine the posted speed limit.

Deciding the importance of the various factors in determining speed limits is complex and many studies have been conducted to assist with this. One study, *Review and Analysis of Posted Speed Limits and Speed Limit Setting Practices in British Columbia* [21] was undertaken on behalf of the province's Ministry of Transportation and published in the spring of 2003. It reviewed speed limits throughout the province and compared them to speed limits set in "other countries with mountainous terrain such as Austria, Finland, France, Italy, etc."[22] The study includes references to speed limits and speed limit setting practices in the U.S., as well as a table comparing the speed limits in over 20 countries.[23] In the Executive Summary are several statements of particular interest to us, as follows:

- *"Speed limits are primarily set for safety reasons, i.e., to reach a balance between travel time and crash risk, and to provide a basis for enforcement of inappropriate speeding behaviour."*[24]

- *"Maximum speed limits posted on fixed-message signs are based on ideal traffic, environmental, and road conditions."*[22]

- *"When less than ideal conditions exist, the driver must adjust their vehicle speed that is appropriate for conditions."*[22]

Another study on speed limit setting practices was undertaken by the Transportation Association of Canada (TAC) and was published in December 2009. The report *Canadian Guidelines for Establishing Posted Speed Limits*[25] reviews the practices of road agencies in Canada, the United Kingdom, Australia, New Zealand and the U.S.[26] The report noted:

- *"The risks associated with the road determine the appropriate posted speed limit. The higher the level of risk, the lower the recommended posted speed limit."*[27]

- *"Important factors to consider when establishing speed limits are the road geometry, alignment, adjacent land use, number of access points, operating speeds, pedestrian presence, heavy vehicle presence, traffic volumes and accident records."*[28]

The report outlines 11 criteria upon which to base posted speed limits. The criteria are:

- horizontal alignment, i.e. curves in highway
- vertical alignment, i.e. highway grades
- average lane widths
- roadside hazards, i.e. hazards beside the highway
- pedestrian exposure
- cyclist exposure
- pavement surface
- number of intersections with public roads
- number of intersections with private access driveways
- number of interchanges
- on-street parking.[29]

The speed limit signs posted alongside roads generally refer to the maximum speed that is to be driven, unless indicated otherwise. This is identified in B.C.'s *Motor Vehicle Act*, section 146 (3):

> *"146 (3) If the minister responsible for the administration of the Transportation Act has caused a sign to be erected or placed on a highway limiting the rate of speed of motor vehicles or a category of motor vehicles driven or operated on that portion of the highway, a person must not, when the sign is in place on the highway, drive or operate a vehicle on that portion of the highway at a greater rate of speed than that indicated on the sign for that category of motor vehicle."[30]*

In the U.S., the Department of Transportation's Federal Highway Administration (FHWA) publishes a manual covering all aspects of signs, signals, line painting and other such measures "used to regulate, warn, or guide traffic."[31] The *Manual on Uniform Traffic Control Devices* includes specific requirements for establishing speed limits for sections of a highway, described as speed zones:

"Speed zones (other than statutory speed limits) shall only be established on the basis of an engineering study that has been performed in accordance with traffic engineering practices."[32]

We see, therefore, that determining the speed limits posted on the streets and highways throughout Canada and the U.S. is given extensive attention. Speed limits are without question one of the most crucial aspects of road safety.

4.4.2.1. Summary: Posted Speed Limits

The following are some of the more important considerations for setting posted speed limits in Canada and the U.S.:

- Posted speed limits are established by the responsible road agency only after careful consideration of many factors and in accordance with established practices.

- The posted speed limits are the maximum speeds to be driven, unless indicated otherwise.

- The posted speed limits are based upon ideal traffic, environmental and road conditions. When conditions are less than ideal, a driver must reduce their speed according to the conditions.

- The higher the speed of travel, the higher the risk. To drive in excess of the posted speed limit is, therefore, to increase the risk to the driver and to everyone else who is using the same street or highway.

- Exceeding the posted or statutory speed limit violates the law and denies the wisdom and reasons used to establish the speed limits.

- When setting speed limits, road agencies accept there are risks on the roads and attempt "to reach a balance between travel time and crash risk."[24]

A great deal of attention is given to establishing the speed limits posted throughout Canada and the U.S. One of the main considerations is the risk associated with speed: the higher the speed the greater the risk of collisions, injuries and fatalities. Exceeding the posted speed limit therefore increases the risks on the roadways. These risks apply not only to the driver of the speeding vehicle, but also to passengers in that vehicle and any others using the roads. As we continue our discussions, the need to comply with the posted speed limits will become increasingly apparent.

Of particular note is the need "to reach a balance between travel time and crash risk"[24] when establishing speed limits. This is crucial to understanding road safety. For the first time we see one of the major conflicts of interest road agencies have regarding safety. Our streets and highways are built to get people and goods from one location to another. On one hand is the need to keep travel time as short as possible, which is accomplished by maintaining speeds as high as possible. On the other is the need to keep speeds as slow as possible to reduce the likelihood and severity of collisions. The fact that road agencies strive to reach a "balance" between these two conflicting interests is a clear indication that public safety is being sacrificed by the desire and "need" to move people and goods as rapidly as possible. Based on the statistics in Chapter 1, we pay a very high price in Canada and the U. S. for our desire and need to be highly mobile.

4.5 Sight Distance and Stopping Sight Distance

In road design, several terms are used to describe being able to see far enough ahead to allow motorists to stop, if required. Two of these terms are sight distance and stopping sight distance. It is useful to see a definition of these terms:

"Sight distance is the length of the roadway ahead that is visible to the driver."[33]

"Stopping sight distance is the distance necessary for a vehicle traveling at or near the design speed to stop before reaching a stationary object in its path."[34]

When we drive, it is essential that we are able to see far enough ahead to be able to stop in time to avoid a collision. Our sight distance and stopping sight distance are important safety considerations on the roadways.

Many people have probably never thought about the process involved in stopping a vehicle quickly. There are actually two stages. The first is the time required for a driver to make a decision to stop and the second is the time for the driver to bring their vehicle to a stop through braking action. We need to examine both of these stages.

4.5.1 Brake Reaction Time (Perception and Reaction Time)

To stop a vehicle, the driver must first decide that they need to stop. To make this decision, the driver must be able to see there is an object or problem ahead. Once the driver identifies a problem, they must decide what to do. One option may be to reduce speed, another may be to swerve and a third may be to stop as quickly as possible. Regardless, the driver must make a decision on what to do once an object comes into view. If the driver decides it is necessary to stop, they must then place their foot onto the brake pedal to begin the vehicle's braking action.

The time that passes from the instant an object comes into view to the moment the driver has placed their foot onto the brake pedal is referred to as the "brake reaction time,"[33] or the "perception and reaction time."[35] The driver's brake reaction time (perception and reaction time) varies according to a number of factors, some of the more important being: the specific situation, the visibility, the attentiveness of the driver, the driver's eyesight and reflexes, and the driver's ability to make a decision. If there is any confusion about the nature of the problem ahead, such as a fallen tree, an animal, rocks etc., it could easily delay the driver's decision to stop.[36]

To determine the distance a vehicle will travel during this period, road designers must place a limit on a driver's brake reaction time (perception and reaction time). Both the AASHTO and the TAC use a time of 2.5 seconds for a driver's brake reaction time (perception and reaction time).[37, 38] If a driver is inattentive, most if not all of the 2.5 seconds could easily be consumed before that driver is even aware of an object ahead and of a possible need to stop urgently. Likewise, if a driver is exceeding the speed limit, their vehicle may advance too far before they are able to apply the brakes, making a collision inevitable. Driver attentiveness and adherence to the speed limit are crucial to being able to stop a vehicle in a timely manner, especially when there is limited sight distance.

4.5.2 Braking Distance

The second stage of stopping a vehicle suddenly involves the time and distance required to bring a vehicle to a stop through braking. The braking distance is considered to be the distance a vehicle will travel from the moment the driver places their foot onto the brake pedal, until the vehicle stops.[39] The distance required to stop a vehicle by braking depends upon a number of factors, including: the speed at time of braking, whether the highway is flat or on a grade, the vehicle's braking system, and, especially in winter conditions, the condition of the vehicle's tires and the road surface.

4.6 Calculating Stopping Sight Distance

To properly understand road hazards it is essential to be aware of how a vehicle's speed influences the distance required to stop in a sudden and unexpected situation.

We have seen that there are two stages involved with stopping a vehicle, the driver's brake reaction time (perception and reaction time) and the braking distance. The total distance required to stop a vehicle in a sudden and unexpected situation is, therefore, the sum of the two distances described by these terms:

(1) "the distance traversed by the vehicle from the instant the driver sights an object necessitating a stop to the instant the brakes are applied"[33]

(2) "the distance needed to stop the vehicle from the instant brake application begins."[33]

The sum of these distances is known as the stopping sight distance.[33]

Both the TAC and the AASHTO have developed tables in their design reference guides that approximate the stopping sight distance for vehicles travelling at various speeds. Table 4.1 shows the approximate stopping sight distance in the AASHTO's *A Policy on Geometric Design of Highways and Streets.*[37]

Table 4.1: Stopping Sight Distance on Level Roadways[37]

Design Speed	Brake Reaction Distance[*]	Braking Distance on Level	Stopping Sight Distance	
			Calculated	Design
(km/h)	(m)	(m)	(m)	(m)
20	13.9	4.6	18.5	20
30	20.9	10.3	31.2	35
40	27.8	18.4	46.2	50
50	34.8	28.7	63.5	65
60	41.7	41.3	83.0	85
70	48.7	56.2	104.9	105
80	55.6	73.4	129.0	130
90	62.6	92.9	155.5	160
100	69.5	114.7	184.2	185
110	76.5	138.8	215.3	220
120	83.4	165.2	248.6	250
130	90.4	193.8	284.2	285

Brake reaction distance predicated on a time of 2.5 s

(Source: From A Policy on Geometric Design of Highways and Streets, 6th Edition, 2011 by the American Association of State Highway and Transportation Officials, Washington, DC. Table 3-1, page 3–4. Used by permission.)

This table shows the stopping sight distance at various speeds, i.e. the sum of the brake reaction distance and the braking distance. Under the heading, Stopping Sight Distance, in Table 4.1 are two columns, one identified as Calculated and the other as Design. The Calculated Stopping Sight Distance is the sum of the figures under Brake Reaction Distance and Braking Distance, both of which are calculated. The figures in the column headed Design are simply the figures in the Calculated column rounded up to become the recommended Stopping Sight Distance for designers to use when designing a (level) road at the respective speed.

Let us now examine how the calculations are made to determine how far a vehicle will travel during both the brake reaction distance and the braking distance.

4.6.1 Calculating Brake Reaction Distance

We have seen that both the AASHTO and the TAC allow 2.5 seconds for the driver's brake reaction time (perception and reaction time). The distance a vehicle will travel during this interval is a simple multiplication of the vehicle's speed at the moment the driver saw a need to stop, by the time that elapsed before the driver placed their foot onto the brake pedal.

To determine the distance a vehicle will travel during the driver's brake reaction time, we need to convert the vehicle's speed from kilometers per hour (or miles per hour) into meters per second (or feet per second). Table 3.2 (a) in Chapter 3 provides the conversion of speed in kilometers per hour to meters per second. We see from this table that at 50 km/h, a vehicle is travelling at 13.9 m/s. In the 2.5 seconds required for a driver's brake reaction time, a vehicle travelling at 50 km/h will advance 13.9 m/s x 2.5 s = 34.75 m, which is rounded off to 34.8 m. If we look at the figures in Table 4.1, under the heading Brake Reaction Distance, we see that at a design speed of 50 km/h, the brake reaction distance is the same 34.8 m we have just calculated. The calculation of the brake reaction distance is therefore quite simple; it only requires us to know the speed of the vehicle (in meters/second or feet/second) at the moment the driver saw the need to stop, and then multiply it by the amount of time allowed (2.5 seconds) for the driver to place their foot onto the brake pedal.

4.6.2 Calculating Braking Distance

The calculation of the braking distance for a vehicle at a specific speed is more complex than the calculation of the brake reaction distance. To understand the complexities of calculating the braking distance it is necessary to diverge for a moment to discuss the physics of moving objects.

A moving object is considered to possess energy. A motor vehicle gets its motion and, therefore, its energy from the fuel igniting within its engine, which accelerates the vehicle until it reaches certain speeds. Just as it takes energy for the vehicle to reach certain speeds, it takes energy to stop the vehicle, which the driver does by applying the vehicle's brakes. The amount of energy a vehicle possesses due to its speed is known as "kinetic energy," often referred to as the "energy of motion."[40] An object's kinetic energy can be calculated, if we know the mass (weight) and speed of the object, using the equation:

$$E_{kin} = \tfrac{1}{2}\, mv^2$$ *where E_{kin} is the kinetic energy, m is the mass (weight) of the object and v^2 is its velocity squared.[40]*

From this equation, we see that the kinetic energy of an object depends upon the square of its velocity. This is where things get interesting. If a vehicle is travelling at, say, 50 kilometers per hour, its kinetic energy will be:

$$E_{kin} = \tfrac{1}{2}\, m \times (50km/h)^2 = \tfrac{1}{2}\, m \times 2500\ km^2/h^2.$$

If the speed of the vehicle doubles to 100 kilometers per hour, its kinetic energy will increase to:

$$E_{kin} = \tfrac{1}{2}\, m \times (100km/h)^2 = \tfrac{1}{2}\, m \times 10,000\ km^2/h^2.$$

Looking at the second part of the equation (the velocity part), we see that by doubling the speed of the vehicle, its kinetic energy becomes four times greater than it was at the lower speed (10,000 versus 2,500). To stop a vehicle moving at 100 kilometers per hour, it will take four times more braking energy than if the vehicle was moving at half that speed, or at 50 kilometers per hour. This has huge implications for the braking distances of vehicles travelling at different speeds.

This basic discussion on kinetic energy is entirely supported by the data in Table 4.1. We see in this table, under the column Braking Distance on Level, that at a (design) speed of 20 km/h, the braking distance is calculated to be 4.6 m. At double this speed, or at 40 km/h, the braking distance is 18.4 m, exactly four times the braking distance required for a vehicle going at 20 km/h, or at half the speed. At 80 km/h, the braking distance is 73.4 m, again four times the distance required to stop a vehicle going at half the speed.

From this we can see that if a motorist doubles their speed, it will take 4 times the distance to stop the vehicle by braking than it would take at the lower speed. The braking distance therefore increases exponentially with the speed of a vehicle. Allowing for both brake reaction distance and braking distance, we see from Table 4.1 that if a person is driving at 130 km/h on a highway where the posted speed limit is 100 km/h, the approximate stopping distance is a full 100 meters greater than if the driver was adhering to the speed limit. This is yet further proof of the need to refrain from exceeding the posted speed limits and the need to be attentive at all times when driving.

4.6.3 Summary: Calculating Stopping Sight Distance

Roads are designed to allow drivers to see sufficiently far ahead, so they are able to stop in time to avoid colliding with obstructions. The distance that designers allow is based upon the intended speed of travel for that road. We see also that there are two stages involved with stopping a vehicle, the driver's perception and reaction time and the time it takes to stop once the brakes have been applied. During both of these stages, the distance vehicles advance increases with speed. Of particular significance to our safety is the fact that if we double our speed, it will take four times the distance to stop through braking action.

Our examination of the stopping sight distance shows the need to keep to the speed limits that are posted. To exceed the speed limit is to risk not being able to see objects ahead within the time and distance available to avoid a collision. Exceeding the speed limit, driving too fast for conditions or being inattentive may simply rob us of the time we need to stop, to prevent colliding with obstructions—vehicles, bicyclists, pedestrians, animals, rocks, trees etc.—on the roadway ahead.

4.7 Traffic Control Devices

Traffic control devices are the signs, light signals, road markings and other tools used to direct and control the movement of people using our streets and highways, including motorists, bicyclists and pedestrians. The posted speed limit signs we discussed are but one of numerous traffic control devices used to direct and control the movement of traffic.

The Federal Highway Administration (FHWA) publishes the extensive *Manual on Uniform Traffic Control Devices* (MUTCD), which details every conceivable requirement for the traffic control devices used on U.S. roadways.[41] The FHWA advises:

> *"The MUTCD…is approved as the national standard for designing, applying, and planning traffic control devices."*[42]

Having a national standard for traffic control devices means these devices are all used in the same way across the country. The U.S. Department of Transportation and the FHWA can be rightfully proud that such a comprehensive document exists. It would be valuable for everyone to briefly review this manual, which is available on line at: http://mutcd.fhwa.dot.gov/pdfs/2009r1r2/mutcd2009r1r2edition.pdf

Canada has a similar but less extensive manual for traffic control devices, the *Manual of Uniform Traffic Control Devices for Canada* (MUTCDC) produced by the Transportation Association of Canada (TAC).[43] While the U.S. manual is available online, unfortunately, the Canadian manual is not.

Traffic control devices are hugely important for the smooth, efficient and safe movement of everyone using our roads. However, what is apparent when reviewing the FHWA's *MUTCD* is how complex the subject is. From cover to cover, this manual is 862 pages in length. It identifies hundreds of different signs, as well as numerous light control systems and line painting schemes. While standardization is tremendously helpful in reducing confusion among road users, the complexity of the signage can easily lead to confusion. For example, when travelling along a highway at 28 meters or 88 feet per second, possibly in the dark, in adverse conditions and in heavy traffic, it is very easy to understand how a motorist could become confused with the intended directions from one of the many traffic control devices located on, beside or above the highway. Confusion leads to errors and at the speeds people commonly drive on our roadways, even the simplest of errors can cause collisions.

Even though a tremendous amount of effort has gone into standardizing traffic control devices there will, nevertheless, be differences with these devices. For example, signs in Quebec may be in French. Speed limit signs in the U.S. are often identified in miles per hour, while in Canada they are in kilometers per hour. Speed limit signs in the U.S. may identify minimum speed limits, reduced night time speed limits or reduced truck speed limits. On a broader scale, in several countries across the world vehicles are driven on the left side of the roads, not on the right. This raises potentially lethal situations for travellers from Canada or the U.S. Similarly, when people from countries that travel on the left side of the road visit Canada or the U.S., they could easily be a hazard to themselves and to others.

Traffic control devices are a necessary part of our roads. They direct people on how to use the streets, highways and freeways properly and safely, as they are intended to be used. However, even experienced, attentive road users could, at times, have difficulty following the directions set out by traffic control devices, especially in poor light, heavy traffic or during adverse road or weather conditions. Inexperience and a lack of attention magnify these problems. At the speeds people commonly travel, if any road user fails to properly follow the directions set out by traffic control devices, it could be fatal. It is therefore important that all road users proceed with caution at all times, particularly when conditions are less than ideal.

4.8 Widths of Traffic Lanes

The width of lanes on our streets, highways and freeways is particularly significant to road safety. There are several types of lanes. The lanes that vehicles travel upon at the posted speed limits are usually referred to as traffic lanes or travel lanes. But there are also "Special Purpose Lanes," which include: parking lanes (used for vehicles to park beside a traffic lane), passing lanes, climbing lanes (used for slower traffic on steeper grades), right-turn and left-turn lanes, and others.[44] The *TAC Guide* allows for the width of these special purpose lanes to be up to 0.2 m narrower than the adjacent traffic lane, in certain circumstances.[44]

The width of traffic lanes depends to a certain extent upon the intended use of the roadway. The *TAC Guide* states:

> *"Lane widths are dependent upon design speed and the volume of traffic the roadway is intended to carry, and the number and types of trucks on the roadway."[45]*

The widths of traffic lanes recommended in the *TAC Guide* vary from 3.0 meters to 3.7 meters (approximately 10 to 12 feet), with various exceptions noted in the guide.[46]

The widths of traffic lanes for streets, highways and freeways within the U.S. are generally similar to those recommended for Canada. The AASHTO publication *A Policy on Geometric Design of Highways and Streets*, states:

"The lane width of a roadway influences the comfort of driving, operational characteristics, and, in some situations, the likelihood of crashes. Lane widths of 2.7 to 3.6 m [9 to 12 ft] are generally used, with a 3.6-m [12-ft] lane predominant on most high-speed, high-volume highways."[47]

"Lanes 3.0 m [10 ft] wide are acceptable on low-speed facilities, and lanes 2.7 m [9 ft] wide may be appropriate on low-volume roads in rural and residential areas."[47]

4.8.1 Summary: Widths of Traffic Lanes

We see from our brief review of the widths of traffic lanes that lane widths are generally similar throughout Canada and the U.S. The AASHTO publication *A Policy on Geometric Design of Highways and Streets* allows for lanes between 2.7 m (9 ft.), for low-volume roads in rural and residential areas, and 3.6 m (12 ft.) on high-speed, high-volume highways. In Canada, traffic lanes vary between 3.0 m and 3.7 m. Special purpose lanes for parking, passing, climbing, right-turns and left-turns may be 0.2 m narrower than the adjacent traffic lane. These dimensions are of great significance to road safety and will be discussed further in our later chapters.

4.9 Shoulders

The shoulder on a street, highway or freeway is another component of our roads that greatly impacts our safety. When we refer to the shoulder, we refer to the relatively level area on the side of a roadway, outside of the traffic lane(s). A shoulder can be paved or gravel and is used by motorists, cyclists or pedestrians. Many city streets do not have shoulders, due to the restricted areas within municipalities, or the need to have parking lanes or sidewalks beside the traffic lanes. However, as soon as we come onto higher speed highways and freeways, there are usually shoulders outside the traffic lanes.

Anyone who has driven a street or highway without a proper shoulder knows how intimidating it can be, especially if the edge of the road surface drops off sharply. Bridges and tunnels can be equally intimidating because they are immovable structures very close to traffic lanes where motorists often travel at high speeds. It is not unusual for bridges and tunnels to have very narrow shoulders, often far narrower than the shoulder on the street, highway or freeway on either side of these structures. Guard rails and concrete abutments, when placed within the width of the shoulder, introduce restrictions that can also be dangerous to road users.

Shoulders are a particularly important feature of higher speed highways and have multiple purposes, some being:

- They provide structural support for traffic lanes.

- They can provide space for motorists to stop their vehicles safely off the traffic lanes, for emergencies, maintenance or other reasons.

- They can increase the margin for error by providing motorists space for movement should they intentionally or unintentionally leave their traffic lane.

- They provide space for pedestrians or bicyclists.

- They can improve motorists' unobstructed visibility (sight distance), provided the shoulders are not covered with high snow banks or occupied by parked vehicles.

Shoulders are therefore a significant component of any road system. It is important to our understanding of road safety to examine the features of shoulders that are, or can be, hazardous.

4.9.1 Shoulders: Widths

Throughout Canada and the U.S., the widths of shoulders vary considerably depending upon a number of considerations, including: vehicle speed, traffic volume, truck traffic, the region through which the highway is constructed, the presence of pedestrians and bicyclists, and the location of guardrails and similar structures. The

Transportation Association of Canada's *Geometric Design Guide for Canadian Roads* (*TAC Guide*) recommends shoulders of between 1.0 m and 3.0 m, depending upon the roadway's use and purpose.[48] In the U.S., the American Association of State Highway and Transportation Officials' (AASHTO's) *A Policy on Geometric Design of Highways and Streets* recommends shoulders of the following widths:

> *"A minimum shoulder width of 0.6 m [2 ft] should be considered for low-volume highways, and a 1.8- to 2.4-m [6- to 8-ft] shoulder width is preferable. Heavily traveled, high-speed highways and highways carrying large numbers of trucks should have usable shoulders at least 3.0 m [10 ft] wide and preferably 3.6 m [12 ft] ."[49]*

We see there can be a large variation in the widths of shoulders. This lack of consistency can create hazards to all road users, as we shall better understand in our discussions to follow.

4.9.2 Shoulders: Cost and Space Constraints

It is often not a case of constructing a shoulder to the desired width, but of doing so within the limitations imposed by costs or the space available for road construction. This is identified in *A Policy on Geometric Design of Highways and Streets* as follows:

- *"Desirably, a vehicle stopped on the shoulder should clear the edge of the traveled way by at least 0.3 m [1 ft], and preferably by 0.6 m [2 ft]. These dimensions have led to the adoption of 3.0 m [10 ft] as the normal shoulder width that is preferred along higher speed, higher volume facilities. In difficult terrain and on low-volume highways, shoulders of this width may not be practical."[49]*

- *"Partial shoulders are sometimes used where full shoulders are unduly costly, such as on long (over 60 m [200 ft]) bridges or in mountainous terrain."[50]*

- *"It is not always economically practical to provide wide shoulders continuously along the highway, especially where the alignment passes through deep rock cuts or where other conditions limit the cross-section width."[51]*

Road users need to recognize that shoulders may be narrower than desired because of constraints imposed by costs or space. These situations may exist on low-volume highways, on bridges, overpasses and in tunnels. They may also exist through rock cuts and in mountainous terrain. And, as we will see in section 4.9.4, these situations may also exist where guard rails or concrete barriers have been placed within the width of the shoulder. In all these situations, all road users must recognize the potential hazards arising from shoulders having restricted widths.

4.9.3 Shoulders: City Streets

We have already noted that many city streets do not have shoulders, which has implications for public safety. It is not uncommon for streets within rural areas to have deep ditches on either side of the roadway. These ditches can be filled with water and become death traps to anyone who fails to remain on the road surface. Here, a simple error can become fatal.

Vehicles parked beside busy streets can also create hazards, as they can severely restrict the visibility and prevent motorists, bicyclists and pedestrians from seeing each other. In such situations, all road users need to pay particular attention to their surroundings and to be especially cautious.

4.9.4 Shoulders: Guard Rails and Concrete Barriers

Guardrails, concrete barriers and similar structures are often placed beside a roadway to prevent motorists, especially, from unintentionally driving off the roadway. Unfortunately, in some jurisdictions, at least in Canada, these structures are frequently placed within the width of the shoulder, drastically reducing the usable width of shoulders, often at sudden and random locations. Such situations are strongly discouraged in the policies, recommendations and guidelines set out in the AASHTO's *A Policy on Geometric Design of Highways and Streets*, as follows:

- *"Where roadside barriers, walls, or other vertical elements are present, it is desirable to provide a graded shoulder wide enough that the vertical elements will be offset a minimum of 0.6 m [2 ft] from the outer edge of the usable shoulder."*[50]

- *"On low-volume roads, roadside barriers may be placed at the outer edge of the shoulder, however, a minimum clearance of 1.2 m [4 ft] should be provided from the traveled way to the barrier."*[50]

- *"Regardless of the width, a shoulder should be continuous."*[50]

- *"The shoulder should be constructed to a uniform width for relatively long stretches of roadway."*[52]

Having guardrails, concrete barriers or similar structures extend onto a shoulder is recognized as being hazardous to road users. Where such hazards exist, hopefully, in the long term, the responsible road agency will find ways to correct these problems. In the short term, we, as individuals using the highways, need to understand that structures extending onto the shoulders are hazardous and that we need to exercise particular caution in these situations.

4.9.5 Shoulders: Bicycle Lanes

Bicyclists are also a consideration in the design and construction of shoulders. In the U.S., *A Policy on Geometric Design of Highways and Streets* makes the following recommendations for high-volume, higher speed highways:

"Where bicycles are to be accommodated on the shoulder, a minimum paved width of 1.2 m [4 ft] should be used."[52]

Under the heading Accommodation of Cyclists in the *Geometric*

Design Guide for Canadian Roads (TAC Guide), the following recommendations and guidelines are set out:

- It is recommended bicyclists have an "envelope" of space 1.0 meter wide for basic riding requirements.[53]

- The *TAC Guide* further states: "Bicycle riders also need adequate clearances to fixed objects and to passing vehicles in addition to the 1.0 m envelope."[53] Specifically:
  - There should be a clearance of 1.0 m from the bicyclist's "envelope" to the edge of the shoulder, or a clearance of between 0.2—0.5 m "to wall, fence, barrier or other fixed object" bordering the shoulder.[54]
  - There should be a minimum clearance between the bicyclist's "envelope" and traffic lanes of 0.5 m for highway speeds of 60 km/h, 1.0 m for highway speeds of 80 km/h, and 1.5 m for highway speeds of 100 km/h.[54]

Regrettably, the bicycle lanes commonly provided along many of our streets and highways are narrower than recommended by design authorities in either the U.S. or Canada. The only short term solution to this problem is for bicyclists, as well as motorists, to recognize that this is unsatisfactory and very hazardous.

It is important for people to exercise and to ride bicycles, and for them to be able to do so in a user friendly environment. All road users should recognize that the road space provided for bicyclists is often far less than what is considered to be safe. It is only fair, therefore, that motorists show respect and caution when approaching bicyclists, something many motorists often fail to do. At the same time, bicyclists need to be equally considerate and respectful of motorists.

4.9.6 Summary: Shoulders

We have seen that shoulders, where they exist, are not standard. On city streets and even on some highways, there is often no shoulder at all. On bridges and tunnels, it is common for shoulders to be far narrower than those on the street, highway or freeway on either side of these structures. Especially in mountainous terrain or through rock cuts, shoulders may be narrower than in more open areas. Guardrails, concrete abutments and similar structures may be placed within the width of the shoulder, thereby creating restrictions to motorists, bicyclists and pedestrians. Shoulders may or may not be paved and they may not be wide enough to allow motorists to safely stop their vehicles fully off the traffic lanes. Further, the width of shoulders may or may not be sufficient for bicyclists or pedestrians to use safely and have adequate clearances from motor vehicle traffic. In addition, as we shall see in Chapter 6, "Hazards of Winter Driving," in spite of the importance of shoulders, it is not uncommon for shoulders to be unusable for long periods during winter months, due to highway winter maintenance practices.

We see that there are many hazardous features of shoulders including:

- inconsistent widths or no shoulder at all

- the possibility of concrete barriers and similar structures being placed within the shoulder

- reduced widths on many bridges, tunnels and through rock cuts

- the often inadequate width to allow motorists to pull off the highway safely

- the often inadequate width to properly accommodate bicyclists or pedestrians

- the frequent lack of proper winter maintenance to the shoulders (covered in Chapter 6).

All road users should fully understand the hazards that the shoulder on any street, highway or freeway may present. As individuals, our purpose is not to correct the shortfalls that created these hazards; rather, it is to recognize the features of shoulders that are inherently hazardous and to take preventive measures. Particularly when shoulders are less than ideal, road users need to proceed with greater caution, more attention and less speed.

4.10 Rumble Strips

Although motorists are expected to remain within their own traffic lane, drivers often stray unintentionally from their lane and drive onto the shoulder, into the lane of adjacent traffic or, on undivided roads, into the lane of approaching traffic. As a means of alerting drivers that they have strayed from their lane, many higher speed highways now have what are referred to as rumble strips along the edges of traffic lanes, including along the centerline of undivided highways and between the traffic lane and the shoulder of highways. Vehicles passing over these corrugated raised or grooved patterns on the pavement surface create sufficient noise and vibrations to alert drivers that they have strayed from their traffic lane. Rumble strips can also serve to warn bicyclists they are getting too close to the traffic lanes occupied by motor vehicles.

The simple fact that rumble strips are such a common feature of highways brings to our attention two highly significant issues about using shoulders:

1. It is not uncommon for drivers to stray unintentionally from their traffic lane and, in the process, to use the shoulder to extend the width of their lane.
2. Shoulders are an extremely important part of any highway because they help to increase the small margin for error that exists on our roads.

That rumble strips are in place on many highways confirms the need to ensure shoulders are as safe as possible, in summer and winter, since motorists often stray from their travel lanes, intentionally and unintentionally.

4.11 Roadside Hazards

The constant focus of our discussions is the risk of being involved in a traffic collision. Often when we think of collisions, we think of incidents wherein one vehicle collides with another vehicle, a motorcyclist or a pedestrian. However, many collisions result from vehicles leaving the roadway and striking natural or man-made hazards beside the road, referred to as roadside hazards. Natural roadside hazards include rivers, lakes or streams, trees, boulders, cliffs and rock faces. Man-made hazards include other vehicles (either moving or parked), telephone poles, buildings and structures such as bridges and tunnels. The consequences of a motorist, motorcyclist or bicyclist leaving the roadway and colliding with a roadside hazard are often extremely serious.

Of all the types of collisions, one of the most terrifying is a "head-on" collision, wherein a vehicle travelling in one direction collides with a vehicle travelling in the opposite direction. Head-on collisions are almost always very serious and often result in fatalities. Particularly on undivided streets and highways, motorists must be constantly attentive to the possibility that an on-coming vehicle may leave its lane and enter theirs. Similarly, drivers must constantly guard against their vehicle entering the lane of an approaching vehicle.

Highway authorities take various measures to reduce the risks of vehicles unintentionally leaving the roadway by providing, for example, guard rails and rumble strips. Divided highways are also of great benefit for preventing head-on collisions. As individuals, our best defence is to remain in control of our own vehicle at all times and to be attentive to others who may lose control of their vehicle. In adverse conditions, especially during winter months, the many problems that arise increase the potential for losing control of our vehicle and encountering a roadside hazard.

Roadside hazards are fundamental and inherent features of roads worldwide that threaten the safety of all road users. People using our streets and highways need to be aware of the threats that roadside hazards pose to their safety and well-being. The simplest error could result in a motorist, motorcyclist or bicyclist colliding with a roadside hazard, the penalty for which could be serious injury or death. The margin for error on our roadways is often extremely small.

4.12 Chapter Summary: Road Design and Operation

In this chapter we reviewed many, relatively complex subjects relating to the design and operation of our streets and highways. It is useful to review in point form the subjects we addressed in this chapter:

- Roadway Design and Intended Use
- Jurisdiction
- Geometric Design of Roads
- Speed Limits
    - Statutory Speed Limits
    - Posted Speed Limits
- Sight Distance and Stopping Sight Distance
    - Brake Reaction Time, or Perception and Reaction Time
    - Braking Distance
- Calculation of Stopping Sight Distance
    - Brake Reaction Distance
    - Braking Distance
    - Kinetic Energy
- Traffic Control Devices
- Widths of Traffic Lanes
- Shoulders
    - Shoulder Width
    - Cost and Space Constraints
    - City Streets
    - Guard Rails and Concrete Barriers
    - Bicycle Lanes
- Rumble Strips
- Roadside Hazards

Our review of these subjects provides us with invaluable insight into the complexities of road safety. Although it is generally accepted that human behaviour is at fault for many of the collisions, injuries and deaths occurring on our roads, we see there is far more to road safety than simply the inappropriate behaviour of some road users. As we are beginning to see, there are many features of our roads that can be inherently hazardous, including:

- posted speed limits
- sight distance and stopping sight distance
- kinetic energy of motor vehicles
- complexities of traffic control devices
- unregulated widths and features of many shoulders
- actual widths of bicycle lanes versus recommended widths
- roadside hazards that exist beside our streets and highways
- widths of traffic lanes (examined in detail in later chapters)

Unfortunately, rarely is the public advised or informed of the many hazards inherent to the very design and operation of our streets and highways. As we shall see in our following chapters, there are also hazards associated with motor vehicles and the standards to which our roads are maintained, especially in winter months. Failure to bring these matters to the public's attention is one of the fundamental problems with road safety in Canada and the U.S. How can the public defend themselves from hazards they do not properly understand? Clearly, they cannot. We hope this book will help provide the public, especially our youth, with a broader understanding of road safety than currently exists.

As individuals, we cannot change the ways that our roads are designed or operated, but we can at least understand the hazards associated with them, and to then conduct ourselves in a way that mitigates the risks these hazards present. The hazardous features of our roads reinforce our need to comply with the laws, rules and regulations governing their use.

In our next three chapters we shall review other components of road safety, including motor vehicles, highway maintenance and the behaviour of people using our roadways. Let us now explore the hazards associated with motor vehicles.

FIVE

Motor Vehicles

5.0 Introduction

In this chapter we shall focus primarily on the dimensions and weights of passenger vehicles and transport trucks. Our purpose is to identify how the physical features of these various types of vehicles potentially affect our safety on the roads. We make no attempt to analyze the technical features of motor vehicles, including seat belts, airbags, interior padding, braking systems, steering, suspension systems, transmissions, engines, tires and so forth. We shall proceed on the basis that all motor vehicles are similarly designed and manufactured.

In this chapter and throughout this book, when we refer to motor vehicles we are referring to either passenger vehicles or transport trucks, and do not include motorcycles, scooters or snowmobiles, unless stated otherwise.

5.1 Passenger Vehicles

5.1.1 Passenger Vehicles: Dimensions

In 2008 and 2009 a study of different vehicle dimensions was undertaken for the City of Calgary, Alberta to determine the optimum dimensions for parking stalls.[1] Bunt & Associates, conducted the study, as described:

"Bunt & Associates undertook a review of the current (2008 and 2009) vehicle fleet to establish an appropriate design vehicle for the Calgary market. In all, 3,225 vehicles models, comprising of 785 Cars, 1068 SUVs, 74 Minivans and 1298 Pick-up Trucks were analyzed. Based upon the selected sample size, a total of 289 vehicle lengths, 169 vehicle widths and 226 vehicle heights were analyzed."[2]

From the data gathered in this study, an average length, width and height of all types of passenger vehicles was determined, with the results shown on Table 5.1.[3] Of course, these are average dimensions, which means that many passenger vehicles will be somewhat shorter or longer than the average, wider or narrower, or a different height. For our purposes, these average dimensions give us an adequate understanding of the size of passenger vehicles. Anyone interested in the dimensions of their own vehicle may simply take their own measurements, or obtain them from manufacturer's specifications, often available in brochures or online.

Table 5.1: Average Passenger Vehicle Dimensions[3]

	Length	Width*	Height
Average (metric)	5.02 meters	1.98 meters	1.76 meters
Average (imperial)	16.5 feet	6.5 feet	5.75 feet

** Excludes added width resulting from exterior rear view mirrors.*

(Source: [metric dimensions] E. Dada and M. Furuya: Bunt & Associates. Parking Dimensions. The Canadian Parking Association. The Parker, Q2 2010. Table 2, page 2. http://canadianparking.ca/files/ParkingDimensions_eng.pdf)

One important consideration is whether the width includes or excludes the exterior rear view mirrors. This is a particularly significant consideration with transport trucks and, to a lesser extent, with passenger vehicles. Table 5.2 shows how much width is added to a sedan, SUV and pick-up truck when the exterior rear view mirrors are added, according to one manufacture's specifications. We see from these figures that including rear view mirrors increases the average width of a passenger vehicle by roughly 0.33 meter or just over one foot. We shall discuss the significance of this later in this chapter.

5.1.2 Passenger Vehicles: Weights

There are different weight classifications of vehicles, one of which is the vehicle's "curb weight." The curb weight of a vehicle is its weight as it comes off the assembly line, plus the added weight of the lubricants and fluids required to make the vehicle operable. It excludes the driver's weight and that of passengers or luggage.[4] The curb weights of three mid-sized passenger vehicles, obtained from the manufacturer's specifications, are shown in Table 5.2. We see from these figures that a very rough, average curb weight of a passenger vehicle is just over 2,000 kilograms, approximately 4,500 pounds.

Table 5.2: Weights Of Mid-Sized Passenger Vehicles and Added Width With Rear View Mirrors

	Vehicle Curb Weight	Added Width With Rear View Mirrors
2013 Ford Taurus (Sedan)[5]		
Approx. (imperial)	4,035 lb.	10 in.
Approx. (metric)*	1,832 kg	0.25 m
2013 Ford Explorer (SUV)[6]		
Approx. (imperial)	4,534 lb.	11 in.
Approx. (metric)*	2,058 kg	0.28 m
2013 Ford-150 (Pick-up)		
Approx. (imperial)	4,925 lb.[7]	18 in.[8]
Approx. (metric)*	2,236 kg	0.46 m
Average Weight (imperial)	4,498 lb.	13 in. (average)
Average Weight (metric)*	2,042 kg	0.33 m (average)

*Converted from imperial units, see Conversion Factors, Chapter 3, Table 3.1

(Source: 2013 Ford Taurus, 2013 Ford Explorer, 2013 Ford-150. Courtesy Ford Motor Company.)

5.1.3 Summary: Passenger Vehicles

Table 5.3 summarizes the average dimensions and weights of passenger vehicles, according to the information we have gathered. It includes the average width of passenger vehicles with and without rear view mirrors.

Table 5.3: Average Dimensions and Weights of Passenger Vehicles[*]

Average Passenger Vehicle Length:	5.0 m	16.5 ft.
Average Passenger Vehicle Width:		
Excluding Exterior Rear View Mirrors:	2.0 m	6.5 ft.
Including Exterior Rear View Mirrors:	2.3 m	7.6 ft.
Average Passenger Vehicle Height:	1.8 m	5.8 ft.
Average Passenger Vehicle Weight:[**]	2,040 kg	4,500 lb.

Information taken from Tables 5.1 and 5.2, figures rounded.
**Curb Weight*

5.2 Transport Trucks

Transport trucks have a dominating presence on many of our roads, so it is important that we understand the implications of the relative sizes and weights of these vehicles. Let us begin by examining some of the regulations pertaining to these often massive vehicles.

5.2.1 Transport Trucks: Regulatory Authority

Regulations in Canada and the U.S. governing the allowable sizes and weights of transport trucks are explained in the following brief summaries:

Canada:

"The provinces and territories have authority for establishing vehicle weight and dimension limits on roads within their jurisdiction (except federal owned roads in national parks, national defense installations etc.). The

provincial and territorial governments also have authority for issuing special permits for oversize and/or overweight loads, movement of selected commodities and other permit provisions which depart from normally regulated limits."[9]

United States:

"In the United States the federal government has authority for mandating minimum and/or maximum size and weight limits for vehicles travelling on the Interstate system and minimum size limits on other portions of the state highway systems on the national truck network."[10]

"The state governments have full responsibility for establishing size and weight limits for highways within their jurisdiction which are not part of the national truck network."[10]

The regulations governing the dimensions and weights of transport trucks include many complexities. This is well identified in a report titled *Heavy Truck Weight and Dimension Limits in Canada,* as follows:

"The regulation of heavy truck weights and dimensions is one of the most complex areas of transportation regulation. Attempting to summarize in a meaningful way the weight and dimension limits of heavy trucks is extremely difficult."[11]

In spite of the difficulty to "summarize in a meaningful way" the weights and dimensions of transport trucks, it is important for us to attempt to do so. Transport trucks often make up a significant percentage of the traffic on our roadways and they are often driven at high speeds in an aggressive manner, by drivers intent upon reaching their destinations on schedule. To properly assess the threat transport trucks present to those using the highways, it is important to understand the sizes and weights of these commercial vehicles.

5.2.2. Transport Trucks: Dimensions, Weights and Number of Axles

Some transport trucks are essentially just large vans where the driver's cabin and cargo carrying part of the vehicle are on the same frame (chassis). Other transport trucks consist of a separate truck (or tractor) which may be connected to one, two or even three trailers. There are infinite tractor-trailer combinations, all resulting in significantly different variations in especially the lengths and weights.

Due to the large variations in the lengths and weights of transport trucks, averaging them would indeed have little significance to our discussions. Therefore, for us to come to an understanding of their sizes, we need to examine several of the most common configurations of these vehicles. One convenient source of information is the report *Heavy Truck Weight and Dimension Limits for Interprovincial Operations in Canada.*[12] This publication identifies the maximum dimensions and weights of several configurations of transport vehicles commonly used throughout Canada. Although these dimensions and weights may exceed regulatory limits for some provinces or states in Canada or the U.S., they provide us with a useful guide on the general maximum sizes and weights of transport trucks. This publication shall therefore be our main source of information on this subject.

As we proceed to examine the dimensions and weights of transport vehicles, we need to do so with a note of caution that the figures are not "carved in stone." Regulations allow for special permits to be issued for oversize and/or overweight loads. In addition, certain provincial, state or federal regulations in Canada or the U.S. may allow vehicles to exceed the sizes and weights of the transport trucks we examine. The configurations of trucks we examine are therefore approximations of the larger vehicles allowed on highways throughout Canada and the U.S.

Tables 5.4 through 5.7 provide us with the dimensions and weights of four configurations of transport trucks: "Straight Trucks," which are simply large vans where the engine, cabin and cargo carrying portion of the vehicle are one unit; "Tractor Semitrailers," where the truck or tractor pulls one trailer; "B Train Doubles," where the truck or tractor pulls two trailers; and "Long Combination Vehicles (LCVs) - Turnpike Doubles," which are extra-length vehicles intended for transporting large volumes of lighter products. The information for the first three configurations is taken from the report *Heavy Truck Weight and Dimension Limits for Interprovincial Operations in Canada*.[12] Information for the fourth configuration, Turnpike Double, is taken from British Columbia's "Long Combination Vehicles Program," which specifies the maximum length and weight for this classification of transport truck.[13]

5.2.2.1 Transport Trucks: Width

Tables 5.4 through 5.7 reveal that the width of each configuration of transport truck is the same, that being 2.6 meters (8 feet 6 inches). In fact, regulations throughout Canada place a limit of 2.6 meters on motor vehicles.[14] In the U.S., federal regulations also place a maximum width of 2.6 meters or 102 inches (8 feet-6 inches) on commercial motor vehicles using the National Network of highways.[15] This is the width that is normally allowed for transport trucks, but it must be remembered there may be exceptions or special permits that allow for wider loads.[15, 9]

Of great importance is that the width of 2.6 meters does not include exterior rear view mirrors.[16, 17] In Canada, rear view mirrors may extend 30 cm (12 inches) beyond each side of the regulated width of a motor vehicle.[16] Although federal regulations in the U.S. do not appear to be specific with the maximum distance rear view mirrors may extend, the State of California is clear on this matter, limiting mirrors to extend a maximum of 10 inches (approximately 25 cm) from either side of a vehicle.[18]

Exterior rear view mirrors are, of course, solid objects. On the highways, truck drivers, especially, must allow for the added width of mirrors both on their vehicles and on those of oncoming or adjacent vehicles. Rear view mirrors effectively increase the standard width of transport trucks in Canada from 2.6 meters to as much as 3.2 meters, and slightly less in states such as California, where exterior mirrors may only extend 10 inches. We shall discuss the implications of this more fully, later.

Table 5.4: Dimensions and Weights: Straight Truck

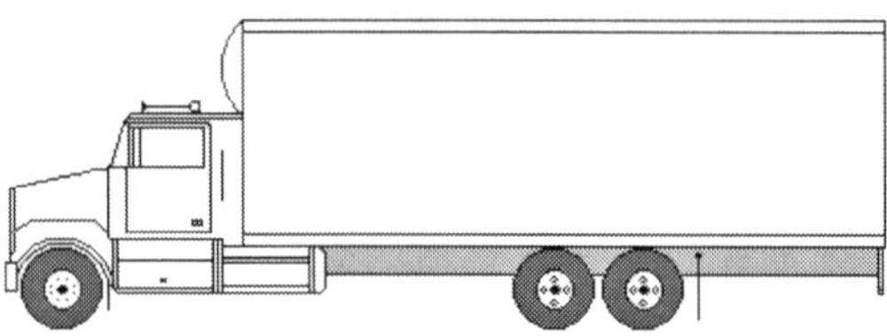

Straight Truck (with 3 axles)[19]

Maximum Overall Width: 2.6 meters*
Maximum Overall Height: 4.15 meters
Maximum Overall Length: 12.5 meters
Maximum Gross Vehicle Weight: 24,250 kg with 3 axles.
*Excludes the added width of exterior rear view mirrors.

(Source: Council of Ministers and Deputy Ministers Responsible of Transportation and Highway Safety. Heavy Truck Weight and Dimension Limits for Interprovincial Operations in Canada. Summary Information, December 2011. Straight Truck, pages 18–19.)

Table 5.5: Dimensions and Weights: Tractor Semitrailer

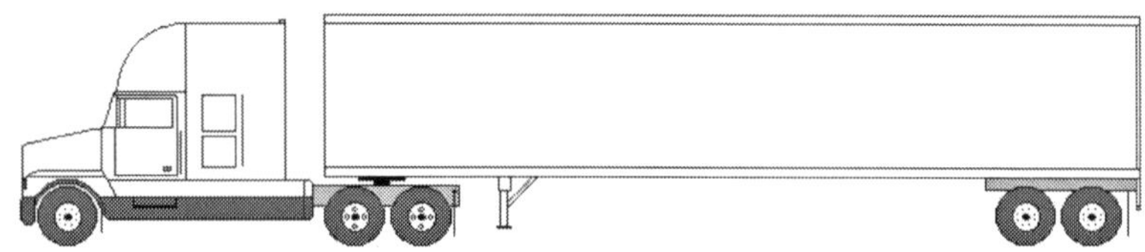

Tractor Semitrailer (with 5 axles)[20]

Maximum Overall Width: 2.6 meters*
Maximum Overall Height: 4.15 meters
Maximum Overall Length: 23 meters
Maximum Gross Vehicle Weight: 39,500 kg with 5 axles.
*Excludes the added width of exterior rear view mirrors.

(Source: Council of Ministers and Deputy Ministers Responsible of Transportation and Highway Safety. Heavy Truck Weight and Dimension Limits for Interprovincial Operations in Canada. Summary Information, December 2011. Tractor Semitrailer, pages 10-11.)

Table 5.6: Dimensions and Weights: B Train Double

B Train Double (with 8 axles)[21]

Maximum Overall Width: 2.6 meters*
Maximum Overall Height: 4.15 meters
Maximum Overall Length: 25 meters
Maximum Gross Vehicle Weight: 62,500 kg with 8 axles.
*Excludes the added width of exterior rear view mirrors.

(Source: Council of Ministers and Deputy Ministers Responsible of Transportation and Highway Safety. Heavy Truck Weight and Dimension Limits for Interprovincial Operations in Canada. Summary Information, December 2011. B Train Double, pages 14-15.)

Table 5.7: Dimensions and Weights: LCV-Turnpike Double

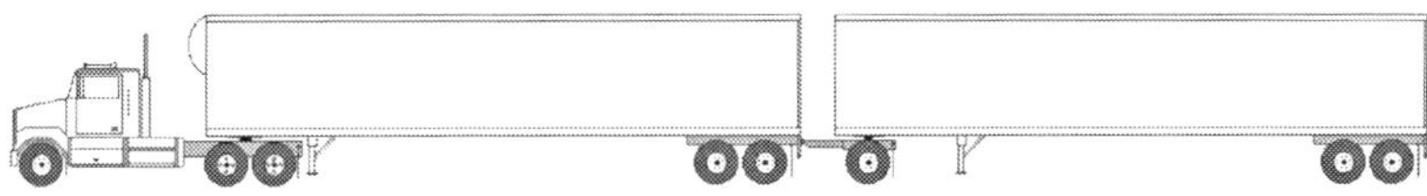

Turnpike Double (with 8 or more axles)[13]

Maximum Overall Width: 2.6 meters*[22]
Maximum Overall Height: 4.15 meters[23]
Maximum Overall Length: 41 meters[13]
Maximum Gross Vehicle Weight: 63,500 kg with 8 or more axles.[13]
*Excludes the added width of exterior rear view mirrors.

(Sources: Width and Height: Province of BC. Commercial Transport Act. Commercial Transport Regulations © Queen's Printer, Victoria, British Columbia, Canada. Page 13. Accessed September 25, 2012. http://www.bclaws.ca/EPLibraries/bclaws_new/document/ID/freeside/30_78

Length and weight: BC Ministry of Transportation and Infrastructure. Long Combination Vehicles Program Weights and Dimensions. Turnpike Doubles. Page 2. Accessed September 25, 2012. http://www.th.gov.bc.ca/cvse/LCV/weights_dimensions.htm)

5.2.2.2 Transport Trucks: Height

Referring to the various configurations of transport trucks shown in Tables 5.4 through 5.7, we see the maximum height of each vehicle configuration is 4.15 meters. This is the standard limit for the height of transport trucks in most of Canada.[14] In the U.S., regulations governing the height of commercial motor vehicles (CMVs) are as follows:

> *"There is no Federal height requirement for CMVs. Thus, States may set their own height restrictions. Most height limits range from 13 feet, 6 inches (4.11 meters) to 14 feet (4.27 meters), with exceptions granted for lower clearance on particular roads."*[24]

As with the width of transport trucks, we see that the height of these vehicles is similar throughout Canada and the U.S.

5.2.2.3 Transport Trucks: Length and Weight

Whereas the width and height of transport vehicles are generally consistent in Canada and the U.S., the lengths or weights of these vehicles vary considerably, making the subject highly complex. However, it is not necessary for us to get into these complexities. Rather, it is adequate to simply refer to the four truck configurations we have been examining to provide us with the information we need on the approximate maximum dimensions and weights of commercial motor vehicles.

The lengths and weights of the four configurations of transport trucks shown in Tables 5.4 through 5.7 are summarized in Table 5.8. The summary includes the number of axles for each truck configuration. Let us examine why the number of axles on transport trucks is significant.

5.2.2.4 Transport Trucks: Number of Axles

Whereas most passenger vehicles have only two axles and a total of four tires with one tire on the end of each axle, transport trucks can have eight or more axles and often have two tires on each end of each axle. The exception to this is the steering axle under the cabin portion of the truck that normally has only one tire on each end of that axle. A transport truck with five axles often has 18 tires. A transport truck with eight axles often has a total of 30 tires.

The main significance of the number of axles is the number of wheels that throw water, slush or snow onto adjacent or oncoming vehicles. The longer a transport truck and the greater the number of axles, the worse this problem becomes when the truck passes us or as we pass it. Now let us refer to Table 5.8 "Summary of Transport Truck Lengths, Weights and Number of Axles."

Table 5.8 highlights the *range* in the lengths and weights of various configurations of transport trucks.

Table 5.8: Summary of Transport Truck Lengths, Weights and Number of Axles*

Configuration	Length	Weight (GVW)	# of Axles
Straight Truck*	12.5 m (41.0 ft.)	24,250 kg (53,500 lb.)	3
Tractor Semitrailer*	23 m (75.5 ft.)	39,500 kg (87,100 lb.)	5
B Train Double*	25 m (82.0 ft.)	62,500 kg (137,800 lb.)	8
LCV-Turnpike Double*	41 m (134.5 ft.)	63,500 kg (140,000 lb.)	8 or more

Metric Information from Tables 5.4, 5.5, 5.6 and 5.7. Conversion to Imperial Units using factors from Table 3.1, Chapter 3. Figures rounded.

Even the smaller Straight Truck with three axles may be over 12 meters long (over 40 feet) and weigh, with cargo (Gross Vehicle Weight or GVW), in the order of 24,000 kg or 24 metric tonnes (roughly 26.5 imperial tons). The commonly used five-axle Tractor Semitrailer is almost twice the length of a Straight Truck with a GVW just less than 40,000 kg. The B Train Double, with eight axles, may be marginally longer than a five-axle Tractor Semitrailer, but could have a GVW approaching 62.5 metric tonnes. The Turnpike Double, a Long Combination Vehicle with eight or more axles and built to carry bulky but lighter cargo, can be over 40 meters long (roughly 135 feet) with a weight similar to the maximum GVW of the B Train Double.

All these dimensions, weights and numbers of axles can become a bit bewildering. However, there is one important message: transport trucks are massive in comparison to the sizes and weights of passenger vehicles. We now need to evaluate the information we have gathered on the dimensions and weights of passenger vehicles and transport trucks.

5.3 Significance of Dimensions and Weights of Motor Vehicles

Table 5.9 (a) provides the dimensions and weights of passenger vehicles and transport trucks in metric units, while Table 5.9 (b) provides this information in imperial units.

Table 5.9 (a): Summary of Motor Vehicle Dimensions and Weights[*]

Metric Units					
Motor Vehicle	Width meters	Height meters	Length meters	Overall Size cu.m	Weight kg
Passenger Vehicles (Averages)	2.0	1.8	5.0	18	2,040
Straight Truck	2.6	4.15	12.5	135	24,250
Tractor Semitrailer	2.6	4.15	23	248	39,500
B Train Double	2.6	4.15	25	270	62,500
LCV (Turnpike Double)	2.6	4.15	41	442	63,500

Information from Tables 5.3 through 5.8. Overall size = width x height x length.

Table 5.9 (b): Summary of Motor Vehicle Dimensions and Weights[*]

Imperial Units					
Motor Vehicle	Width feet	Height feet	Length feet	Overall Size Cu.ft.	Weight lb.
Passenger Vehicles (Averages)	6.5	5.8	16.5	622	4,500
Straight Truck	8.5	13.6	41.0	4,740	53,500
Tractor Semitrailer	8.5	13.6	75.5	8,728	87,100
B Train Double	8.5	13.6	82.0	9,480	137,800
LCV (Turnpike Double)	8.5	13.6	134.5	15,548	140,000

Passenger vehicle data taken from Table 5.3. Truck data converted from Table 5.9 (a) to imperial units using conversion factors from Table 3.1 Chapter 3. (1 m = 3.281ft.; 1 kg = 2.205 lbs.) Overall size = width x height x length.

Included in these tables is a column identifying the Overall Size of each vehicle—simply the multiplication of the vehicle's width, height and length. This measurement gives us an additional perspective of the relative sizes of different vehicle classifications.

With the information provided in these tables we are now in a position to examine how the dimensions and weights of passenger vehicles and transport trucks relate to road safety.

5.3.1 Significance of Overall Sizes and Weights of Motor Vehicles

Our first observation about the dimensions and weights of motor vehicles shown in Tables 5.9 (a) and (b) is the monstrous sizes and weights of transport trucks, especially when compared to passenger vehicles. Transport trucks are 8 to 25 times the overall size of the average passenger vehicle and can be 12 to 30 times its weight. At any speed, transport trucks have the potential to cause immense damage to anything in their path. Any collision between any vehicle and a transport truck has the potential for devastating consequences. It is vitally important for passenger vehicle drivers to stay well clear of transport trucks. At the same time, it is essential for transport truck drivers to avoid taking advantage of the size and weight of their vehicles.

It must also be observed that even though passenger vehicles are much smaller and lighter, they are capable of causing terrible damage to occupants or anything in their path at virtually any speed. Seat belts, airbags and other safety features of passenger vehicles do not eliminate the risks of injury or death in collisions, they only reduce them. Motorcyclists, bicyclists and pedestrians are especially vulnerable in a collision with any passenger vehicle and even more so with a transport truck. As we learned in Chapter 3, our delicate human bodies are not designed to withstand an impact from a motor vehicle.

In the ideal world, passenger vehicles would not be required to share roads with transport trucks, but this is unlikely to happen. As individuals, our best defense is to be constantly aware of the sizes and weights of passenger vehicles and transport trucks and of the destruction they are capable of causing. Every motor vehicle should be considered hazardous at any speed, especially if it is not being driven properly and safely.

5.3.2 Significance of Motor Vehicle Width

Our first observation is that transport trucks are considerably wider than the average passenger vehicle. We see that transport trucks are 2.6 meters wide compared to passenger vehicles that are approximately 2 meters wide. Transport trucks are therefore roughly 30% wider than the average passenger vehicle. This percentage becomes even greater when the exterior rear view mirrors are included.

The greatest significance of the widths of passenger vehicles and transport trucks is the amount of space they occupy within the limited widths of traffic lanes. In section 4.8 of Chapter 4, we reviewed the widths of traffic lanes and saw that in Canada and the U.S. they vary according to the intended use of the roadway. Lower volume, lower speed roads with little to no truck traffic are generally about 3.0 meters wide.[25, 26] Modern highways and freeways intended for higher speed, higher volume traffic usually have traffic lanes 3.6 meters wide in the U.S. and 3.7 meters in Canada.[25, 26]

Table 5.10 shows the widths of motor vehicles in comparison to the widths of traffic lanes. Note that the widths of the motor vehicles shown in Table 5.10 do not include the added width of exterior rear view mirrors for either passenger vehicles or transport trucks.

Table 5.10: Widths of Motor Vehicles and Traffic Lanes

(a) Lower volume, lower speed roads with little to no truck traffic

Vehicle	Vehicle Width[*]	Lane Width[**]
Passenger Vehicles	2.0 m (6.5 ft.)	
	}	3.0 m (10.0 ft.)
Transport Trucks	2.6 m (8.5 ft.)	

(b) Higher volume, higher speed, principal arterials

Vehicle	Vehicle Width[*]	Lane Width[**]
Passenger Vehicles	2.0 m (6.5 ft.)	
	}	3.6/3.7 m (12.0 ft.)
Transport Trucks	2.6 m (8.5 ft.)	

*Vehicle Width taken from Tables 5.9 (a) and 5.9 (b). Widths exclude exterior rear view mirrors.

(**Source: Lane Width: Transportation Association of Canada (TAC). Geometric Design Guide for Canadian Roads. Table 2.2.2.1 and 2.2.2.3, pages 2.2.2.1 and 2.2.2.2. From A Policy on Geometric Design of Highways and Streets, 6th Edition, 2011, by the American Association of State Highway and Transportation Officials, Washington, DC. Section 4.3, page 4–7. Used by permission.) See also Chapter 4, section 4.8.

The widths of both passenger vehicles and transport trucks in comparison to the widths of traffic lanes are fundamental to our safety on the roads and it is therefore important for us to examine this subject thoroughly.

5.3.2.1 Motor Vehicles in Narrow Traffic Lanes

5.3.2.1a Passenger Vehicles

Referring to Table 5.10, passenger vehicles have an average width of around 2.0 meters, excluding exterior rear view mirrors, compared to lane widths of 3.0 meters on lower volume, lower speed roads with little to no truck traffic. This means that traffic lanes on narrower roadways are approximately one meter wider than the average passenger vehicle. If a passenger vehicle is in the center of a 3.0-meter-wide lane, there will be roughly 0.5 meters, less than 2 feet, of space on either side of that vehicle within the traffic lane.

Since we are reviewing lower speed, lower volume roads, let us consider the speed of a passenger vehicle travelling at 50 km/h (roughly 30 mi./hr.). As we saw in Chapter 3, Table 3.2 (a) and (b), a vehicle travelling at 50 km/h is travelling at 13.9 meters per second. A vehicle travelling at 30 mi./hr. is travelling at 44 feet per second. With only 0.5 meters of space on either side of a passenger vehicle within a 3.0-meter-wide traffic lane, it takes but a fraction of a second for a vehicle travelling at 13.9 meters per second to veer into a line of parked vehicles, into oncoming traffic, or into pedestrians or bicyclists beside the road. We see, therefore, that on municipal streets, travelling at speed limits common for such areas, the widths of passenger vehicles combined with the widths of traffic lanes allows very little room for error and very little time for drivers to recover from either their own errors, or those of others. At the speeds commonly travelled, the margin for error is very small for passenger vehicles on city streets.

5.3.2.1b Transport Trucks

On occasion, transport trucks travel on city streets. However, as we have seen, transport trucks are 2.6 meters wide and city streets are generally only 3.0 meters wide. Allowing for exterior rear view mirrors extending upwards to 0.3 meters from either side, transport trucks have an effective width of up to 3.2 meters. The effective width of transport trucks is therefore wider than the traffic lanes on many city streets. From a safety perspective, motorists, pedestrians and cyclists need to be very attentive anytime they encounter a transport truck on any city street. There is essentially no margin for error when transport trucks are driven on city streets.

5.3.2.2 Motor Vehicles in Wider Traffic Lanes

5.3.2.2a. Passenger Vehicles

On higher speed, higher volume highways, traffic lanes are commonly 3.6 to 3.7 meters (12 feet) wide in the U.S. and Canada respectively, compared to passenger vehicles, which are on average, approximately 2.0 meters (approx. 6.5 feet) wide. When centered in wider traffic lanes, passenger vehicles have less than 1 meter (approx. 3 feet) on either side, excluding exterior rear view mirrors.

We again refer to the speeds vehicles are travelling at, but in this case, since we are examining lane widths on higher speed highways, we need to consider speeds in the range of 100 km/h or, say, 60 mi./hr. Referring to Tables 3.2 (a) and (b) in Chapter 3, we see that at 100 km/h a vehicle is travelling at 28 m/s, or 88 ft./sec. at 60 mi./hr. With less than 1 m of space on either side of a passenger vehicle on 3.6- or 3.7-meter-wide traffic lanes, it again takes but a fraction of a second at normal highway speeds for drivers of passenger vehicles to veer onto a shoulder, into an adjacent traffic lane or into oncoming traffic.

From a safety perspective, the added width on 3.6- or 3.7-meter traffic lanes on higher speed, higher volume highways does not necessarily reduce the risks of collisions, since the speed is usually so much greater than on streets with narrower lanes. Again, even on highways with wider lanes, there is very little time and very little space to correct for any errors made by anyone. In but a fraction of a second, any error can turn into a disaster. Compounding the hazards on higher speed highways is the presence of transport trucks, which occupy most of the width of their traffic lanes.

The margin for error for passenger vehicles on highways and freeways is very small.

5.3.2.2b Transport Trucks

Although traffic lanes 3.6 to 3.7 meters (12 feet) wide are intended for higher speed, higher volume traffic, including truck traffic, we immediately see that there is barely room for transport trucks, even in these wider traffic lanes. As we noted previously, regulations allow exterior rear view mirrors to extend from either side of transport trucks by as much as 0.3 meters (12 inches) in Canada and slightly less (10 inches) in states such as California. This brings the effective width of transport trucks to as much as 3.2 meters (10.5 feet) compared to the 3.6 to 3.7 meter (12 feet) width of traffic lanes on higher speed, higher volume highways. At these effective widths, transport trucks almost totally occupy the full width of traffic lanes on our highways and freeways. Especially when two transport trucks are side by side on a highway, either travelling in the same direction or in opposite directions, their drivers must make room for one another. This forces truck drivers to hug the outside of their respective traffic lane and, as a result, places these massive vehicles very close to the space normally occupied by other motorists, motorcyclists, pedestrians or bicyclists.

Clearly, the width of transport trucks is a significant risk to people using the highways. Again, as with passenger vehicles, there is very little time and very little space for errors on the highways, especially when transport trucks are involved.

5.3.3 Significance of Motor Vehicle Height

Transport trucks have a maximum height of 4.15 meters. Passenger vehicles have an average height of roughly 1.8 meters. This makes transport trucks close to 2½ times the height of the average passenger vehicle and raises several significant safety considerations.

5.3.3.1 Water, Slush or Snow Thrown from Tires

- The lower a vehicle, the more a driver's visibility is affected by water, slush or snow thrown from the wheels of adjacent or oncoming vehicles. Conversely, the higher a vehicle the less a driver's visibility is affected by these occurrences.

- The height of the cabin portion of transport trucks helps place drivers above the height the water, slush or snow are normally thrown from the wheels of adjacent or oncoming vehicles. Transport truck drivers are therefore less affected by these adverse conditions and may not find it necessary to reduce their speed to the same extent as people driving (lower) passenger vehicles. This could result in transport trucks constantly overtaking passenger vehicles during adverse conditions. In such situations, passenger vehicle drivers will have to choose between driving faster than they are comfortable with, or suffering the problems created when transport trucks pass them, throwing water, slush or snow from their tires onto the windshields of the much smaller passenger vehicles.

5.3.3.2 Visibility

- The height of a vehicle may restrict the visibility of others using the highways. The higher the vehicle, the greater the risk of it obstructing the visibility of others.

- The height of transport trucks can obscure the driver's ability to see pedestrians in front of them, as New York City's experience demonstrates:

"Because of the height of large trucks, it can be difficult for truck drivers to see what is happening directly in front of their vehicles. This has contributed to a significant number of pedestrian deaths in New York City."[27]

5.3.3.3 Height of Undercarriages (Chassis) of Transport Trucks

- One terrifying feature of many transport trucks is that their undercarriages or chassis are often exposed and are a great risk to people in passenger vehicles if a collision occurs. The problem is that the undercarriages of transport trucks are sufficiently high to allow for the lower portions of many passenger vehicles to fit beneath the framework of the truck in either rear-end or side collisions. If a passenger vehicle runs into the back or side of a transport truck, unless the truck is protected with an end or side guard, the windshield and upper portion of the smaller vehicle will experience the full impact of the collision, as the lower portion of the vehicle slides beneath the undercarriage of the truck—with dreadful consequences. Some, but not all trucks are equipped with guards to reduce these hazards. As individuals, all we can do is to be aware that these hazards exist and keep our distance, as best we can, from all transport trucks.

5.3.3.4 Center of Gravity and Rollover

- Very often, the higher a vehicle the higher its center of gravity will be, making it potentially more susceptible to rollovers on the highway. Because of the seriousness of rollovers, the National Highway Traffic Safety Administration (NHTSA) has developed a rating system for the rollover potential of vehicles as a part of its "New Car Assessment Program" (NCAP). The NHTSA states the following:

> *"The National Highway Traffic Safety Administration's New Car Assessment Program (NCAP) created the 5-Star Safety Ratings Program to provide consumers with information about the crash protection and rollover safety of new vehicles beyond what is required by Federal Law. One star is the lowest rating; 5 stars is the highest. More stars equal safer cars."*[28]

The NHTSA has a website that allows individuals to check the rollover rating of their vehicle, provided it is a 1990 model or newer. The site is: http://www.safercar.gov/Safety+Ratings

Motorists should refer to this site to determine the rollover rating for the vehicle they drive or intend to purchase. The potential for motor vehicles to rollover is yet another of the many hazards to road users.

5.3.4 Significance of Motor Vehicle Length

The lengths of motor vehicles can have serious implications for our safety on the roadways, as follows:

- On roads with one lane only in each direction, it can be very difficult and very dangerous to pass transport trucks. We see from the information in Tables 5.9 (a) and (b) that Straight Trucks are at least twice as long as the average passenger vehicle; Tractor Semitrailers and B Train Doubles are more than four times as long and the exceptionally long Turnpike Doubles are approximately eight times as long. Passing a transport truck not only takes more time than passing a much shorter passenger vehicle, but it also requires a longer distance. This makes it imperative for motorists to be able to quickly assess the time and distance required to pass the particular configuration of transport truck ahead.

- When passing longer vehicles, drivers must be careful not to allow their speeds to become excessive in the often limited distance and time available to pass these vehicles.

- Yet another problem related to the length of transport trucks is the number of axles. As Table 5.8 shows, some transport trucks have eight axles or more, with the outer tires from each axle all potentially throwing water, slush or snow onto an adjacent or passing vehicle. This can severely reduce motorists' visibility, possibly for extended periods of time. Given the limited width of traffic lanes and the amount of space occupied by motor vehicles, reduced visibility can be extremely hazardous, especially when travelling at higher speeds beside mammoth transport trucks. Motorists should take every precautionary measure possible to avoid such situations.

- Many passenger vehicles have the capacity to pull trailers, which can significantly add to the vehicle's overall length. Passing passenger vehicles pulling trailers can pose many of the same problems as passing transport trucks.

- Motorists driving passenger vehicles pulling trailers may lack experience in operating long vehicles. These drivers need to recognize their lack of experience and take precautions accordingly. This could particularly apply to senior citizens who, in their retirement, purchase or rent large motor homes for the first time and venture onto the highways in situations they are unfamiliar. Others using the highways should recognize that motor homes and passenger vehicles pulling trailers may be driven by drivers who lack experience.

5.4 Miscellaneous Motor-Vehicle-Related Hazards

In addition to the hazards arising from the dimensions, weights and numbers of axles of motor vehicles, there are several miscellaneous features of motor vehicles that could also affect the safety of those using our streets and highways.

5.4.1 Convertibles

Convertibles with fabric tops leave occupants very exposed, should the vehicle be in a major collision such as a rollover. Of course, this applies particularly when the top is in the retracted position, although it could also apply when the top is closed. Some convertibles have retractable metal tops that likely offer greater protection when closed. In our personal check lists of ways to reduce our risks of injury or death on the highways, we certainly need to include the added risks of being in a convertible.

5.4.2. Power

The engines of many passenger vehicles have tremendous power, allowing vehicles to accelerate rapidly and to attain high rates of speed within short periods of time. Although high powered vehicles appeal to many motorists, these vehicles need to be used with great respect and caution. Excessive power can easily cause a driver to lose control of their vehicle when accelerating too rapidly. Excessive power can also allow drivers to quickly attain speeds far in excess of the posted speed limits. When overtaking and passing a vehicle, motorists driving high powered vehicles need to take particular care that they do not gain too much speed while passing. When the road surface is covered with ice, snow, slush or water, excessive power can be especially hazardous, even to experienced drivers. During adverse road conditions, too much power applied to the drive system can easily cause tires to lose traction and drivers to lose control of their vehicles.

Whenever a person purchases a vehicle they should consider that excessive power could be hazardous. Purchasing a muscle car for a son or daughter's high school graduation gift could prove to be the worst gift imaginable.

5.4.3 Speed

As obvious as it may seem, we would be remiss not to specifically stress that every motor vehicle is hazardous to all road users, simply because it moves. The larger, the heavier and the faster a vehicle moves, the more hazardous it potentially becomes.

5.4.4 The Deadly Comforts of Motor Vehicles

There are many very attractive and appealing features of modern motor vehicles. However, several of these features could also prove to be hazardous to the unwary. The following are some vehicle luxuries that could result in drivers becoming drowsy, falling asleep or becoming inattentive to their driving:

- beautifully designed interiors with upholstery of the finest quality, with seats that are usually adjustable to anyone's liking and are frequently heated

- wonderful sound systems that help drivers relax after a hard day at the office

- sound-proofing that makes the noises from outside the vehicle muffled and quiet

- good suspension systems that allow occupants to travel very smoothly over most road surfaces

- cruise control, which should never be used in adverse road or weather conditions or when the driver is feeling tired.

It is the often luxurious, comfortable interiors of vehicles that can easily lull drivers into a false sense of security. Everything within a vehicle can seem perfect, thereby insulating and isolating drivers and passengers from the harsh realities associated with high speeds, congested roads or adverse conditions. Any of these features could easily prove to be hazardous, unless used wisely.

5.4.5 Turbulence

The movement of a vehicle disturbs the air, causing turbulence. Generally, the larger a vehicle and the faster it is travelling, the greater the turbulence it creates. On gravel roads, this turbulence is often sufficient to create enough dust to seriously affect the visibility of other motorists using the highway. If the highway is covered with water or snow, especially dry snow, the turbulence often creates a plume or cloud of spray or snow beside, behind and above the vehicle, which could engulf approaching, adjacent or following vehicles. Such situations can be extremely dangerous.

As an object moves through the air, the disturbed air can be similar to a sudden and unexpected gust of wind sufficient to shake another vehicle, or to cause a bicyclist or pedestrian to lose balance. The turbulence created by vehicles can also cause dust, dirt or rocks to be tossed into the air and into the faces and eyes of pedestrians or bicyclists. This turbulence can also cause gravel to fly into the windshields of adjacent or approaching vehicles.

Overall, the turbulence created by vehicles should be recognized as being one of the many hazards created by motor vehicles of all sizes.

5.5 Chapter Summary: Motor Vehicles

Our review and analysis of motor vehicles explains why all motor vehicles are potentially a threat to our safety. Motor vehicles are large, powerful machines capable of doing incredible damage if involved in a collision. The human body is no match for the size, weight and composition of any motor vehicle. At the same time passenger vehicles are no match for the sizes and weights of transport trucks.

Especially, we see many hazards associated with transport trucks. Transport trucks can dominate our roadways with their often immense size and weight. We can see that the sizes and weights of transport trucks make it essential for motorists to be cautious whenever these large vehicles are present. At the same time, drivers of transport trucks must recognize the vulnerability of the much smaller passenger vehicles. There is every opportunity for the drivers of transport trucks to become bullies on our roadways, since other road users are virtually defenseless against their actions. Courtesy and consideration are of paramount importance to sharing public roadways. This applies to all road users.

We must understand that:

- As soon as a motor vehicle begins to move, it has the potential to inflict damage to anything or anyone in its path. Any collision involving a motor vehicle is potentially serious.

- The larger a motor vehicle and the faster it is moving:
  - the greater the impact will be to anyone involved in a collision
  - the more time and distance it will take to stop the vehicle, in order to prevent a collision
  - the less time and the less space there is to correct for the errors caused by any road user.

Vulnerable road users, those without a protective shell around them, including pedestrians, bicyclists and motorcyclists, need to be constantly aware of their vulnerability when on the roads. As we saw in

Chapter 3, most people are killed if they are hit by a car travelling at 50 km/h and above.[29]

Having a protective shell, such as being inside a motor vehicle, by no means ensures a person will be adequately protected from injury or death in a collision. The weights of motor vehicles and the speeds at which they travel mean the impacts in collisions could be, and often are, sufficient to cause injury or death to the occupants. As we saw in Chapter 3, an occupant of a motor vehicle is unlikely to survive an uncushioned impact at speeds in excess of 30 km/h.[30]

Our review of the various classifications and configurations of motor vehicles allows us to better understand the complexities of road safety and to understand the numerous hazards associated with the dimensions and weights of the vehicles. Again, as with our examination of road design and operation, we see there is far more to road safety than simply ensuring the people using the roads behave appropriately. We see that the sizes and weights of motor vehicles, especially transport trucks, combined with the widths of our traffic lanes and the distances we travel every second, give all road users a very small margin for error. On our streets and highways, at the speeds commonly travelled, there is very little time and very little space to correct for our errors or the errors of others. These hazards exist during ideal road and weather conditions and, as we will learn in our following chapters, become far greater in adverse conditions.

SIX

Hazards of Winter Driving

6.0 Introduction

In many regions throughout Canada and the United States, temperatures often dip below freezing in the early fall and continue to do so periodically until late spring. With freezing temperatures, frost occurs and this can quickly turn sidewalks, streets and roads into slippery, treacherous surfaces. With freezing temperatures, puddles can turn into what is sometimes referred to as "black ice," catching drivers unaware and possibly causing them to lose control of their vehicles. Within very short periods of time, freezing temperatures can also turn rain-soaked surfaces into the equivalent of skating rinks or bobsled runs, rendering road users almost helpless. Of course, temperatures below the freezing level also cause precipitation to be in the form of slush or snow, both of which can be lethal to road users.

Although the calendar identifies winter as being a three-month period, winter driving conditions can extend over a 6-, 7- or even an 8-month period. For clarity, when we refer to winter months, winter driving or winter maintenance, we are referring to the period when temperatures fall below the freezing level. As soon as freezing temperatures start occurring, all road users need to be aware that winter driving conditions may exist.

In this chapter, we shall focus on the road hazards that exist during adverse winter conditions. Closely related to adverse winter conditions is the subject of roadway winter maintenance.

6.1 Roadway Winter Maintenance

We saw in Chapter 4 that each province, state and municipality is responsible for maintaining the roads within their jurisdiction. Maintaining roads in winter months includes: removing freshly fallen snow and compacted snow and ice from the traffic lanes and shoulders; placing sand, salt or chemicals to provide vehicle traction; monitoring and reporting on the weather and road conditions. Although Mother Nature controls the weather—temperatures, fog, rain, sleet, snow, wind—road agencies have a great deal of control over road conditions. Roadway winter maintenance and the need for all road users to adjust to the variable conditions that inevitably arise during winter months are major components of road safety.

Large differences in climate, weather and geography exists throughout Canada and the U.S. Population densities also vary extensively, resulting in some regions requiring vast freeway systems and others requiring only two-lane, two-way highways. Winter maintenance requirements vary according to the climate, weather, geography, the amount of traffic and the purpose of the road system.

Motorists need to understand that in winter months it takes time for maintenance crews to remove freshly fallen snow and compacted snow and ice from streets and highways. It also takes time to spread sand, salt or other "winter abrasives" on the roads. Since winter maintenance cannot be performed instantaneously, it must be undertaken on a priority basis. A top priority for snow removal must be roads serving hospitals and schools, and highways with large volumes of traffic. The placement of sand, salt or other chemicals required for vehicle traction must also be undertaken on a priority basis, with hills and sharp corners receiving attention before straight and level sections of the roadways. Although safety is always a prime consideration for winter maintenance, the reality is that costs are also a determining factor.

It would be a huge undertaking, and well beyond our needs in this book, to examine the winter maintenance practices throughout different jurisdictions in Canada and the U.S. However, it will be of great value to examine the winter maintenance practices of at least one province or state, as a means of understanding some of the complexities and hazards inherent to winter driving. One road agency whose winter maintenance practices are worthy of examination is the province of British Columbia:

- Many areas within B.C. have relatively severe winters, resulting from the northern latitude of this vast province, the moisture created by the bordering Pacific Ocean and the large number of mountain ranges dominating the landscape.

- Significant variations in the climate and weather patterns often result in drastically different highway conditions during much of the fall, winter and spring. Whereas the relatively mild and wet coastal areas are frequently above freezing, the temperatures of the interior of the province are often well below freezing, creating variable highway conditions for extended periods.

- In B.C. a wide variety of highway systems service different populations. Freeways of the southern coastal areas lead to the interior of the province, extend through mountain passes and turn into two-lane highways. Highway corridors extend to all regions of the province, connecting areas that have different precipitation, different temperatures and different highway maintenance requirements.

- B.C. is a large province (948,600 sq. km [366,255 sq. mi.[1]]), making its highway maintenance program of considerable significance to Canada and the U.S.

These factors make British Columbia's highway winter maintenance program deserving of close examination.

6.2 British Columbia's Highway Maintenance Program: Maintenance Agreements

Since 1988, highways in B.C. have been maintained by private contractors.[2] In order to administer the program, the provincial government has divided the province into 28 Service Areas,[3] each maintained under a separate Highway Maintenance Agreement.[4] B.C.'s Highway Maintenance Agreements require contractors to provide all labour, equipment and materials necessary to undertake highway maintenance in accordance with Highway Maintenance Specifications.[5] The agreements are for 10 years. The annual payment is based upon a lump-sum price bid by the contractor for the first year of the 10-year contract.[3] After the first year, there may be payment increases due to changes in price indices or possible changes to the contract itself.[3] However, no additional payments will be made for winter maintenance work if winters are more severe than anticipated when the contractor submitted their bid.[6] The provincial Ministry of Transportation and Infrastructure monitors and audits the contractor's work to ensure compliance with the terms and conditions of the agreement and adherence to maintenance specifications.[3]

We shall now review and analyze B.C.'s Highway Maintenance Agreements and then B.C.'s (Winter) Maintenance Specifications.

6.2.1 Privatizing Highway Maintenance

One of the main considerations with B.C.'s Highway Maintenance Program was the decision to privatize maintenance work in 1988.[2] It meant that private contractors were contracted to do highway maintenance work, through a bid process, rather than have B.C. government employees continue to do this work. This is not an unusual decision, as governments attempt to make all forms of public services more efficient and competitive, to balance their budgets and to leave as much work as possible to free enterprise.

However, having private contractors do maintenance work, instead of government employees, introduces complexities such as the payment process, the administration and supervision of highway maintenance work and, to a certain extent, the details within maintenance specifications. We shall examine some of the complexities of highway maintenance that are unique to having private contractors perform the maintenance of public streets and highways. One of the most important features of B.C.'s Maintenance Agreements with private contractors is the payment process through "lump-sum" contracts.

6.2.2 Lump-Sum Contracts

A lump-sum contract is one in which a contractor agrees to undertake certain specified works for a fixed amount. In B.C.'s Highway Maintenance Agreements, contractors submit their lump-sum amount to provide the labour, equipment and materials required to undertake highway maintenance according to maintenance specifications.

One of the most appealing features of lump-sum contracts is the owner, or in this case the B.C. Government, knows the amount the works are going to cost once the contract is awarded. This helps governments in their attempt to balance their budgets.

However, from the perspective of the travelling public, there are two inherent risks with lump-sum contracts for winter maintenance work. One risk pertains to the fact that Mother Nature alone decides the extent of slush, snow and freezing temperatures. If Mother Nature delivers a severe winter, it could put the contractor in the difficult situation of having underestimated the costs to do winter maintenance. In severe winters, the potential exists for a contractor to attempt to reduce their expenses as much as possible by reducing the amount of labour, equipment and materials they use to undertake highway winter maintenance. Such cost cutting measures would inevitably result in road maintenance being reduced to minimum standards, if not below minimum standards, to the detriment of the travelling public.

Another risk to the public with lump-sum contracts for highway winter maintenance relates to any contractor who wishes to maximize profits. To make a profit in a lump-sum contract, a contractor must keep expenses below the fixed contract amount. The lower the expenses, the greater will be the profit. Should a contractor wish to reduce the costs of winter maintenance work as a means of increasing profits, these cost cutting measures will result in a minimum level of highway maintenance, potentially creating severe hazards to the travelling public.

An alternative to a lump-sum contract is known as a "cost-plus" contract. In a cost-plus contract, a contractor is paid a base amount plus additional amounts for the work actually performed. In highway winter maintenance work, this means that a contractor would receive payment for the amount of labour, equipment and materials required for snow removal, placement of winter abrasives and so forth, as required, according to the severity of the winter. This method of payment would remove the contractor's risk of underestimating winter maintenance requirements and would remove the public's risk of the contractor taking cost cutting measures. It would also remove the risks to the public of the contractor attempting to increase profits by reducing the amount of labour, equipment and materials used to perform winter maintenance. Overall, a cost-plus contract appears to be a more appropriate form of contract for highway winter maintenance, primarily for the safety of the travelling public.

However, there are disadvantages to cost-plus contracts. One is the difficulty to accurately record the contractor's expenses. Another is that cost-plus contracts remove the incentive for contractors to be efficient and cost effective. A third potential disadvantage is the potential for the contractor to submit dishonest expense claims or to "over-do" actual maintenance requirements. All three of these potential problems are likely amongst the reasons cost-plus contracts are not used by the B.C. Government in their Highway Maintenance Agreements.

Highway maintenance programs, therefore, involve political decisions. This will be the case for any municipal, provincial, state or federal road agency. The responsible agency needs to decide if they want government employees or private contractors to maintain highways within their jurisdiction. If private contractors are to be used, then a method of payment needs to be determined along with an appropriate manner of contract supervision. The standards to which the highways are maintained, especially during winter months, will depend upon the wisdom of the political decisions made by the respective road agency. The highway maintenance program will have a direct bearing on the standard of snow removal and on the extent to which the next corner on the roadway has been sanded or salted. Road safety and the hazards of winter driving depend on making sound political decisions and enforcing them.

6.2.3 10-Year Agreements

We noted previously that B.C.'s Highway Maintenance Agreements are 10-year, lump-sum contracts with private contractors.[3] In these agreements, contractors are required to submit their bids to perform highway maintenance, including winter maintenance, for the 10-year contract period. The length of these contracts increases the difficulty for contractors to accurately predict winter maintenance requirements.

No one can control, or has a way of predicting, what Mother Nature will do over an extended period of time. It is difficult to find a weather forecast that can accurately predict the weather several weeks ahead, let alone for an entire decade. Weather is often cyclical in nature and therefore difficult to predict. Even the history of highway maintenance requirements may be a poor guide for future requirements, especially today with global warming affecting climates worldwide. There is the potential, therefore, for contractors to make poor estimations of winter maintenance requirements, particularly for a 10-year contract period.

The weaknesses of lump-sum agreements with private contractors for winter maintenance work are, therefore, magnified by the fact that these contracts span 10-year-periods. If contractors estimate the severity of winters poorly, this could affect their financial ability to fulfill their obligations for the full length of the contract. The travelling public must be aware of the potential for these situations to develop with highway winter maintenance. Clearly, the standards to which highways are maintained will be affected by the highway maintenance program the responsible road agency uses.

6.2.4 Ministry Responsibilities

It is the B.C. Ministry of Transportation and Infrastructure's responsibility to monitor the work of the Highway Maintenance

Contractor to ensure contractual obligations are met. This includes ensuring the contractor is undertaking highway maintenance according to the maintenance specifications.[3]

Contract enforcement can be very demanding, especially if the contractor is being "difficult," such as when needing to reduce expenses or wishing to increase profits. The province's 28 Maintenance Service Areas are extensive. Hundreds of kilometers of roadways have to be maintained, 24 hours a day, seven days a week. Weather and highway conditions can change quickly. Properly monitoring a contractor's work could, therefore, be difficult at the best of times.

Regardless of the extent of ministry supervision, numerous events could develop to prevent contractors from completing maintenance on sections of the roadways. Maintenance crews could run out of winter abrasives and need to return to the yard for additional materials. A snow plow might be involved in a collision, or have a mechanical problem resulting in snow removal operations ceasing until a replacement vehicle is available. An equipment operator could become suddenly ill and be unable to continue. These and numerous other problems could result in the roadways not being maintained to the standards expected, in spite of ministry officials overseeing the work.

Problems like these could occur in any winter maintenance program. Poor winter maintenance could have several causes: poor supervision, a contractor's wish to reduce expenses and/or increase profits, or the untimely shortage of winter abrasives, loss of equipment or employee illness. What the travelling public needs to recognize is that there are no guarantees the streets and highways will be maintained to the standards set out in contract documents.

6.2.5 Summary: B.C.'s Highway Maintenance Agreements

Our review and analysis of B.C.'s Highway Maintenance Agreements provides an insight into some of the administrative complexities of highway winter maintenance, as well as the realities of having winter maintenance work conducted according to agreements or specifications. Each highway jurisdiction has its own program to oversee winter maintenance work. Whatever the program, it will inevitably be less than perfect. For many, often complex reasons, roads might not be maintained to the standards expected. People using the streets and highways should always be aware of this possibility.

6.3 British Columbia's Highway Maintenance Program: Maintenance Specifications

B.C.'s Highway Maintenance Contractors, as we have seen, are required to undertake highway maintenance according to maintenance specifications.[5] We shall now examine these specifications so that we gain an understanding of the numerous hazards that potentially exist during adverse winter conditions. It is worth noting that these are the maintenance specifications for only one province and that each province, state and municipality throughout Canada and the U.S. will have its own maintenance specifications for its respective jurisdiction.

6.3.1 Highway Classifications

B.C.'s highways are classified according to the volume of traffic and the highway's importance.[7] In summer, highways are classified through a numbering sequence, whereby highways with the highest use (vehicles per day) are Class 1 highways, followed by Class 2, Class 3 etc. down to Class 8, in descending order of use. In the winter, highways are classified by letter designations according to both traffic volumes and priorities. Class A highways have the greatest use and highest priority. These are followed by Class B highways and so forth, in descending order. The standards to which a highway is maintained in B.C. vary according to its classification.

Many motorists will likely not know the classification of the highway (or highways) they intend to travel, nor are they likely to know the maintenance standards for different highway classifications. As a result, they will often not know the level of maintenance to expect during winter months. What motorists do need to know is that highway winter maintenance varies according to the highway classification and that when they turn onto another street or highway, they may be turning onto a roadway maintained to standards totally different from the roadway they are presently driving on. These are yet further hazards of winter driving.

6.3.2 Maximum Allowable Accumulations of Snow

B.C.'s Highway Maintenance Specifications require contractors to ensure accumulations of freshly fallen snow remain below specified levels, according to the highway's classification. For highways with more than one lane in each direction, there are varying maximum accumulations of snow allowed for the different lanes, as the numbers in Table 6.1 show.

Table 6.1: Snowfalls: Maximum Allowable Accumulations [8]

Class A highway: One lane each direction: 4.0 cm
                Second lanes: 8.0 cm
                All Others: 12.0 cm
Class B highway: One lane each direction: 6.0 cm
                Second lanes: 10.0 cm
                All Others: 16.0 cm
Class C highway: One lane each direction: 10.0 cm
                Second lanes: n/a
Class D highway: One lane each direction: 15.0 cm
                Second lanes: n/a.
Class E highway: One lane each direction: 25.0 cm
                Second lanes: n/a.

(Source: Adapted from British Columbia Ministry of Transportation, Schedule "21," Maintenance Specifications, February 2003, Chapter 3-300, Section 3.1.1a)i), page 3. http://www.th.gov.bc.ca/BCHighways/contracts/maintenance/Schedule_21_Maintenance_Specifications.pdf)

The figures in Table 6.1 show the significant variations in the maximum allowable accumulations of snow that are permitted on adjacent lanes of multi-lane highways and on highways of different classifications. A number of hazards could arise from this practice.

- Vehicles travelling on loose snow will often compact it, resulting in what is referred to as compacted snow on the road surface. This compacted snow can become highly rutted from vehicles having different weights and tire sizes. The greater the depth of snow, the deeper the ruts can become. On Class A and Class B highways, where snow is allowed to reach different depths on adjacent lanes, the ruts on one lane could be considerably worse than on the adjacent lane. The conditions on one lane may then demand a slower speed than on the adjacent lane, creating a potentially serious problem when switching lanes.

- Another problem with allowing snow accumulations of different depths on adjacent lanes is that a ridge could develop between the compacted snow on one lane and that on an adjacent lane. This ridge could toss a vehicle from its path, possibly causing it to leave the highway or to collide with an adjacent or oncoming vehicle.

- Another potential problem with having snow reach different levels on different lanes, or on highways of different classifications relates to the turbulence created by vehicles (see Chapter 5). The turbulence a moving vehicle produces can create a plume of snow that can severely obstruct the visibility of adjacent or oncoming motorists. The greater the depth of snow, the worse the problem. Motorists must be attentive to the problems vehicle turbulence creates, and know that visibility may vary according to the classification of the highway and the condition of the adjacent lane.

A number of hazards could, therefore, exist when snow is allowed to reach different levels on adjacent traffic lanes, or on highways with different classifications. These hazards will exist to varying degrees throughout any highway system, any time there are snowfalls. Recognizing these hazards will help motorists manage their risk in winter driving conditions.

6.3.3 Time to Remove Compacted Snow or Ice
When snowfalls occur, highway traffic will often compact the snow before crews are able to remove it. In some cases, the compacted

snow will turn into ice, much like the snow on sidewalks often turns to ice if it is walked upon before being shovelled. B.C.'s Highway Maintenance Specifications identify the amount of time contractors have to remove compacted snow or ice from all travelled lanes with paved highway surfaces. This is measured from the time of the last measurable snowfall and is shown on Table 6.2.

Table 6.2: Removal of Compacted Snow or Ice, All Travelled Lanes[9]

Class A highway: 2 days
Class B highway: 3 days
Class C highway: 7 days
Class D highway: 21 days

(Source: Adapted from British Columbia Ministry of Transportation, Schedule "21," Maintenance Specifications, February 2003, Chapter 3-300, Section 3.1.1 c), page 4. http://www.th.gov.bc.ca/BCHighways/contracts/maintenance/Schedule_21_Maintenance_Specifications.pdf)

As noted earlier, B.C. is divided into 28 Service Areas with private contractors responsible for highway maintenance in each of the different areas. B.C. is a large province and each Service Area is extensive. This could easily result in snowfalls occurring at different times within the same Service Area. Even more likely is that snowfalls will occur at different times in adjacent Service Areas. As snowfalls occur, clean-up operations begin. The possibility exists, therefore, that snow removal operations could be at different stages within one Service Area, let alone in adjacent Service Areas. This possibility increases because there is a significant variation in the time allowed for removing compacted snow or ice from highways of different classifications.

The condition of traffic lanes therefore depends upon a large number of variables. These include the amount of snowfall, when the snowfalls started and ended, the stage of snow removal operations, the classification of the highway and the time allowed for contractors to remove compacted snow or ice from the road surface. It is entirely possible for motorists who are travelling from one region to another, within the province, to be driving on bare pavement at one moment and suddenly to be driving on compacted snow and/or ice. As motorists drive anywhere in the winter, in any province or any state, they must be constantly conscious that highway conditions could change drastically at any time, as dictated by Mother Nature and highway maintenance programs and specifications.

6.3.4 Removal of Snow and Ice From Shoulders

B.C.'s Highway Maintenance Specifications specify that, commencing from the time of the last measurable snowfall, contractors must push snow and ice beyond the shoulder edge within the times listed in Table 6.3.

Table 6.3: Removal of Snow and Ice From Shoulders[10]

Class A highway: 4 days
Class B highway: 6 days
Class C highway: 10 days
Class D highway: 24 days

(Source: Adapted from British Columbia Ministry of Transportation, Schedule "21," Maintenance Specifications, February 2003, Chapter 3-300, Section 3.1.1 e), page 4. http://www.th.gov.bc.ca/BCHighways/contracts/maintenance/Schedule_21_Maintenance_Specifications.pdf)

We saw in Chapter 4 the importance of shoulders on a highway. We see from Table 6.3 that contractors are allowed from 4 to 24 days to remove snow and ice from the shoulders for Class A through to Class D highways, respectively. The time is measured from the last snowfall. If it continues to snow, as it frequently does in B.C., this keeps extending the time required for contractors to remove snow and ice from the shoulders, which means that the shoulders could be covered in, possibly, deep snow or ice for long periods. Some of the accumulation of snow or ice on the shoulders could result from plowing the traffic lanes. As a result, motorists will not have a usable shoulder throughout these periods, which introduces a number of serious hazards:

- If shoulders are not properly cleared of snow and ice, they could be badly rutted. Driving onto such a surface from, possibly, a well plowed and sanded traffic lane could be very dangerous, especially if the motorist is travelling at a significant speed. The presence of snow, ice and, possibly, ruts on the shoulders could cause a vehicle to be deflected into adjacent or oncoming traffic, or off the shoulder and into obstacles (roadside hazards) bordering the highway.

- One of the main purposes of shoulders is to provide a space for motorists to safely stop off the traffic lanes, if necessary, for emergency, maintenance or other reasons. When snow and ice are not removed from the shoulders and motorists are unable to stop off the highway, it effectively removes this highway safety feature.

- Shoulders have another purpose—to provide additional space when motorists intentionally or unintentionally leave their traffic lanes. If the shoulders are covered with an appreciable amount of snow or ice, it could be dangerous for motorists to drive onto them. As discussed in Chapter 4, rumble strips placed on the edge of shoulders of many highways alert drivers that they are no longer totally within their traffic lane. That rumble strips now exist clearly indicates that it is quite common for motorists to leave their traffic lanes and to drive, at least partially, onto the shoulder. This would suggest that it is essential for shoulders to be properly cleared of snow and ice, not only for intentional use, but equally for unintentional use by motorists.

- When highways are covered with freshly fallen snow or compacted snow and/or ice, it is often very difficult, if not impossible, to see the line painting on the highway that identifies the edges of the travel lanes, the centerline and the edge of the shoulders. On such occasions, it is virtually impossible for motorists to be certain they are properly within their lane. This raises two distinct possibilities: 1. Drivers stay closer to the edge of their traffic lane, either to avoid being in an adjacent lane or to avoid being in the lane of oncoming traffic. 2. Drivers stay away from the shoulder, knowing it is not a safe place to drive.

Drivers are in a terribly difficult situation under these circumstances. They cannot identify the exact location of their lanes, they must avoid oncoming and adjacent traffic, and they cannot drive onto the shoulder of the highway because the condition of the shoulder might be treacherous.

- Most people who have spent time on snow know how difficult it can be, at times, to distinguish the features of the terrain ahead. Alpine skiers often experience this on ski hills when the light becomes what is referred to as "flat light." Under such light conditions, it can become difficult for skiers to identify bumps and hollows in the snow, thereby increasing the hazards.

  Flat light situations can occur on the highways, especially when they are covered in freshly fallen snow, or even compacted snow and ice. In these light conditions, it can be difficult for drivers to distinguish between their traffic lane and the shoulder. If the shoulders are not safe to be driven upon and the light is flat, very hazardous situations could easily develop, as drivers could unknowingly stray onto the shoulder.

Many hazards could therefore develop when the shoulders are not properly cleared on a timely basis. The best way to eliminate these hazards is to ensure the shoulders are maintained to the same standard as the adjacent traffic lane. This should include not only the timely removal of freshly fallen snow, but also the removal of compacted snow and ice. Likewise, the shoulders should be treated with winter abrasives to the same extent as the adjacent traffic lane.

Regardless of maintenance specifications, motorists must recognize that the shoulders of a highway may be unsuitable to drive upon during winter conditions, and/or may be considerably more hazardous to drive upon than the adjacent traffic lane. Further, motorists must be aware that it may be difficult to identify the edge of the shoulder due to freshly fallen snow, compacted snow and ice or flat light. Even though shoulders are considered an essential part of highways, they may only be safe to use in the summer, which illustrates both the increased hazards of winter driving and the need for drivers to proceed more cautiously in winter conditions.

6.3.5 Removal of Sight Distance Obstructions

B.C.'s Highway Maintenance Specifications require snow and ice that obstructs "Sight Distance" to be removed by contractors within specified times, beginning when snow removal on adjacent highways is completed. These times are shown in Table 6.4.

Table 6.4: Removal of Sight Distance Obstructions [11]

Class A highway: 3 days
Class B highway: 5 days
Class C highway: 8 days
Class D highway: 12 days
Class E highway: 20 days

(Source: Adapted from British Columbia Ministry of Transportation, Schedule "21," Maintenance Specifications, February 2003, Chapter 3-320, Section 3.1.1 a) (vi), page 3. http://www.th.gov.bc.ca/BCHighways/contracts/maintenance/Schedule_21_ Maintenance_Specifications.pdf)

We saw in Chapter 4 the importance of sight distance and stopping sight distance on our roadways. Motorists must be able to see far enough ahead to be able to stop their vehicles in time to prevent colliding with an object in their path. The posted speed limit must coincide with the stopping sight distance for all sections of a highway. The fact that accumulations of snow resulting from snow plowing could obstruct a motorist's vision introduces yet more hazards for all highway users.

In winter months, the pavement surface will often not allow motorists to stop in the time and distance in which it is possible to stop in summer. If a motorist must come to a sudden stop, braking can be extremely treacherous on slippery surfaces. If the driver is not very careful, sudden braking can throw their vehicle into a spin and cause them to lose control. Therefore, any obstruction to a motorist's vision on a highway, especially in winter months, could be extremely hazardous, as it could result in the driver not having sufficient visibility, traction or time to stop suddenly to prevent a collision.

Where snow banks or other obstructions exist beside a highway, motorists must understand that these may reduce their visibility sufficiently to prevent them from seeing an object in time to stop. Obstructions to sight distance, combined with slippery road surfaces, are yet further hazards of winter driving.

6.3.6 Application of Winter Abrasives

Spreading salt, sand or chemicals on road surfaces to improve vehicle traction on slippery road surfaces is fundamental to road safety during winter months. B.C.'s Highway Maintenance Specifications therefore specify the times allowed for maintenance contractors to place winter abrasives on road surfaces to allow for the safe and efficient movement of traffic, during winter conditions.[12] Applying winter abrasives is prioritized according to the classification of the highway. A high priority is also given to hills and curves, mountain passes, high elevation areas and locations known to be unsafe.[13]

B.C.'s Maintenance Specifications stipulate the response times for contractors to restore traction to highways during and after snowfalls, commencing from "the time the deficiency was detected by or reported to the Contractor."[14] The response times are as follows:

1. From beginning and/or during snowfalls:[15]

- Hills with more than a 5% gradient (one lane in each direction) and curves less than 60 kilometers per hour must have traction restored within 60 minutes on Class A highways and within 90 minutes to 4 hours on Class B to Class D highways, respectively.
- School zones and intersections must have traction restored within 90 minutes on Class A highways and within 2 to 6 hours on Class B to Class D highways, respectively.
- All other locations must have traction restored within 2 hours on Class A highways and within 3 to 8 hours on Class B to Class D highways, respectively.

Motorists need to understand that during snowfalls, contractors are not expected to restore traction to all highway surfaces immediately. The highest priorities are given to steeper grades, sharper curves, school zones and intersections. During snowfalls, slippery conditions could exist on many sections of the highways.

2. After snowfalls:[16]

- Hills (all lanes) and all curves must have traction restored within 5 hours on Class A highways and within 8 hours to 48 hours on Class B to Class D highways, respectively.
- All other locations must have traction restored within 24 hours on Class A highways, within 36 hours on Class B highways, within 3 days on Class C highways and "as required" on Class D highways.

Motorists must understand that there are limitations to the extent that traction will be restored to road surfaces both during and after snowfalls. In cases where snowfalls continue day after day, it will be particularly difficult to anticipate with any certainty the condition of the road surface at any time and at any location. After snow storms, it could be days before traction is restored to all sections of all highways.

In addition to contractors having a time range for dealing with slippery surfaces based upon the classification of the roadway and when snowfalls took place, it is important to note that contractors also have a responsibility to deal with slippery surfaces from "the time the deficiency was detected by or reported to the Contractor."[14] This is an important distinction. Application of winter abrasives may not commence until either the contractor or someone else has observed and reported that slippery conditions exist. Potentially, motorists could be headed toward treacherous road conditions that have not yet been detected by or reported to the contractor. Or the conditions may have been previously identified or reported, but the maintenance contractor has not yet been able to attend to the problem. In either case, the road conditions ahead could be treacherous and will remain in this condition until highway crews have dealt with the problem. These are the harsh realities of winter driving.

On a final note, recognizing the public's role in reporting hazardous highway conditions is important. If anyone notices hazardous conditions, they have a responsibility to report the conditions to the highway maintenance contractor, to the police or to the responsible road agency.

6.3.7 Freezing Rain and Black Ice

B.C.'s Maintenance Specifications require all highway locations affected by freezing rain and black ice to have traction restored within 2 hours on Class A highways and within 3 to 6 hours on Class B to Class D highways, respectively.[17] These treacherous conditions can develop quickly and unexpectedly, as identified in the following situations:

- Particularly at night, rain-soaked surfaces can become glazed sheets of ice if the temperatures suddenly drop below freezing.

- After periods with temperatures well below freezing, if temperatures rise above freezing and cause precipitation to fall as rain, the rain water can freeze as it comes into contact with the frozen pavement, covering the pavement with a glazed sheet of ice.

Freezing rain conditions can develop within minutes, perhaps around the next corner, resulting in extremely treacherous road conditions and catching unwary motorists totally by surprise. The temperature gauges provided within many motor vehicles are wonderful features, as they assist motorists in knowing the outside temperature, which can be critically important during winter driving. However, even when temperatures rise above freezing, road surfaces could remain frozen, resulting in potentially treacherous conditions at any time during winter months.

Whereas a road could be mostly bare and dry, patches of water might remain in shaded areas, in depressions on the road surface or where water drains across the highway. These isolated areas on the road surface could freeze or remain frozen, resulting in what is referred to as "black ice." All road users should fear such sections on the roadways because they are often difficult to see and are often unexpected.

The problem with the term black ice is that it has the connotation of being an unusual event that no one could reasonably have expected. Ice is, of course, not black. Ice is clear and it is the black road surface beneath the ice that leads to this term. Further, it is not unusual to have temperatures change from above freezing to below freezing at any time during winter months. Nor is it unusual to have isolated dips, hollows or depressions on a road surface, or to have water draining at times across the roadway. Shaded areas exist on most roadways and remain wet for longer periods. Although maintenance crews strive to fill potholes and depressions on the road surface and strive to prevent water from draining across a roadway, it is not always possible to eliminate these problems. Motorists therefore need to be constantly alert to the possibility of black ice anywhere, any time during winter months.

Freezing rain conditions and the presence of black ice are yet additional hazards of winter driving.

6.3.8 Rest Areas

B.C.'s Highway Maintenance Specifications require contractors to "maintain Rest Area access roads and parking lots in accordance with all specifications for roads of one Classification lower than the adjacent Highway."[18] This means that rest areas will be maintained to lower standards than the adjoining highway.

During winter months when the shoulders can be unsuitable for use due to a lack of winter maintenance, rest areas offer one of the few places for motorists to pull off the highway. When motorists leave a highway and enter a rest area, they will need to reduce their speed and come to a stop within a relatively short distance. However, if rest areas are not maintained to the same standards as the adjoining highway, motorists could experience conditions they are not expecting and suddenly find they are unable to properly steer or stop in the space available. Additional winter driving hazards therefore exist any time rest areas are maintained to a lower standard than the adjoining highway,

6.3.9 Travel Advisory Notices

B.C.'s Highway Maintenance Specifications require contractors to monitor weather and highway conditions and to "prepare and release traffic advisories approved by the Province, where Highway closures, lane closures and/or weather conditions are unsafe or have the potential to become unsafe for Highway Users."[19]

The public needs to be aware of where and how to obtain traffic advisory notices for the areas they intend to travel during adverse winter conditions. In B.C., they are available through DRIVE BC, online at http://www.drivebc.ca/.

6.4 British Columbia's Highway Maintenance Program: Service Areas

As we noted earlier, the province of British Columbia is divided into 28 Service Areas (see section 6.2), each of which has a private contractor responsible for highway maintenance on behalf of the provincial government. A map identifying the boundaries of the service areas is available online at[20] http://www.th.gov.bc.ca/bchighways/contracts/maintenance/hwy_maint_boundary_maps.htm.

B.C. is a large province with diverse geography and a wide range of climates, temperatures and associated weather. Rarely, if ever, is the weather the same at any given moment throughout the entire province. This is especially true in winter. When motorists take extended journeys throughout B.C. in winter, not only do they travel through the diverse areas that B.C. offers, but they also travel through different Service Areas maintained by different contractors. In spite of the requirement to adhere to the same Maintenance Specifications, contractors differ. They all have different employees and may use different materials and equipment to do maintenance work. In addition, it is inevitable that contractors will be at different stages of their winter maintenance obligations at any one time.

When driving from Vancouver to Prince George at the centre of the province, motorists pass through eight Service Areas. Travelling from Vancouver to Banff, Alberta, takes a traveller through six Service Areas. Travelling from the province's capital, Victoria, on southern Vancouver Island, to Prince Rupert on the north coast of B.C., entails passing through approximately 13 Services Areas, depending upon the route chosen.

It would not be unusual, therefore, for motorists travelling any appreciable distance during winter months in B.C. to encounter vastly different highway conditions numerous times during a day's travel. Even when travelling shorter distances, it is entirely possible for motorists to experience vastly different highway conditions as they enter the Service Areas of different contractors who are at different stages with their highway maintenance obligations.

Driving anywhere in adverse winter conditions can be treacherous and can be particularly dangerous when conditions change frequently and suddenly. Any time highway conditions change, for any reason, motorists must adjust their driving to the changing conditions. The more conditions change, the greater the potential for errors. Motorists must take into consideration the realistic possibility of frequent changes in highway conditions during winter months.

6.5 Hazards of Winter Driving: Margin for Error

In Chapter 5 we compared the widths of motor vehicles to the widths of traffic lanes. We saw that there is a small margin for error on our highways because, at the speeds we drive, it takes only a fraction of a second for a vehicle to veer into an adjacent lane, into oncoming traffic or off the shoulder.

We stressed the importance of using both roads and motor vehicles in the manner in which they are designed and are intended to be used. Road and motor vehicle design demands that road surfaces have proper traction and motorists have proper visibility. Without proper traction and proper visibility, it is impossible to drive safely on the limited widths of our roadways, especially at the speeds we commonly travel.

During winter conditions, the hazards can be extreme at times and the only sure way of avoiding a collision will be to remain off the roadways. However, if we must use the roadways during adverse conditions, it is essential that we reduce our speeds to ensure we can maintain proper control of our vehicle, given the existing traction and visibility. Not only will reducing our speed in adverse conditions allow us to maintain better control, but it will also lessen the impact that will result should we be involved in a collision. Less speed = better control of our vehicle = less impact in a collision = less risk of injury or death. Obvious and simple. Sadly, however, many people fail to recognize these simple facts. They insist upon driving according to the posted speed limits in spite of adverse conditions. In Chapter 4 we noted the following:

- *"Maximum speed limits posted on fixed-message signs are based on ideal traffic, environmental, and road conditions."*[21]

- *"When less than ideal conditions exist, the driver must adjust their vehicle speed that is appropriate for conditions."*[21]

Road conditions in winter months significantly increase the risks of a motorist losing control of their vehicle. The small margin for error that exists on our roadways does not allow for vehicles to slide out of control, or for motorists to drive at normal speeds with reduced visibility. It is imperative that motorists reduce their speed when adverse conditions exist.

6.6 Police Enforcement During Adverse Winter Conditions

During summer months, it is common to encounter police enforcing the speed limits within our municipalities and on the highways.

However, in the winter months and during adverse conditions, rarely does one see the police pulling motorists over and issuing tickets to people driving too fast for the road or weather conditions. It is therefore apparent that speed is not controlled or enforced by the police to the same extent during adverse conditions as it is during ideal conditions.

Unfortunately, society does not seem capable of functioning properly without police to enforce the laws governing proper conduct. This appears to be the case on our roadways during adverse conditions when many people drive at speeds far in excess of what is appropriate for the conditions. Reduced speed enforcement by the police during adverse conditions is, therefore, another hazard that exists during the winter months.

6.7 Chapter Summary: Hazards of Winter Driving

Our review and analysis of B.C.'s Highway Winter Maintenance Program has allowed us to see many of the complexities and hazards that could arise from the manner in which road agencies decide to undertake their winter maintenance obligations. The hazards associated with winter maintenance practices will by no means be limited to highways in B.C., but will exist to varying degrees on all highways throughout Canada and the U.S., wherever and whenever temperatures fall below the freezing level.

We have seen that, for numerous reasons, road conditions during winter months can vary significantly and can be hazardous and unpredictable. The following list summarizes the reasons:

- Mother Nature controls the weather—temperatures, fog, rain, sleet, snow, wind—resulting in adverse winter conditions extending for long durations in many regions of Canada and the U.S.
- Highway winter maintenance depends upon both the standards (specifications) governing maintenance and upon the costs of doing the work.
- The standards to which roads are maintained could be negatively

influenced by contractors needing to reduce expenses or wishing to maximize profits.

- Numerous problems could arise that prevent crews from undertaking maintenance work as intended (equipment breakdowns, sickness, injury etc.).
- Maintenance crews cannot perform all maintenance requirements instantaneously.
- Certain sections of a highway such as hills, sharp corners, and hospital and school zones have a higher maintenance priority than the remaining sections of that particular street or highway.
- Maintenance specifications vary for different classifications of roads.
- At any given time, maintenance crews may be at different stages of snow removal and other operations.
- Weather and temperatures change quickly and storm systems vary in intensity and location.
- Black ice could exist on any road surface, at any location and at any time, during or after freezing conditions.
- Shoulders may or may not be useable.
- Rest areas may not be maintained to appropriate standards.
- Hazardous conditions may not have been reported or maintenance crews may not have been able to deal with specific problems.
- Speed is not controlled or enforced by the police during adverse winter conditions to the same extent as it is during summer conditions.

We saw in Chapters 4 and 5 the hazards inherent to the design and operation of our roads and to the sizes and weights of motor vehicles. We see now the additional hazards inherent to highway winter maintenance practices and to adverse road and weather conditions. Winter conditions often result in our streets and highways being treacherous to even the most cautious and experienced road users. Our safety on the roads depends not only upon the standards to which our streets or highways are maintained, but also on the stage to which maintenance work has progressed. The small margin for error that exists on our roads does not tolerate motorists sliding uncontrollably on slippery road surfaces. Whereas speed limit signs are posted to advise motorists of the maximum safe driving speed in ideal conditions, in adverse conditions there are no such signs to guide motorists.

Thus we see further the complexities of road safety and the importance of understanding the numerous hazards that exist, so we can reduce our risks on the roads. As individuals, our best defence against the hazardous and unpredictable conditions that arise during winter months is to understand the hazards and to proceed very cautiously. This applies to all road users.

In the following two chapters, we will come to a better understanding of the extent and complexities of the hazards associated with adverse road and weather conditions.

SEVEN

Contributing Factors of Collisions

7.0 Introduction

We have now examined our roads and motor vehicles, as well as the highway winter maintenance practices of one major road authority, and have developed an understanding of the hazards that are inherent to these aspects of our roadways. In this chapter, we turn our attention to statistics on what are referred to as the "contributing factors of collisions." As we shall see, these statistics offer a unique and valuable insight into road hazards that arise from human behaviour, environmental factors and vehicle condition. Our objectives remain the same: we wish to identify and understand the many hazards on our roads and, in the process, come to an understanding of what we need to do to reduce our risks of being involved in a traffic collision.

7.1 Contributing Factors of Injury and Fatal Collisions

Statistics are recorded and compiled for different purposes. As we saw in Chapter 1, statistics are gathered to identify the numbers of collisions, injuries and deaths occurring on the roadways, as well as the resulting costs. There are also statistics compiled to determine the contributing factors of collisions. These are based upon an assessment, made by qualified people, of the probable cause or causes of any specific collision. We will now review statistics pertaining to the contributing factors of collisions, specifically those collisions that result in injuries or fatalities.

7.1.1 Source of Reference

Our source of reference for statistics on the contributing factors of traffic collisions is British Columbia's 2007 annual report *Traffic Collision Statistics.*[1] This report is useful for several reasons:

- It is relatively current.
- It has extensive data on the contributing factors of collisions, which is often lacking in other statistical reports on collisions.
- The information provided is based upon police-attended injury and fatal collisions, which means the statistics are consistent and reliable.[2]

It is to be expected that statistics on the contributing factors of collisions will vary from one jurisdiction to another and from year to year, throughout Canada and the U.S. However, for our purposes, we do not need these statistics to be exact, only to provide us with an indication of the extent of the problems on our roadways. On this basis, the statistical data provided in B.C.'s *Traffic Collision Statistics* provides us with the information we seek.

B.C.'s 2007 *Traffic Collision Statistics* report is based upon the following parameters:[3]

- Estimated B.C. Population (2007): 4,310,000
- Licensed Motor Vehicles: 3,852,365
- Total Vehicles Involved in Collisions: 74,567
- Property Damage Only Collisions: 25,224
- Personal Injury Collisions: 17,914
- Persons Injured: 25,064
- Fatal Collisions: 372
- Persons Killed: 417
- Road Users Killed in Impaired Driving Collisions: 128

- Pedestrians Killed: 74
- Motorcycle Riders Killed: 48

7.1.2 Collection of Statistical Data

The contributing factors of collisions included in B.C.'s *Traffic Collision Statistics* are taken from police reports on injury and fatal collisions.[2] These reports identify the factors that police determined were most likely to have caused the collision(s).[4] Very often, there is more than one contributing factor in a collision. For example, the driver of a motor vehicle may have been driving too fast for conditions when striking a pedestrian. At the time, the road conditions may have been wet or even icy and the pedestrian may have been intoxicated. In such a situation, the police would note all three contributing factors on their collision reports, namely "Driving too Fast for Conditions," "Alcohol" and "Road Condition." When more than one motor vehicle is involved in a collision, the contributing factors for all the vehicles involved are included in the police report. If two vehicles are involved in a collision and both drivers are considered to have been intoxicated, "Ability Impaired by Alcohol" will be "scored" twice, thus allowing statistics to properly reflect the frequency of any contributing factor.

In B.C.'s *Traffic Collision Statistics,* each contributing factor is given the same importance as any other, meaning that no assessment is made on which factor may have been more important than another.[4] Records will then show the number of collisions that involved, for example, "Exceeding the speed limit" or "Ability Impaired by Alcohol" or "Pedestrian Error/Confusion" and so forth. Records will also show the total number of times (frequency) that each factor was reported to have contributed to a collision. Police reports recorded in this manner allow a great deal of information to be extracted and analyzed.

7.2 Percentage of Collisions Involving Each Contributing Factor

B.C.'s 2007 *Traffic Collision Statistics* report lists the main contributing factors of injury and fatal collisions and shows the percentage of collisions that involved each factor. Table 7.1 is taken from the list provided in the report.[5] We see that "Driver Inattentive" was a contributing factor in over 34% of the injury and fatal collisions that year. "Driver Error/Confusion" was a contributing factor in over 20% of these collisions. There are 30 factors listed with "Other" and "Unknown" also shown. "Speed" is shown as one factor, but includes the three types of speeding-related offences, namely "Exceeding the speed limit," "Driving too fast for conditions" and "Excessive speed" (40 km/h or more over the speed limit). "Alcohol" is also shown as one factor, but includes both "Alcohol suspected" and "Ability impaired." Similarly, "Drugs" is shown as one factor, but includes both "Drugs suspected" and "Ability impaired." It is worth noting that the total percentage of the contributing factors shown in Table 7.1 exceeds 100%. The reason is that very often there is more than one contributing factor in a collision and, therefore, at times, the percentages are duplicated.

The list of contributing factors shown in Table 7.1 offers a valuable insight into some of the major causes of collisions.

7.3 Contributing Factors Grouped According to Category

As a means of analyzing the causes of collisions, B.C.'s 2007 *Traffic Collision Statistics* places the factors contributing to injury and fatal collisions into one of three main categories, namely "Human Factors," "Environmental Factors" and "Vehicle Condition Factors."[6] Human Factors are in turn divided into "Human Action" and "Human Condition." The contributing factors placed into in each of these categories are shown in Tables 7.2, 7.3 and 7.4. Table 7.5 summarizes the information provided in Tables 7.2 through 7.4.

In each category, B.C.'s *Traffic Collision Statistics* report identifies the number of times (frequency) each contributing factor was reported during the year. There were 18,286 injury and fatal collisions in B.C. in 2007.[3] Throughout the year, records show that 34,365* contributing factors were identified in the 18,286 injury and fatal collisions, approximately two contributing factors for each collision that occured.[6]

** (Note: In B.C.'s 2007 **Traffic Collision Statistics,** the text identifies this figure as 34,385, whereas several of the report's tables use the figure of 34,365.[6,7] Here, we shall use the lower figure.)*

7.4 Review and Analysis: Contributing Factors of Collisions

As we are beginning to see, the statistical data on the contributing factors of injury and fatal collisions provides us with great insight into some of the causes of collisions. We shall now examine the information contained in Tables 7.1 through 7.5.

7.4.1 The Most Significant Contributing Factors

A review of the contributing factors of injury and fatal collisions reveals that some factors are far more significant than others. For example, we see from Table 7.1 that Driver Inattentive was considered to be a contributing factor in more than 34% of the collisions that occurred in B.C. in 2007, while other factors contributed to less than 1% of collisions. Further, from Tables 7.2, 7.3 and 7.4 we see that several contributing factors were reported thousands of times, while others were reported relatively infrequently.

To understand the greatest risks to our safety, we need to identify those contributing factors that were most commonly reported. Tables 7.2 through 7.4 show that a relatively small number of the contributing factors were reported more than 1,000 times. Using this figure as an arbitrary benchmark, Table 7.6 lists those factors contributing to injury and fatal collisions that were reported more than 1,000 times. The percentage of collisions involving each of the contributing factors, as taken from Table 7.1, is shown beside each of the factors.

Also included on Table 7.6 is "Adverse Driving Conditions," which shows the combined frequency of "Road Condition" and "Weather." This is a significant subject that will be discussed later in this chapter as well as in Chapter 8.

Table 7.1 Contributing Factors of Injury and Fatal Collisions: Percent of Collisions Involving Each Factor[5]

Contributing Factor		% of Total Collisions[*]
1. Driver Inattentive		34.33%
2. Driver Error/Confusion		20.61%
3. Speed: Exceeding Speed Limit	6.58%	
Driving too Fast For Conditions	12.54%	
Excessive Speed**	0.83%	
Speed Total	19.95%	
4. Failing to Yield Right of Way		14.70%
5. Road Condition (Ice/Snow/Slush/Water)		14.47%
6. Alcohol (Suspected and Ability Impaired)		11.68%
7. Following too Closely		8.68%
8. Weather (Fog/Sleet/Rain/Snow)		7.80%
9. Ignoring Traffic Control Device		6.44%
10. Improper Turning		4.48%
11. Driver Internal/External Distraction		3.34%
12. Driving on Wrong Side of Road		2.82%
13. Wild Animal		2.42%
14. Fell Asleep		2.24%
15. Avoiding Veh/Ped/Cycle		2.07%
16. Pedestrian Error/Confusion		2.06%
17. Drugs (Suspected and Ability Impaired)		1.85%
18. Improper Passing		1.70%
19. Sunlight Glare		1.46%
20. Cutting In		1.39%
21. Extreme Fatigue		1.06%
22. Defective Tires		1.06%
23. Roadside Hazard		0.98%
24. Illness		0.90%
25. Backing Unsafely		0.89%
26. Site Line Obstruction		0.84%
27. Obstruction/Debris on Road		0.73%
28. Unconscious		0.72%
29. Defective Brakes		0.69%
30. Road/Intersection Design		0.68%
31. Other		14.19%
32. Unknown		8.97%

Total injury and fatal collisions in B.C. in 2007: 18,286[7]

**Excessive Speed means driving 40 km/h or more over the speed limit.*

(Source: Reprinted from the 2007 Traffic Collision Statistics with permission from ICBC. Section 3, Table 3.06, page 16. http://www.icbc.com/road-safety/safety-research/traffic-coll-stats-2007.pdf)

Table 7.2: Human Contributing Factors and Their Frequency[8]

a. Human Action	Frequency	b. Human Condition	Frequency
Driver Error/Confusion	3,953	Driver Inattentive	6,684
Speed Total*	3,732	Alcohol Total**	2,164
Fail to Yield		Driver Distraction	627
Right of Way	2,754	Fell Asleep	411
Following too Closely	1,725	Drug Total***	346
Ignoring Traffic		Extreme Fatigue	194
Control Device	1,229	Illness	164
Improper Turning	832	Unconscious	134
Driving on Wrong		Physical Disability	66
Side of Road	528	Ability Impaired by	
Pedestrian Error/Confusion	412	Medication	58
Avoiding Veh/Ped/Cycle	408	Deceased Prior to	
Improper Passing	320	Collision	12
Cutting In	264	Frequency Total:	10,860
Backing Unsafely	165		
Use of Com/Video Equip.	64		
Failing to Signal	63		
Ignoring Officer/			
Flagman/Guard	57		
Failure to Secure			
Stopped Vehicle	41		
Frequency Total:	16,547		

Total Frequency - Human Action:	16,547
Total Frequency - Human Condition:	10,860
Total Frequency - Human Factors:	27,407
Total of reported contributing factors:	34,365

% Human Factors: 27,407/34,365 = Approx. 80% of reported factors.

Total injury and fatal collisions in B.C. in 2007: 18,286

Speed Total includes: Exceeding Speed Limit, Driving too Fast For Conditions and Excessive Speed (40km/h or more over the speed limit).

**Alcohol Total includes: Ability Impaired by Alcohol and Alcohol Suspected.*

***Drug Total includes Drugs suspected and Ability Impaired by Drugs.*

Table 7.3: Enviromental Contributing Factors and Their Frequency[9]

Environmental Factor	Frequency
Road Condition (Ice/Snow/Slush/Water)	3,007
Weather (Fog/Sleet/Rain/Snow)	1,684
Wild Animal	454
Sunlight Glare	290
Roadside Hazard	186
Site Line Obstruction	174
Obstruction/Debris on Road	144
Road/Intersection Design	143
Domestic Animal	70
Roadway Surface Defects	69
Previous Traffic Collision	62
Defective/Inoperative Traffic Control Device	37
Artificial Glare	28
Insufficient Worksite/Construction Traffic Control	24
Frequency Total:	6,372

Total Frequency - Environmental: 6,372

Total of reported contributing factors: 34,365

% Environment factors: 6,372/34,365 = Approx. 19% of reported factors.

Total injury and fatal collisions in B.C. in 2007: 18,286

Table 7.4: Vehicle Condition Contributing Factors and Their Frequency[10]

Vehicle Condition	Frequency	Vehicle Condition	Frequency
Defective Tires	193	Defective Suspension	13
Defective Brakes	127	Trailer Brakes	10
Defective Engine	38	Defective Windshield	9
Defective Headlights	33	Defective Tow Hitch	7
No Driver	32	Dangerous Goods	6
Windows Obstructed	31	Illegal Vehicle Modifications	6
Insecure Load	30	Defective Brakelights	4
Defective Steering	22	Oversize Vehicle	4
Defective Accelerator	18	Defective Turn Signals	3

Total Frequency - Vehicle Condition: 586
Total of reported contributing factors: 34,365
% Vehicle Condition: 586/34,365 = Approx. 2% of reported factors.
Total injury and fatal collisions in B.C. in 2007: 18,286.

(Source: Reprinted from the 2007 Traffic Collision Statistics with permission from ICBC. Section 3, Table 3.05, page 15. http://www.icbc.com/road-safety/safety-research/traffic-coll-stats-2007.pdf)

Table 7.5: Summary of Contributing Factor Categories[*]

Category	Total Factors Reported	% of Total Factors (Rounded)
Human Factors		
Human Action	16,547	48 %
Human Condition	10,860	32 %
Total Human Factors	27,407	80 %
Environmental Condition	6,372	19 %
Vehicle Condition	586	2%
Total Factors Reported:	34,365	

*Information from Tables 7.2, 7.3 and 7.4.

Table 7.6: Most Frequently Reported Contributing Factors

Contributing Factor	Frequency[*]	% of Collisions[**]
1. Driver Inattentive	6,684	34.33%
(ADVERSE DRIVING CONDITIONS[***]	4,691[***]	22.27%)[***]
2. Driver Error/Confusion	3,953	20.61%
3. Speed Total[****]	3,732	19.95%
4. **Road Condition** (Ice/Snow/Slush/Water)	3,007[***]	14.47%[***]
5. Failing to Yield Right of Way	2,754	14.70%
6. Alcohol Total[*****]	2,164	11.68%
7. Following too Closely	1,725	8.68%
8. **Weather (Fog/Sleet/Rain/Snow)**	1,684[***]	7.80%[***]
9. Ignoring Traffic Control Device	1,229	6.44%
Total:	26,932	

Total reported contributing factors: 34,365

% of 9 contributing factors listed: 26,932/34,365 = 78% of all reported factors

Total injury and fatal collisions in B.C. in 2007: 18,286

[*]*Information from Tables 7.2, 7.3 and 7.4.*

[**] *Information from Table 7.1.*

[***] *ADVERSE DRIVING CONDITIONS is the combined total of Road Condition and Weather (Contributing Factors #4 and #8 of this Table).*

[****]*Speed Total includes: Exceeding Speed Limit, Driving too Fast For Conditions and Excessive Speed (40km/h or more over the speed limit).*

[*****]*Alcohol Total includes: Ability Impaired by Alcohol and Alcohol Suspected.*

Table 7.6 shows that nine contributing factors were reported 26,932 times (Adverse Driving Conditions is not included in this total, since it is already accounted for in Road Condition and Weather). The total of all reported contributing factors in 2007 in B.C. was 34,365, meaning that approximately 78% of all reported contributing factors (26,932 of 34,365) resulted from only nine different factors. The factors shown on Table 7.6 are amongst the worst causes of collisions on our roadways. These relatively few contributing factors keep occurring and reoccurring, contributing to the majority of roadway injuries and deaths.

7.4.2 Human, Environmental and Vehicle Condition Contributing Factors

As noted earlier, B.C.'s 2007 *Traffic Collision Statistics* report divides the factors contributing to injury and fatal collisions into three categories. We now need to examine each of these categories, which we do by starting with the least significant of the categories, namely, Vehicle Condition.

7.4.2.1 Vehicle Condition Contributing Factors

Table 7.4 shows that of the 34,365 contributing factors reported in B.C. in 2007, "only" 586, or roughly 2%, of those are related to Vehicle Condition (vehicle disrepair). Relative to the other categories, namely Environmental and Human—with total reported factors of 6,372 and 27,407 respectively—we see there are many problems of far greater significance to our safety than the condition of motor vehicles. The fact that only 2% of the reported contributing factors of injury and fatal collisions were related to Vehicle Condition indicates the problems on our roadways are *not*, in large part, the result of poorly maintained motor vehicles.

It is important to note, however, that the contributing factors of collisions resulting from Vehicle Condition should not be confused with the hazards of motor vehicles discussed in Chapter 5. The hazards we identified there—the width, height, lengths, weights and number of axles of motor vehicles, etc.—are related to the inherent features of motor vehicles as they come off the assembly lines, which are different from the hazards resulting specifically from poor vehicle maintenance.

7.4.2.2. Environmental Contributing Factors

Table 7.3 identifies the contributing factors included in the category of Environmental Factors in B.C.'s 2007 *Traffic Collision Statistics* report. The most significant contributing factors in this category and the number of times each was reported, were: Road Condition (Ice/Snow/Slush/Water) (3,007), Weather (Fog/Sleet/Rain/Snow) (1,684), Wild Animal (454), Sunlight Glare (290).

Although both Wild Animal and Sunlight Glare are reported relatively infrequently, they are, nevertheless, significant. We see that Wild Animal is reported to be a contributing factor almost as frequently as all forms of Vehicle Condition, which we saw in our previous discussions were reported a total of 586 times in B.C. in 2007. Sunlight Glare is a contributing factor almost half as often as all the problems with Vehicle Condition. Therefore, although Wild Animal and Sunlight Glare are far less significant than many other contributing factors of collisions, their significance is comparable to the entire Vehicle Condition category.

The two most frequently reported contributing factors in the Environmental Condition category are Road Condition and Weather. We see from Table 7.6 that both factors are amongst the most frequently reported of all contributing factors of collisions. These factors therefore deserve further review.

7.4.2.2a Adverse Road Conditions

In B.C. in 2007, Road Condition—ice, snow, slush and water—was reported to be a contributing factor of injury and fatal collisions 3,007 times, making this one of the worst road safety problems. As we saw in Chapter 6, road conditions in winter months can be extremely hazardous and unpredictable, for many reasons, which helps us understand why adverse road conditions are so often contributing factors of collisions. Statistics indicate the need for utmost caution any time the condition of the road surface is affected by ice, snow, slush or water.

7.4.2.2b Adverse Weather

Weather—fog, sleet, rain and snow—was reported to be a contributing factor of collisions 1,684 times. To add perspective to this number, most people are aware from news reports that alcohol abuse is a very serious problem on our roadways. Alcohol was reported to be a contributing factor of collisions 2,164 times. Comparing these statistics, we see that adverse weather was a contributing factor of collisions almost as frequently as alcohol was. Adverse weather, therefore, must be recognized as being a major hazard on our roads.

7.4.2.2c Adverse Driving Conditions

As we have just seen, in B.C. in 2007, adverse road conditions and adverse weather were reported to be contributing factors of injury and fatal collisions 3,007 times and 1,684 times respectively. When combined, these adverse conditions were reported a total of 4,691 (3,007 +1,684) times. Table 7.6 shows that Adverse Driving Conditions, the combination of Road Condition and Weather, would be the second most frequently reported contributing factor of injury and fatal collisions, second only to Driver Inattentive.

It is important to recognize that adverse road and weather conditions occur at limited times throughout the year. It is reasonable to project that if adverse conditions existed 365 days of the year, they would result in a much higher percentage of collisions, injuries and deaths on our highways. This then places the significance of adverse conditions at another level. On a day-to-day basis, Adverse Driving Conditions, consisting of adverse road and weather conditions, must therefore be recognized as being one of the worst road safety hazards. Anytime traction is affected by ice, snow, slush or water on the road surface, or anytime visibility is affected by fog, sleet, rain or snow, everyone using the roadways must use extreme caution. Such conditions result in a very high percentage of collisions. No one, but no one, should underestimate the risks of adverse road or weather conditions to road safety.

7.4.2.3 Human Contributing Factors

Table 7.2 identifies the Human Contributing Factors, where we see that 27,407 of the 34,365 contributing factors reported in B.C. in 2007 were attributed to either Human Action or Human Condition. In other words, the condition or various actions of the people using our streets and highways account for nearly 80% of the reported contributing factors of collisions. Reviewing the contributing factors from this perspective makes the problems on our roads painfully apparent. Through their actions and through their condition, people are considered to be contributing factors in the majority of collisions, injuries and deaths that occur on our streets and highways.

We shall review this matter in greater detail in our following chapter.

7.5 Chapter Summary: Contributing Factors of Collisions

Our review and analysis of British Columbia's 2007 *Traffic Collision Statistics* determined the following:

- A large percentage of collisions result from a relatively small number of contributing factors (see Table 7.1 and 7.6).

- The most frequently reported contributing factors of injury and fatal collisions are:
  - Driver Inattentive
  - Driver Error/Confusion
  - Exceeding the Speed Limit and Driving too Fast for Conditions
  - Road Condition
  - Failing to Yield Right of Way
  - Alcohol
  - Following too Closely
  - Weather
  - Ignoring Traffic Control Device.

  Close to 80% of all reported contributing factors of injury and fatal collisions result from these nine factors (see Tables 7.1 through 7.6).

- By far the majority of the contributing factors of collisions result from either Human Action or Human Condition (see Tables 7.2 and 7.5).

- Contributing factors related to Vehicle Condition indicate the problems on our highways are not, in large part, the result of poorly maintained motor vehicles (see Table 7.4 and 7.5).

- Whenever and where ever they occur, Adverse Driving Conditions, consisting of Road Condition (Ice/Snow/Slush/Water) and Weather (Fog/Sleet/Rain/Snow) are a terrible threat to the safety of all road users (see Table 7.3 and 7.6).

The statistics on the contributing factors of collisions have immense value to our understanding of the hazards on our roads. By reviewing these statistics, we have come a long way in reaching our objective of identifying and understanding the causes of collisions. By understanding the causes, we can strive to avoid making those mistakes that so often result in collisions.

In our next chapter we shall examine what we refer to as the Underlying Causes of Collisions. This will add greatly to our overall understanding of the causes of collisions and allow us to better understand what we need to do to reduce our risks of being involved in a traffic collision.

EIGHT

Underlying Causes of Collisions

8.0 Introduction

In the previous chapter we reviewed statistics on the contributing factors of injury and fatal collisions. From this review, we gained an understanding of some of the greatest threats to our safety on our streets and highways. We saw that Driver Inattentive, Driver Error/ Confusion, Speed, Road Condition, Failing to Yield Right of Way, Alcohol, Following too Closely, Weather and Ignoring Traffic Control Device are common problems on our roads and are amongst the most frequently reported contributing factors of collisions.

However, the contributing factors of collisions do not tell the full story about the causes of collisions. What remains to be explained is *why* the various contributing factors of collisions so often cause or contribute to collisions. For example, we know from statistics that Driver Inattentive is a major factor in collisions, but *why* is this? Why do Driver Error/Confusion, Speed, Alcohol and Following too Closely so frequently result in injury and fatal collisions? Why does Adverse Driving Conditions, consisting of adverse road and weather conditions, so frequently contribute to collisions?

In order for us to fully understand the hazards that exist on our roads, we need to understand the underlying reasons the major contributing factors of collisions occur so frequently. In this chapter we shall, therefore, examine the components of our roadways to develop a deeper understanding of what we refer to as "the underlying causes of collisions."

8.1 Underlying Hazards of Our Streets and Highways

We know from our previous chapter that human behaviour and adverse road and weather conditions are contributing factors in the majority of the collisions, injuries and deaths occurring on our roads. Our question is: Why do certain human behaviours and adverse conditions so often result in collisions? To answer this question, we need to examine the various components of our roadways.

8.1.1 City Streets

In chapters 4 and 5, we examined the widths of traffic lanes and motor vehicles. Let us review several of our findings:

- In Canada and the U.S., the traffic lanes on city streets are generally 3.0 meters wide (see section 4.8, Chapter 4).[1,2]

- Passenger vehicles—sedans, SUVs, minivans and pick-up trucks—have an average width of approximately 2.0 meters, excluding exterior rear view mirrors (see Table 5.1, Chapter 5).[3] This means a passenger vehicle travelling in the center of its lane on city streets has only 0.5 meters of spare room on either side, within its lane.

- Transport trucks are 2.6 meters wide, excluding exterior rear view mirrors, and have an effective width of up to 3.2 meters when their exterior rear view mirrors are considered (see Section 5.2, Chapter 5).[4,5] Transport trucks, therefore, occupy virtually the entire width of lanes on many city streets.

- As we saw in Chapter 4, the speed limits on city streets are generally 40–50 km/h, except for school zones and playgrounds where speed limits are generally 30 km/h. At 50 km/h, vehicles travel 13.9 meters every second (see Table 3.2(a)) on traffic lanes only 3.0 meters wide.

We see that due to the widths of city traffic lanes, the widths of passenger vehicles and transport trucks, and the speeds we commonly drive within our cities, it takes only a fraction of a second for a motorist to veer into an adjacent lane, into a line of vehicles parked beside the street or into the lane of on-coming traffic. There is, indeed, a very small margin for error on our streets and very little time to correct for the errors made by anyone.

Still further:

- City streets often have vehicles parked along one or both sides of the traffic lanes, thereby potentially limiting the visibility of drivers, pedestrians and bicyclists from one another.

- There are intersections, stop signs and traffic lights all demanding that drivers be able to reduce their speeds or stop at a moment's notice.

- City streets are used day and night, in all weather and road conditions. Visibility can often be restricted. With restricted visibility, vehicles, motorcycles, pedestrians and bicyclists are often difficult to see. Lighting at night is often poor. In the rain at night, partially blinded by the headlights of on-coming traffic, a motorist could have difficulty in seeing anything or anyone on the road ahead. At such times, seeing the directions of traffic control devices may also be difficult.

- There are the constant movements of other vehicles, pedestrians and bicyclists, with everyone fixed upon their own purpose.

- Children are frequently present within school zones and at playgrounds, and they often play on the streets in their neighbourhoods.

In short, there are many features of our city streets that are inherently hazardous. It is partially due to these features that collisions occur when drivers are not attentive, make errors or are confused. With the small margin for error, combined with the multitude of activities often occurring on our city streets at all hours and in all conditions, we must recognize our city streets as an underlying cause of collisions.

8.1.2 Highways and Freeways

A fundamental hazard of highways and freeways—like that of city streets—is the relatively narrow width of traffic lanes in relation to the widths of passenger vehicles and transport trucks. Here is a quick refresher:

- In Canada and the U.S., traffic lanes on highways and freeways are generally 3.6 to 3.7 meters wide (see section 4.8, Chapter 4).[1,2]

- Passenger vehicles, with an average width of approximately 2.0 meters, excluding the exterior rear view mirrors, have approximately 0.8 meters of spare room on either side when centered within a traffic lane on highways and freeways.

- Transport trucks, with an effective width of up to 3.2 meters when the exterior rear view mirrors are included (see Section 5.2, Chapter 5), have essentially no spare room within a traffic lane on highways and freeways.[4,5]

- When travelling at 100 kilometers per hour, which is common on highways and freeways throughout Canada and the U.S., vehicles move at 27.8 meters per second (see Table 3.2(a)).

These figures highlight the very small margin for error on our highways and freeways, due to the speeds commonly driven, the widths of traffic lanes, the widths of passenger vehicles and especially the widths of transport trucks. When collisions occur at the speeds commonly driven on highways and freeways, the impacts are usually severe. That massive transport trucks are hurtling along our highways and freeways with such small margins for error should make all road users concerned for their safety. That there are often large numbers of transport trucks on roads used by the general public should cause further concern.

Our highways and freeways have additional features that are inherently hazardous:

- They are often congested with traffic, have corners, hills, merging traffic, passing lanes, turning lanes, intersections and stop lights, all of which require that drivers be constantly prepared to adjust their speed or direction of travel.

- They often have a multitude of traffic control devices placed above, alongside or on the pavement surface, all dictating the speed and direction required. People using the highways and freeways are required to be attentive to such directions, while travelling at high rates of speed, often in adverse conditions and heavy traffic.

- When driving in the rain at night time, the headlights of on-coming traffic can be as blinding as the sun, vastly reducing the ability of drivers to see objects on the roadway ahead.

- Highways and freeways are designed to provide drivers with adequate site distance to be able to stop in time to prevent a collision.[6] However, there may be insufficient distance and time for motorists to stop if they are exceeding the posted speed limit or are not fully attentive or if adverse conditions are affecting visibility or vehicle traction.

With these inherently hazardous features, our highways and freeways, similar to our city streets, must be recognized as being an underlying cause of collisions, injuries and deaths. Very simply, at the speeds commonly driven, the small margin for error on our roadways cannot tolerate behaviours such as Driver Inattentive, Driver Error/ Confusion, Failing to Yield Right of Way and Ignoring Traffic Control Device. Similarly, the small margin for error available, combined with the variety of activities taking place day and night, in all conditions, does not tolerate road users who are under the influence of alcohol or drugs, who exceed the speed limit or drive too fast for conditions. During adverse road and weather conditions, our streets and highways become more treacherous. Our streets, highways and freeways must themselves, therefore, be recognized as being underlying causes of collisions.

8.1.3 Intersections

Intersections are one of the most hazardous locations on our roadways. This is where vehicles and pedestrians cross at right angles to one another, making a collision inevitable unless everyone does what they are supposed to do. Statistics are valuable for understanding how hazardous intersections can be. The U.S. National Highway Traffic Safety Administration's (NHTSA's) 2010 report, *Crash Factors in Intersection-Related Crashes: An On-Scene Perspective,* provides the following information:[7]

- In 2008, an estimated 5,811,000 crashes occurred in the U.S.

- Approximately 40%, or about 2,300,000 of the crashes occurred at intersections.

- Of the estimated 2,300,000 crashes at intersections, 7,421 resulted in at least one fatality and 733,000 resulted in one or more occupants suffering injuries.

These statistics alone stress the need to be alert at any intersection. Road users who are inattentive, who are confused or make errors, who fail to yield the right of way, who ignore traffic control devices or who are intoxicated at intersections are a very high risk, not only to themselves, but also to others. The best approach at any intersection is for everyone to proceed cautiously. Intersections, therefore, must also be recognized as an underlying cause of the collisions, injuries and deaths on our roadways.

8.1.4 Shoulders

As we saw in chapters 4 and 6, there are a large number of hazards often associated with shoulders. Some of the most significant hazards we identified were:

- The widths of shoulders vary considerably.

- On city streets and even on some highways it is not uncommon for there to be no shoulder at all. Without shoulders, pedestrians and bicyclists are often forced to be on the traffic lanes used by motorists, exposing these vulnerable road users to the risks of being struck by a motor vehicle.

- The absence of shoulders can be particularly hazardous in rural areas where open ditches frequently exist beside roadways. Ditches can be filled with water and can become death traps to anyone who fails to remain on the road surface.

- Where there are shoulders beside a street or highway, they may not be sufficiently wide to provide bicyclists or pedestrians adequate clearances from rapidly moving motor vehicles.

- On bridges and in tunnels, it is common for shoulders to be much narrower than on the street, highway or freeway on either side of these structures. Particular caution is therefore required when entering these confined spaces.

- Especially in mountainous terrain and through rock cuts, shoulders may be narrower than in more open areas.

- Guardrails, concrete abutments and similar structures may be placed within the width of the shoulder, thereby substantially reducing the shoulder width available to motorists, bicyclists and pedestrians.

- Shoulders may or may not be wide enough to allow motorists to safely stop their vehicles fully off the traffic lanes.

- In spite of the importance of shoulders, during winter months it is not uncommon for shoulders to be unusable or to be in a poor state of repair, due to highway winter maintenance practices.

These features of shoulders all introduce yet more hazards. When shoulders are less than ideal, which they often are, all road users need to proceed with greater caution and more attention. When shoulders are less than ideal, there is the potential for them to be an underlying cause of collisions.

8.1.5 Bicycle Lanes

We also saw in Chapter 4 that bicycle lanes are often far narrower than recommended by authorities (see section 4.9.5). All too frequently, this places bicyclists closer to motor vehicle traffic or roadside obstructions than is desirable, and often results in collisions. Inadequate widths of bicycle lanes must be recognized as being an underlying cause of the collisions, injuries and deaths experienced by bicyclists.

8.1.6 Motor vehicles

In Chapter 5, we reviewed the hazardous features of motor vehicles, with particular emphasis on the width, height, lengths, weights and number of axles of transport trucks. We also identified hazards of motor vehicles arising from excessive power, convertibles, the comforts of motor vehicles, the turbulence created by vehicles and from the mere fact that vehicles move, often at high rates of speed.

We have learned that passenger vehicles and, especially, transport trucks are large, heavy, powerful machines capable of travelling at high rates of speed, on traffic lanes only marginally wider than the vehicles themselves. At the speeds commonly travelled the destructive forces of motor vehicles are enormous. At the speeds commonly travelled, it takes but a second or a fraction of a second for a collision to occur, since the margin for error on our roadways—even in ideal conditions—is so small.

There are numerous features of motor vehicles that are inherently hazardous. Motor vehicles must, therefore, be recognized as a fundamental and underlying cause of the collisions, injuries and deaths that occur so frequently on our roadways.

8.1.7 Roadside Hazards

In section 4.11 of Chapter 4, we discussed the significance of what are referred to as Roadside Hazards, those man-made or natural hazards situated alongside our streets and highways. These include other vehicles (moving or stationary), buildings, telephone poles, structures such as bridges and tunnels, trees, boulders, mountain faces, ravines, lakes, rivers, streams or, simply, open ditches. Unless suitable protection is provided, these roadside hazards seriously threaten the safety of anyone who leaves the roadway, whether they are the occupants of motor vehicles or are motorcyclists, bicyclists or even pedestrians.

Although roadside hazards do not cause collisions, they are an underlying cause of many of the injuries and deaths that occur in collisions.

8.1.8 Improperly Maintained Streets or Highways

In Chapter 6, we examined the maintenance of our streets and highways during winter months. We saw that each road agency is responsible for the maintenance within their jurisdiction, including the removal of snow and ice and the application of abrasives to allow for proper traction in adverse road conditions. We saw the many complexities associated with winter maintenance work and the potential for roadways not to be plowed, salted or sanded to expectations or specifications.

If, following harsh winters, potholes are not filled, and sand is allowed to remain on the roadways for extended periods, this would result in treacherous conditions during the summer months, especially for motorcyclists and bicyclists. Still further, maintenance crews may not have re-painted the lines on roadways, making it difficult for motorists to properly position their vehicles.

There is, therefore, the potential for our streets, highways and freeways to be improperly or inadequately maintained, in both summer and winter months. Improperly maintained streets or highways must be recognized as being, as least potentially, an underlying cause of collisions.

8.1.9 Summary: Underlying Hazards of Our Streets and Highways

From our review of the many hazardous features of our streets, highways, freeways and motor vehicles, we can better understand why certain human behaviours and adverse road and weather conditions frequently contribute to collisions, injuries and deaths. Streets and highways that are often congested with large, heavy and powerful motor vehicles moving rapidly, often in poor light and adverse conditions, are no place for anyone to be inattentive. They are no place for anyone to make errors or to be confused, to exceed the speed limit, to fail to yield the right of way, to be under the influence of alcohol or drugs, to follow another vehicle too closely, to drive too fast for conditions or to ignore traffic control devices.

It is fundamental to our safety to recognize the many hazardous features of our city streets, highways and freeways, intersections, shoulders, bicycle lanes, motor vehicles, roadside hazards, as well as the possibility of improperly maintained roads. These hazardous features exist in ideal conditions and become far worse in adverse road and weather conditions. It is also fundamental to our safety to understand and refrain from behaviours that so frequently contribute to collisions (see Chapter 7).

8.2 The Hazards of Speed

In Chapter 7, speed was identified as being a contributing factor in collisions when motorists were exceeding the speed limit or driving too fast for conditions. However, it is critical to our understanding of speed to understand that any speed, even speeds within the posted speed limits, can contribute to the collisions, injuries and deaths occurring on our roadways. In the following sections we shall therefore review the significance of all speeds on our roadways. Our review of speed shall be from three perspectives: hazards that exist when driving *within* the posted speed limits; hazards that exist when *exceeding* the posted speed limits; hazards that exist when driving *too fast for conditions.*

8.2.1 Hazards When Driving Within the Posted Speed Limits

As soon as a vehicle begins to move, it has the potential to cause damage and do harm. Whether we are the occupants of a motor vehicle, motorcyclists, bicyclists or pedestrians, speed—any speed—is potentially hazardous. It is critical to our understanding of road safety to understand there are numerous hazards created by the speeds we travel at, even when those speeds are *within the posted speed limits.* The following are some of these hazards:

- Small margin for error
  There is a very small margin for error on our streets, highways and freeways, due to the limited widths of our traffic lanes, the widths of motor vehicles and the distance we travel every second—even at speeds within the posted limits.

- Events happen quickly
  Events happen very quickly at the speeds normally travelled on our roadways. Any error has the potential to place the offender in the path of on-coming traffic and to place innocent people in the offender's path.

- Stopping sight distance
  It takes time and distance to stop a vehicle. In other words, even when driving within the posted speed limits, collisions can, and often do, occur.

- Impacts in collisions
  The human body has a limited ability to withstand impacts, so any collision at any speed threatens our safety (see section 3.1). At the speeds motorists, motorcyclists and bicyclists commonly travel, impacts can result in serious or fatal injuries. Vulnerable road users are particularly at risk.

- Errors and confusion
  Our streets and highways are used for multiple purposes, at all hours and in all conditions, giving rise to errors and confusion, which occur at all speeds and which result in collisions.

- Inherent hazards of motor vehicles
  There are hazards inherent in the widths, heights, lengths, weights and number of axles of transport trucks, especially, which are a threat at any speed to all road users.

- Shoulders
  The lack of uniformity and regulations pertaining to the widths of shoulders are inherent hazards, with the potential to threaten the safety of all road users at all speeds.

- Bicycle lanes
  The often substandard width of bicycle lanes threatens the safety of bicyclists at all speeds.

- Roadside hazards
  Roadside hazards are a threat to all road users at all rates of travel.

- Traffic control devices

The complexities of traffic control devices combined with heavy, rapidly moving traffic, often in poor light and adverse conditions, adds considerably to the hazards at all rates of travel.

- Roadway maintenance
The potential for improperly maintained roads is a potential hazard for all road users at all speeds, especially in winter months.

- Adverse conditions
Adverse road and weather conditions that affect traction and visibility are a threat to all road users at all speeds.

- Human behaviour
Human behaviour and a lack of compliance with the laws, rules and regulations governing the safe and proper use of our roadways are a constant threat to the safety of all road users. These threats exist at all rates of travel.

We see, therefore, that there are numerous hazards to all road users, even when users travel within the posted speed limit. Motorists do not need to exceed the speed limit or drive too fast for conditions to make the speed at which they are travelling hazardous. For example, many of the most frequently reported contributing factors of collisions occur even when road users are travelling within the posted speed limits. These include Driver Inattentive, Driver Error/Confusion, Failing to Yield Right of Way, Alcohol, Following too Closely, Weather and Ignoring Traffic Control Device. Speed—any speed—on our roads is potentially hazardous. Never should we consider speed to be hazardous only when we are exceeding the posted speed limits or driving too fast for conditions.

8.2.2 Hazards of Exceeding the Posted Speed Limits

Exceeding the posted speed limit is a major contributing factor of collisions and is a serious hazard to all road users, as we saw in Table 7.1 of Chapter 7. It is important that we fully understand why.

We have learned that hazards exist even when we travel within the posted speed limits. Logically, all the hazards that exist when driving within the speed limits are magnified, compounded and made all the more serious when motorists exceed the posted speed limits. In addition, however, there are hazards specific to exceeding the speed limit that warrant our attention:

- Small margin for error
  We know from previous discussions there is a very small margin for error, due to the distances we are travelling per second, the widths of traffic lanes and the widths of motor vehicles. This small margin for error exists even when we travel within the posted speed limits. The faster we travel, the greater the distance we travel every second, which further reduces the already small margin for error. The small margin for error that exists on our roads is fundamental to the increased hazards that are created—for all road users—when motorists exceed the posted speed limits.

- Basis upon which posted speed limits are established
  The basis upon which speed limits are established, as we saw in Chapter 4, include the following considerations: curves and grades of roadways, lane widths, pavement surface, traffic volume, volume of heavy truck traffic, presence of bicyclists and pedestrians, roadside hazards, number of intersections with public and private access roads, number of interchanges, on-street parking and collision records.[8, 9] Based upon these considerations, the posted speed limit signs indicate the maximum speed that is to be driven, unless indicated otherwise.[10] Exceeding the posted speed limit increases the hazards associated with each factor that is considered when establishing the speed limit.

- Stopping sight distance
  As we saw in section 4.5, roads are designed and speed limits are established based upon the need for drivers to see far enough ahead to be able to stop in time to avoid a collision, if they need

to. Stopping a vehicle involves two stages. The first is the time the driver requires to assess a situation and to decide if it is necessary to stop. The second is the time the driver requires to bring their vehicle to a stop, through braking action. During both stages, the time and distance required to stop a vehicle increases as the speed increases. When drivers exceed the speed limit they may simply be travelling too fast to be able to stop in time to avoid a collision.[11, 12]

- Kinetic energy
A moving vehicle has what is known as kinetic energy.[13] If the speed of a vehicle doubles (for example from 50 to 100 km/hour) its kinetic energy quadruples (see section 4.6). This means that if the speed of a vehicle doubles it will take four times the amount of braking energy to stop that vehicle than it would take at the lower speed. Exceeding the speed limit is serious because it takes much more time and distance to stop the vehicle than it would if the vehicle was travelling within the speed limit. Calculations show that it will normally take a driver approximately 285 meters to stop a vehicle travelling at 130 km/h, as opposed to 185 meters to stop when travelling at 100 km/h (see Table 4.1).[14] In other words, if a motorist is driving at 130 km/h in a zone with a posted speed limit of 100 km/h, it will take that motorist 100 meters more (approximately 20 car lengths) to stop their vehicle, in an unexpected situation, than it would if they were driving within the posted speed limit.

- Impacts in collisions
As we saw in Chapter 3, the human body is very fragile and has a limited ability to withstand impacts without serious injury. Exceeding the speed limit increases the risks of causing a collision, increases the impacts that will occur in a collision and, thereby, increases the risks of seriously injuring or killing anyone involved in the collision.

- Behaviour of others on the roads
The statistics we reviewed in Chapter 7 showed that people using

our streets, highways and motor vehicles are often inattentive, make errors or are confused. In addition, they are, sometimes, intoxicated. Motorists also exceed the speed limits and commit other traffic violations that endanger themselves and other road users. When a motorist is speeding, it becomes all the more difficult to avoid colliding with other people who may not be using the roads properly.

- Inherent hazards of our roads
  As we have seen in previous discussions, many features of our roadways are inherently hazardous (see section 8.1). There are hazards inherent to the widths, heights, lengths, weights and number of axles of motor vehicles. Further, there are hazards inherent to intersections, shoulders, bicycle lanes, roadside hazards and the possibility of improperly maintained roads. In addition, there are complexities associated with traffic control devices and the need for motorists to adhere to the speed and directions indicated by such devices, often in heavy traffic, poor light and adverse conditions. Many features of roadways and motor vehicles are hazardous to those driving within the posted speed limits and become far more hazardous when motorists exceed the speed limits.

- Adverse road and weather conditions
  Adverse conditions exist whenever traction is reduced due to ice, snow, slush or water on the road surface, or whenever visibility is reduced due to fog, sleet, rain, snow or darkness. In these situations, all road users need to be more cautious. Especially during adverse conditions, it becomes extremely hazardous for motorists to exceed the posted speed limits.

- Multiple motorists speeding
  When a number of motorists, possibly the majority, exceed the posted speed limit, it often causes traffic jams to occur behind people who are adhering to the speed limit. Motorists then start to follow too closely, or attempt to pass when it may not be safe to

do so. These traffic jams also encourage those driving within the speed limit to either pull aside, or drive faster than they wish to drive, creating yet more hazards.

Clearly, there are many fundamental reasons why it is hazardous to exceed posted speed limits. Exceeding the speed limit not only breaks the law, but also defies and denies the wisdom and authority of those responsible for setting the speed limits. Motorists, for their own safety, as well as the safety of others, need to use the roads in the manner they are intended to be used, which includes staying within the posted speed limits.

What is particularly troublesome is that so many motorists exceed the speed limits. It happens all the time, everywhere one travels. Try driving within the posted speed limit on a city street, highway or freeway and see how long it is before someone tailgates or passes you. Why is it that so many seemingly honest, law-abiding citizens consider it acceptable to exceed the posted speed limits, thereby breaking the law and placing others' lives at risk? Why do we, as a society in Canada and the U.S., so diligently establish speed limits only to allow drivers to exceed these limits at their own discretion?

People's haste to get from point A to point B as rapidly as possible, blatantly exceeding the speed limits, causes many deaths and injuries throughout Canada and the U.S. every day of every year. Because the majority of motorists may exceed the speed limits does not make it right or safe to do so.

It is clear there are many reasons why exceeding the speed limit is a contributing factor of collisions, injuries and deaths occurring on our streets and highways. Motorists' relentless haste to get to their destinations as rapidly as possible and their lack of compliance with the speed limits are additional underlying causes of collisions.

8.2.3 Hazards of Driving Too Fast For Conditions

In Table 7.1, we saw that Driving too Fast for Conditions was a contributing factor in close to 13% of collisions, in British Columbia in 2007.[15] Road Condition (Ice/Snow/Slush/Water) contributed to almost 15% of collisions and Weather (Fog/Sleet/Rain/Snow) contributed to approximately 8% of collisions.[15] When we combine Road Condition and Weather under the heading of Adverse Driving Conditions we see that adverse conditions were contributing factors in more than 22% of all the collisions that occurred in B.C. in 2007 (see Table 7.6). Since adverse conditions do not exist every day, the percentage of collisions to which they contribute becomes even more significant when compared with statistics on the other causes of collisions that do occur every day, throughout the year. Whenever adverse conditions exist, these conditions are the greatest hazards on the roads. Let us, therefore, examine the implications of Driving too Fast for Conditions.

Driving too Fast for Conditions describes situations when motorists drive too fast to be able to properly control their vehicles, because of limitations imposed by poor traction or poor visibility. As we have repeatedly discussed, in *ideal conditions* there is small margin for error on our roadways. This small margin for error provides little tolerance for drivers who cannot control the speed or direction of their vehicles because they lack proper visibility or proper traction with the road surface. The hazards arising in adverse conditions apply to all road users, including drivers, motorcyclists, bicyclists and pedestrians.

8.2.3.1 What is a Safe Speed in Adverse Driving Conditions

Knowing what is a safe driving speed in adverse conditions is one of the greatest challenges motorists experience. It is accentuated by the fact that road and weather conditions often change very rapidly; a safe speed one moment may be far too fast for the conditions only a second or a minute later.

The posted speed limits are set for ideal road and weather conditions (Chapter 4). When conditions are less than ideal, due to either road conditions or weather, drivers need to reduce their speed, based on the following:

- *"Maximum speed limits posted on fixed-message signs are based on ideal traffic, environmental, and road conditions."[16]*

- *"When less than ideal conditions exist, the driver must adjust their vehicle speed that is appropriate for conditions."[16]*

Driving in ideal conditions can be relatively easy, since there are signs telling us the maximum safe driving speeds. In ideal conditions, our visibility is not severely and suddenly restricted by water, slush or snow tossed onto our windshield from adjacent or oncoming traffic. Neither is our visibility restricted by fog, heavy rain, sleet or snow. In ideal conditions, we can be confident there is adequate traction between our tires and the pavement to allow proper steering and braking. We can be confident that adjacent and on-coming traffic will also have proper traction. We can be confident that the posted speed limit signs advise us of a safe speed to drive around the corner ahead. Overall, we know that it is relatively safe to drive in ideal conditions at the posted speed limits because of the rigorous measures designers and road authorities have taken to establish the speed limits. However, in adverse conditions when driving becomes the most treacherous, there are no signs to advise motorists of a safe driving speed.

Road safety becomes more complicated and more dangerous as soon as *traction is affected* by freezing temperatures and ice, snow, slush or water on the road surface. It becomes more complicated and more dangerous as soon as *visibility is impaired* by fog, sleet, rain, snow or darkness, or by the water, slush or snow being thrown from the tires of adjacent vehicles. Posted speed limits are not applicable in these situations. Rather, it becomes the responsibility of individual drivers to evaluate the conditions and determine for themselves a safe driving speed. The question that immediately arises is: "How does the average motorist know what a safe speed is during adverse conditions?" The answer to this question is not simple.

In answering this question, we refer to posted speed limit signs and note that these provide the *maximum* speeds to be driven, in ideal conditions, on any specific section of a street or highway. If it takes qualified experts to determine a maximum safe speed under ideal conditions, how is the average driver able to make an intelligent appraisal of a safe driving speed during adverse driving conditions? How many drivers have sufficient knowledge and experience to determine with any accuracy how long it will take to stop their vehicle on freshly fallen snow or on compacted snow and ice? How do motorists know how forcefully they can apply the brakes on slippery road surfaces without losing control? How does a motorist know how fast they can drive around the corner ahead when the road surface is covered in snow, slush or ice? How does a driver determine a safe speed without knowing with any certainty the conditions on the next corner, down the next hill or 10 kilometers further along the roadway? How does a motorist know how fast it is safe to drive when visibility and the condition of the road surface are changing rapidly?

8.2.3.2 Choosing a Safe Speed in Adverse Driving Conditions

A fundamental problem with adverse conditions is that many drivers attempt to drive at the *maximum* speed they consider to be safe. However, it is impossible for most motorists to know with any certainty *what a maximum safe speed is* for most adverse conditions. This is likely the clue to this complex and dangerous problem. The clue is the word *maximum*. In winter months and during adverse conditions, motorists can only guess the maximum speed that is safe for the conditions that exist, at the moment. On occasions, motorists may even guess correctly. But what happens a moment later when the conditions on the road have changed? How does a motorist know that the condition of the road surface has changed and that their speed a moment ago is now too fast for the new conditions? During adverse conditions, a safe speed must therefore be less than the maximum speed at which it *may* be safe to drive. Let us consider what this means.

One of the underlying problems with driving in adverse conditions is that most motorists need and/or want to get to their destinations as quickly as possible. Our society is structured upon large masses of people moving rapidly from one location to another every day. We need to get to and from work and want to do so in as little time as possible. We become accustomed to being able to drive at the posted speed limits, which are the *maximum* speeds determined to be safe for our roadways. Now, when temperatures drop below freezing and it starts to snow, we continue to want to get to our destination at the *maximum safe speed.*

However, when driving during adverse conditions, it is extremely risky to attempt to drive at what we *think* is the maximum safe speed. If we do and conditions worsen, as they can do anytime, anywhere, (see Chapter 6) then our speed may suddenly be too fast for the new conditions. Once we realize we are driving too fast for conditions, it is often already too late to reduce our speed. We cannot turn the clock back and correct our mistake. We have lost control of our vehicle. Within a moment we could become yet another collision statistic.

Only one inescapable conclusion can be reached from analyzing driving in adverse conditions and that is we must always drive at a speed *less than* what is likely a maximum safe driving speed for the conditions that exist. Since adverse road or weather conditions can change very quickly, to risk driving at what is likely the maximum safe speed is to risk driving too fast for conditions.

Unfortunately, driving at less than what one considers to be a maximum safe speed in adverse conditions is not what everyone wants to do. Many people are of the mentality that the posted speed limits are the target speeds for any and all conditions. Statistics indicate too many motorists drive at the brink of disaster during adverse conditions. It is these people who so often lose control of their vehicles during adverse conditions, which results in terrible collisions.

From the above, we see the complexities of the hazards that arise during adverse conditions and why Driving too Fast for Conditions is a contributing factor of so many collisions, injuries and deaths on our streets and highways. Driving too fast for the variable conditions that exist during adverse driving conditions is a fundamental cause of collisions.

Hydroplaning

Hydroplaning occurs when water builds up in front of a tire, causing the tire to lose normal contact with the road surface. *Heavy rain, slush or even wet pavement can cause tires to lose proper traction with the road surface, with potentially devastating consequences.*

The American Association of State Highway and Transportation Officials (AASHTO) state in their publication *A Policy on Geometric Design of Highways and Streets*:

> *"Drivers should be expected to exercise caution in wet conditions in a manner similar to operating a vehicle during ice or snow events"*[17]

It is easy to think that adverse driving conditions exist only during winter months. This is not the case. Fog and rain, which may restrict visibility, can occur 12 months of the year. Also, during heavy rain or even when road surfaces are wet, hydroplaning can occur. Adverse driving conditions can therefore extend over the full 12 months of the year.

8.3 Abuse of Alcohol and Drugs

8.3.1 Alcohol

For many years, great efforts have been made, with limited success, to deal with the dreadful problems created by people who drive while under the influence of alcohol. It is important that we examine the extent of the problems created by the abuse of alcohol, primarily on our roads, but also throughout society.

8.3.1.1 Statistics

The extent of the problems on our roads caused from alcohol use and abuse is evident in the statistics from the following sources:

- *Traffic Collision Statistics British Columbia 2007*
  Alcohol was a contributing factor in close to 12% of all injury and fatal collisions,[15] and was a contributing factor in close to 32% of all fatal collisions.[18]

- *Alcohol—Crash problems in Canada: 2010*
  "It can be estimated that in Canada during 2010, 984 persons died in alcohol related crashes."[19]

- *Smashed: A Sober Look at Drinking and Driving*
  "In 2007, roughly 1.84 million Canadians reported that they had driven when they felt they were over the legal limit."[20]

- *NHTSA Traffic Safety Facts 2010*
  There were 10,228 alcohol-impaired driving fatalities in the U.S. in 2010, representing 31% of the total traffic fatalities for the year. [21]

These statistics show that alcohol is a contributing factor in approximately one out of every three traffic fatalities in Canada and the U.S. Between both countries, approximately 11,000 road deaths each year result from alcohol. In addition, tens of thousands of people are injured, many seriously. People who chose to drive a motor vehicle, motorcycle, bicycle or snowmobile, or who chose to be a pedestrian while impaired by alcohol, do so at great risk to themselves and to others.

Tragically, there are other problems associated with the abuse of alcohol, as the following sections show.

8.3.1.2 Costs of Alcohol Abuse

The report, *Smashed: A Sober Look at Drinking and Driving* published by Transport Canada, states:

"Over 1,000 Canadians—impaired and sober—die each year in alcohol-related crashes. In total these crashes cost Canadians over $10.6 billion a year in lost wages, property damage and health-care costs."[20]

8.3.1.3 Alcohol: The Bigger Picture

Unfortunately, the harm done to others by people who abuse alcohol is by no means restricted to our roadways. It extends into every aspect of our lives. The World Health Organization's 2011 *Global status report on alcohol and health* provides insight into the overall problems created by people who abuse alcohol:

- *"An intoxicated person can put people in harm's way by involving them in traffic accidents or violent behavior, or by negatively affecting co-workers, relatives, friends or strangers."*[22]

- *"Intoxicated people commit many crimes where the victims are unknown to the perpetrators, including homicide, robbery, sexual assault and property crimes. The well-being of others can also be affected by verbal threats, noise and nuisance from intoxicated people."*[23]

- *"The impact of alcohol consumption reaches deep into society. Alcohol consumption causes harm far beyond the physical and psychological health of the drinker. It also causes harm to the well-being and health of others."*[24]

What is evident from the WHO's report is that people who abuse alcohol do a great deal of harm to other people in all segments of society. They create far reaching problems that negatively affect many people in many ways, extending to our families, to our places of work and to our roads.

The problems on our roads are, therefore, but one aspect of the overall problems related to alcohol abuse. Not only does alcohol abuse result in close to 11,000 people a year being killed in traffic collisions in Canada and the U.S., and tens of thousands of others being injured, but there is untold harm done to other people in all aspects of society. It seems unrealistic to think that the problems on our roads resulting from alcohol abuse will ever be resolved satisfactorily, until society has learned how to deal more effectively with the bigger picture.

The small margin for error, in combination with the many hazardous features of our roadways does not allow for any road user to be under the influence of alcohol. The use and abuse of alcohol is a major contributing factor of traffic collisions, injuries and deaths, and results in a great deal of harm to others in all aspects of society.

8.3.2 Drugs

The use of drugs, similar to the use and abuse of alcohol, is yet another terrible problem in our society, affecting all aspects of our lives and having devastating consequences on our roads. In Transport Canada's report *Smashed: A Sober Look at Drinking and Driving*, are the following comments about the use of drugs:

> *"Taking drugs before driving—whether they are legal or not—is also dangerous. Drugs and driving are a big problem in Canada: studies show drugs are found in up to 30 percent of drivers killed in crashes."*[25]

Drug use adds to the horrific social problems created from the use and abuse of alcohol and is a major contributing factor of the collisions, injuries and deaths occurring on our streets and highways. The small margin for error on our roads simply does not allow for any road user to be under the influence of either drugs or alcohol.

8.4 Following Too Closely

Following too Closely is another contributing factor of collisions that B.C.'s 2007 *Traffic Collision Statistics* identified. Close to 9% of all injury and fatal collisions (approximately 1 out of 11 collisions) result from motorists following too closely behind another vehicle (see Table 7.1, item 7).[15] The question that comes to mind is: What is a safe distance to follow a vehicle? We need to examine this basic question.

A good reference on the subject of Following too Closely is the Ontario Ministry of Transportation's *Driver's Handbook*. It states:[26]

> *"Maintaining space*
> *As a general rule, drive at the same speed as the traffic around you without going over the speed limit. Leave a cushion of space around your vehicle to let other drivers see you and to avoid a collision.*
> *Whenever you follow another vehicle, you need enough space to stop safely if the other vehicle brakes suddenly. A safe following distance is at least two seconds behind the vehicle in front of you. This lets you see around the vehicle*

ahead and gives you enough distance to stop suddenly.

Do not block the normal and reasonable movement of traffic.

To give yourself a two-second space, follow these steps:

1. Pick a marker on the road ahead, such as a road sign or telephone pole.

2. When the rear of the vehicle ahead passes the marker, count 'one thousand and one, one thousand and two.'

3. When the front of your vehicle reaches the marker, stop counting. If you reach the marker before you count 'one thousand and two,' you are following too closely.

Remember that the two-second rule gives a minimum following distance. It applies only to ideal driving conditions. You will need extra space in certain situations, such as bad weather, when following motorcycles or large trucks, or when carrying a heavy load."[26]

There are actually two parts to the problem of following too closely. One is our need to stay a safe distance behind the vehicle in front of us and the other is to try to prevent the vehicle behind us from following too closely. If a collision occurs, it is equally serious for the vehicle following us to hit us from behind, as it is for us to collide with the vehicle in front.

The problem of following too closely is often referred to as tailgating, which frequently results in what are known as rear-end collisions. Tailgating can be particularly intimidating and hazardous when the perpetrator is a massive transport truck and it is so close that if you need to stop suddenly the result could be deadly.

On higher speed, multi-lane highways and freeways, it can be very difficult to keep a proper spacing, due to other drivers quickly passing and cutting in front of us or tailgating, thereby eliminating the safe zone we are attempting to maintain. No matter how difficult it is to maintain adequate spacing either in front of, or behind us, it is important to do so whenever possible.

Statistics indicate that following too closely or tailgating is a major contributing factor of the collisions, injuries and deaths occurring on our streets and highways. A good guide for the spacing required between vehicles is the 2-second rule, which applies to ideal conditions. During adverse conditions, this spacing should be increased.

8.5 Pedestrian Error/Confusion

Up to this point we have focused much of our attention on the causes of collisions and the hazards relating to drivers. Understanding the hazards pertaining to pedestrians is, however, also important.

According to statistics provided by Transport Canada and the U.S. Department of Transportation, the percentage of pedestrians injured and killed in Canada and the U.S. are similar. In Canada in 2009, pedestrians accounted for approximately 13% of those seriously injured in traffic collisions and 14% of all fatalities.[27] In the U.S. in 2010, 12% of people injured in traffic crashes and 13% of all fatalities were pedestrians.[28] The question we must ask is why are so many pedestrians injured and killed each year on our roads?

In Chapter 5, we reviewed the dimensions and weights of motor vehicles and saw how massive a motor vehicle is in comparison to our relatively small and fragile bodies. Our bodies are no match for the weights and composition of vehicles. In B.C.'s 2007 *Traffic Collision Statistics*, pedestrians accounted for close to 97% of those injured or killed in pedestrian-related traffic collisions.[29] In other words, only 3% of the victims in pedestrian-related collisions were the occupants of the vehicles involved in the collisions. The simple conclusion here is that pedestrians are foolish to "argue" with motorists or motor vehicles because the pedestrian will almost always lose the argument.

Collisions involving pedestrians happen for reasons. Sometimes the pedestrian's actions are at fault and other times the driver's actions are at fault. B.C.'s 2007 *Traffic Collision Statistics* is again helpful in providing statistics on the contributing factors of pedestrian collisions:

- Most significant contributing factors of pedestrian collisions, resulting from pedestrian actions:[29]
  1. Pedestrian error/confusion

   2. Alcohol involvement

   3. Failing to yield right of way

- Most significant contributing factors of pedestrian collisions, resulting from driver actions:[29]

   1. Driver inattentive

   2. Failing to yield right of way

   3. Driver error/confusion

Pedestrians need to be constantly aware that driver behavior will often put their lives in jeopardy. Pedestrians cannot afford to assume that a motorist will stop at a stop sign or traffic light, or stop because they are in a cross-walk. Nor can pedestrians afford to make errors or to be confused while on the streets. A pedestrian should always yield the right of way to a motorist and should never be intoxicated while close to motor vehicle traffic.

Pedestrians can reduce their risks of being involved in a collision by adopting these behaviours:

- Stop, look and listen.

Many years ago, school children were taught to "stop, look and listen" before crossing any street. Today, it appears these teachings are often forgotten, by both the young and the old. Time and again, pedestrians do not take the time to see if vehicles are approaching before crossing the streets or highways at intersections or cross walks. Pedestrians need to understand that it takes time for a driver to react and to bring their vehicle to a stop. If a pedestrian suddenly decides to cross the street or highway, the driver might not have enough time to stop. Pedestrians also need to be aware that it takes only a second or two for a motor vehicle to cross through an intersection, whereas it takes a pedestrian very much longer.

- Ensure motorists see you before you step onto the roadway.

Drivers may not see you. They are often inattentive, make errors, may be confused and may fail to yield the right of way. Pedestrians must be conscious that they may not be easily visible to motorists, due to their dark clothing, poor light or adverse weather. It is in pedestrians' best interests to act defensively around motor vehicles and to ensure motorists can see them before they attempt to cross any street or highway. Pedestrians need to understand that vehicles parked on the sides of streets often obstruct a driver's visibility and may prevent the driver from seeing them until the pedestrian is already well into the cross walk. Once a pedestrian has been struck, it does not really matter who was at fault; what does matter is the pedestrian has been struck and likely injured, possibly seriously and possibly fatally.

- Pay attention to the inherent hazards of our streets and highways. Pedestrians should pay more attention to their safety on the streets and less attention to texting, talking on their cell phones or listening to their head-sets. Pedestrians also need to recognize the many hazardous features of our streets and highways, including the small margin for error that exists.

Pedestrians, similar to bicyclists and motorcyclists, are vulnerable road users and need to behave accordingly. Motorists also need to recognize and respect the vulnerability of pedestrians.

8.6 Miscellaneous Underlying Causes of Collisions

In Chapter 7 we reviewed the contributing factors of collisions as provided by B.C.'s 2007 *Traffic Collision Statistics*. Table 7.2 identified contributing factors arising from "human action" and "human condition." In addition to those human factors already identified, there are several others deserving of our attention.

8.6.1 Driver Inexperience

Being educated in the inherent hazards of our roads and in the proper and safe use of our streets, highways and motor vehicles is one requirement for becoming a safe driver. Another is learning the skills of driving in all conditions, in daylight and in darkness. The skills of driving can only be gained through time and, preferably, under the guidance of mature, experienced drivers. Until drivers gain the proper skills, they need to be particularly cautious.

Driver inexperience must be recognized as being, potentially, an underlying cause of collisions.

8.6.2 The Elderly

As people age, they lose many of the physical and mental abilities they had when they were younger. Eyesight, hearing and reflexes are reduced. Concentration may not be as good. Driving and riding a bicycle or motorcycle becomes more challenging. Elderly pedestrians are particularly vulnerable due to their reduced mobility, their reduced eyesight, hearing, reflexes and balance. It would be inappropriate not to identify the elderly as an underlying cause of collisions, injuries and deaths on our roads.

8.6.3 Herd Mentality

Time and time again, there are news reports throughout Canada and the U.S. of multi-vehicle collisions resulting in serious injuries, fatalities, and millions of dollars in damages. Often the collisions occur in adverse conditions. These tragic events are at least partially the result of what is known as "herd mentality."

The classic example of herd mentality is where buffalo trustingly and naively follow the lead buffalo in a stampede over a cliff. It is not uncommon for similar events to occur on the roads, where drivers carelessly follow one another at rapid speeds, often in terrible driving conditions. Just because others are driving at the posted speed limits when visibility is restricted by heavy snowfall, blowing snow or fog, does not make it right or safe to do so. Just because others are driving rapidly on road surfaces covered with ice or snow, does not make it right or safe to do so. Just because others are on the roadways in severe conditions, does not make it right or safe to be on the streets or highways at all. In severe conditions, it may be best to remain off the roads altogether, until conditions improve.

We all need to refrain from being led astray by people who are using poor judgment on the roads or are partaking in any high-risk driving behaviour. The "leaders" on our streets and highways need to be those who drive safely and behave responsibly. We need to recognize that herd mentality is yet another of the many underlying causes of collisions.

8.6.4 Lacking Road Education

As we are learning, there are numerous hazards on the roads and there is a great deal to know in order to reduce—to the greatest extent possible—the risks of being involved in a collision. To prevent collisions it is essential for the general public to be well-educated on the hazards that exist on our roads and on how to use our streets, highways and motor vehicles properly and safely. This education should start when children are young to ensure they grow up with the proper attitude towards safety on the roads, as pedestrians, bicyclists, passengers or drivers.

The lack of a well-designed road safety educational program in many of our schools, starting from a young age, must be recognized as being one of the fundamental underlying causes of the collisions, injuries and fatalities occurring on our roadways.

8.6.5 Lacking Self-Discipline

It is not sufficient for road users to simply know, from driver training, experience and education, how to use our roadways and motor vehicles properly and safely. They must also have the self-discipline necessary to use sound judgement and restraint on our roadways. Many of the human behaviours that contribute to collisions are, at least partially, a result of road users not disciplining themselves to use our roadways properly and safely. Driver Inattentive, Exceeding the Speed Limit, Driving too Fast for Conditions, Failing to Yield Right of Way, Alcohol, and Ignoring Traffic Control Device are examples of road user behaviour that could be greatly improved through better self-discipline.

A lack of self-discipline by motorists, motorcyclists, bicyclists and pedestrians could easily result in a collision. A lack of self-discipline should therefore be recognized as being, at least potentially, another underlying cause of collisions.

8.6.6 Poor Time Management

We all know people who are always in a rush. They are typically late for work or arrive at the last possible moment. They are also often the last to leave work, as they attempt to complete just one more task before leaving. These people are often late when leaving for a destination, causing them to drive as fast as possible to make up time. This behaviour can simply be the result of poor time management.

Allowing sufficient time to get to our destination is important. If we leave late, we should accept that we will then arrive late at our destination. Under no circumstances should we attempt to drive faster to make up for our late departure. If road or weather conditions are adverse, we should abandon any concern for time and drive only at a speed that is suitable for conditions.

We should recognize that poor time management could be one reason people drive in a high-risk manner. This, then, makes poor time management yet another of the potential underlying causes of collisions.

8.6.7 Use of Electronic Devices

It should now be blatantly obvious just how hazardous it is for drivers and pedestrians to use electronic devices while using the roadways. Time and again, we have seen how critical it is for all road users to be attentive to their actions on the roadways. Driver Inattentive is one of the most frequently reported contributing factors of collisions and was a factor in over 34% of collisions in B.C. in 2007 (see Table 7.1).[15] In addition, Driver Internal/External Distraction was a contributing factor in over 3% of collisions in B.C. in 2007 (see Table 7.1).[15] When road users are not paying proper attention to driving, walking or riding a motorcycle or bicycle, collisions frequently occur.

We have seen that at the speeds we commonly drive, there is a small margin for error. For drivers to be distracted in any way is hazardous. For drivers, using a cell phone or texting a message while driving is a selfish action that puts them, their passengers and other road users at great risk. Similarly, it is hazardous for pedestrians, motorcyclists and bicyclists to use electronic devices.

The use of electronic devices by people using our streets and highways must be recognized as being another fundamental underlying cause of collisions.

8.6.8 Pets in Vehicles

It is not uncommon to see motorists with a dog or cat sitting on their laps as they drive along the streets and highways. Drivers may even have the window open to allow their pet to get fresh air, while the pet sits on their shoulders or lap. Dogs, especially, are active and it is common to see them going from one side of the vehicle's cab to the other, on and off the driver's lap, as they see other dogs or interesting sights.

Although animal lovers will be passionately defensive about having their pets uncaged within their vehicle, such practices should not be tolerated. No one should lose their life or that of their child or grandchild because another person wanted to drive with their pet sitting on their lap. Such practices are yet further underlying causes of the collisions, injuries and deaths occurring on our roads.

8.7 Reducing the Risks of Being Injured or Killed in Collisions

Since the possibility exists for any road user to be involved in a traffic collision at virtually any moment, often for reasons beyond their control, let us focus on how we can reduce our risks of being seriously or fatally injured if we were involved in a collision.

As we saw in Chapter 3, the delicate human body is limited in its ability to withstand impacts. In a collision, the extent of our injuries will depend upon a number of factors, including the speed(s) involved and the extent to which our bodies are protected from the impacts. We have discussed the hazards associated with speed, any speed, on our roads, and we now need to focus on how best to protect ourselves from the impacts that occur in collisions.

8.7.1 Seat Belts

Wearing a seat belt is one of the best defensive measures occupants of motor vehicles can take to reduce the severity of the impacts that occur in collisions. Statistics provided by the U.S. Department of Transportation's NHTSA support the need to be cushioned in the event of a collision or crash, as follows:

Seat Belts/Child Restraints

- *"From 1975 through 2010, NHTSA estimates that seat belts saved the lives of 280,486 passenger vehicle occupants age 5 and older, including 12,546 lives saved in 2010."[30]*

- *"Among children, an estimated 9,611 lives were saved by restraints from 1975 through 2010."[30]*

- *"In 2010, it is estimated that 303 children under age 5 were saved as a result of child restraint use, which includes child safety seats and seat belts."[30]*

Although it would seem natural to use a seat belt at all times, statistics show this is not being done. In the U.S. in 2010, NHTSA's statistics indicate 29% of passenger car occupants involved in fatal crashes were unrestrained.[31] NHTSA's statistics further indicate that:

"In fatal crashes, 78% of passenger vehicle occupants who were totally ejected from vehicles were killed."[31]

Based on these statistics, if anyone wishes to reduce their risks of injury or death on the roadways, one of the first steps must be to "buckle up." It must be recognized that another underlying cause of injuries and deaths on our roadways is that motor vehicle occupants are often not using seat belts or child restraints.

8.7.2 Motorcycles

Our discussion on the hazards of motorcycles can be brief. Everyone who drives a motorcycle or is considering doing so should be aware of the statistics provided by the U.S. Department of Transportation's NHTSA:

> *"Per vehicle mile travelled in 2010, motorcyclists were 30 times more likely than passenger car occupants to die in a motor vehicle traffic crash and 5 times more likely to be injured."*[32]

As we continue to search for ways in which we can reduce our risks of injury or death on our roads, it is apparent that using means of transportation other than a motorcycle will be a step in the right direction. However, for those who insist upon driving a motorcycle in spite of the hazards, the following section on helmets should be of interest.

8.7.3 Helmets

NHTSA also provides some useful information on the use of helmets, as follows:

- *"NHTSA estimates that helmets saved the lives of 1,550 motorcyclists in 2010. If all motorcyclists had worn helmets, an additional 706 lives could have been saved."*[32]

- *"All bicyclists should wear properly fitted bicycle helmets every time they ride. A helmet is the single most effective way to prevent head injury resulting from a bicycle crash."*[33]

Like using seat belts in a motor vehicle, it would seem natural to wear a helmet when riding a motorcycle or bicycle. Again, however, statistics indicate this is not the case. NHTSA's figures indicate that in 2010 in the U.S., "42 percent of fatally injured motorcycle riders and 51 percent of fatally injured motorcycle passengers were not wearing helmets at the time of the crash."[32]

Although wearing a helmet may not be what everyone wants to do, it is a matter of safety. We all want to think that nothing will go wrong, but when something does go wrong, events happen very quickly. When riding a motorcycle or bicycle, we have no protective shell around us, as we do in a motor vehicle. Nor are we wearing seat belts. Therefore, one of our only forms of protection when riding a motorcycle or bicycle is to wear a helmet that will give us some protection to the most vital part of our body—our heads.

We must recognize that not wearing helmets is often an underlying cause of injuries and deaths occurring to motorcyclists and bicyclists.

8.8 Television Commercials

A final subject that warrants attention in this chapter is the television commercials that show beautiful sedans, SUVs or pick-up trucks zooming along streets or highways (or deserts or frozen lakes) with little to no regard for safety or speed limits. The disturbing aspect of these commercials is that they rarely leave the viewer with any appreciation of the hazards associated with the speeds at which the vehicles are travelling. Our youth are growing up watching these commercials and, over the years, associate beautiful vehicles with speed and excitement. This is not the attitude we should wish our children to have when they get behind the wheel for the first time. As such, at least some of the motor vehicle commercials should be recognized as being an underlying cause of collisions.

8.9 Chapter Summary: Underlying Causes of Collisions

The information we have reviewed in this chapter contributes substantially to our understanding of the hazards that exist on our roads and to our understanding of how to reduce our risks of being involved in a traffic collision. The many inherent hazards of our roads make it unsafe for road users to be inattentive, to make errors, to not yield to the right of way, to be under the influence of alcohol or drugs, or to ignore traffic control devices. We can see also that the many hazards inherent to our roads make speed—any speed—potentially hazardous. All speeds on our roads, including speeds within the posted limits, speeds exceeding the posted limits and driving too fast for conditions, are major problems on our roads. Why? Because of the many hazards that exist, the small margin for error that exists on our streets and highways, and because of the severity of the impacts that result from collisions.

To use the roads properly, we can see that it is imperative to fully understand the hazards that exist with our city streets, highways and freeways, intersections, shoulders, bicycle lanes and motor vehicles, and with roadside hazards and roadway maintenance practices. Clearly, it is difficult, if not impossible, for road users to defend themselves from hazards they do not properly understand. As individuals, our best defense is to acquire a proper understanding of the many hazards that exist on our roads and to use the roads with caution at all times. We must use our streets, highways and motor vehicles according to the way they are designed and are intended to be used. This includes complying with the laws, rules and regulations governing their safe and proper use.

8.10 Questions That Remain to be Answered

In view of our findings in this and our previous chapters, several questions remain to be answered:

- With traffic collisions and crashes in Canada and the U.S. resulting in tens of thousands of people dying every year, hundreds of thousands suffering injuries and social and societal costs approaching one trillion dollars ($1,000,000,000,000) a year, why is more not being done to educate the public on the underlying causes of the collisions, injuries and deaths occurring on our roads?

- Why are those responsible for road safety and road safety education not doing more to inform the public of the numerous hazards inherent to our streets, highways and freeways, intersections, shoulders, bicycle lanes, motor vehicles, roadside hazards, winter maintenance practices and of the small margin for error that exists on our roads?

- Why is a well-designed road safety educational program not mandatory in all schools throughout Canada and the U.S.?

- Why are the public and, especially, our youth being denied the opportunity to fully and properly understand the hazards on the roads?

This book, we hope, will stimulate discussions on these and similar questions.

NINE

The Road Safety Revolution

9.0 Introduction

In our previous chapters we examined various components of our roads, in order to identify the hazards that exist to road users. Our ultimate objective has been to understand how we, as individuals, can reduce our risks of being involved in a traffic collision. We saw the hazards inherent to the design, operation and maintenance of our roads and motor vehicles, the hazards resulting from human behaviour, and the hazards resulting from adverse road and weather conditions. Combined, these hazards are largely responsible for the incredible numbers of collisions, injuries and deaths that occur year after year on the streets and highways across Canada, the U.S. and the world. As countries around the world have become more motorized, this carnage has become one of the world's worst problems.[1] The costs resulting from this death and destruction are staggering.

Although many people seem to accept the collisions, injuries and deaths occurring on our roads as the inevitable price we must pay for our standard of living, for our use of motor vehicles and for our mobility, not everyone accepts this fatalistic attitude.[2,3,4,5] There are some people who believe our roads are unnecessarily and unacceptably hazardous and who are no longer willing to tolerate the violence that continues to occur on them.[2,3] There is, in short, a revolution that is occurring in parts of the world in opposition to the death and destruction that is so prevalent on the roads.

9.1 A New Approach to Road Safety

In the 1990s a fundamental shift in the way of thinking about road safety occurred in the Netherlands and in Sweden.[2] Visionaries in these countries recognized that when even minor mistakes are made on the roads, these mistakes often result in collisions, injuries and deaths.[2] They recognized that as human beings we all make mistakes and that collisions are therefore inevitable.[6] What these visionaries would not accept is that when responsible road users make even a minor mistake they at times receive the "death penalty" for their mistake.[6] These visionaries concluded that road users have the right to be safe on the roads and that "travel speeds as well as roads, roadsides and vehicles should be designed and managed to reduce the risk of crashes and prevent serious injury or death to people in the event of a crash."[18]

New road safety strategies were then developed, based upon the visionaries' belief there needed to be a shared responsibility for road safety. Road users would be required to behave responsibly and to abide by the laws, rules and regulations established for the safe and proper use of the roadways. The people designing roads and motor vehicles would be responsible for protecting road users from death or serious injury when collisions inevitably occured.[6] This was a major departure from the attitude that road safety was primarily the road user's responsibility, an archaic attitude that has essentially existed since "the horseless carriage" was invented.[6,8]

Based upon this line of reasoning, both the Netherlands and Sweden adopted new road safety strategies in the 1990s.[2] The Netherlands' strategy for road safety was named the "Sustainable Safety" approach to road safety, while Sweden's was called "Vision Zero."[2] Both visions are revolutionizing the way the world is thinking about road safety. Between 2000 and 2010, Australia and New Zealand also developed new road safety strategies, based upon principles similar to those adopted by the Netherlands and Sweden.[2,3] Australia's "Safe System" approach to road safety formed the basis for its National Road Safety Strategy 2011–2020.[2] New Zealand's "Safer Journeys" strategy formed the basis for its Road Safety Strategy 2010–2020.[3] In addition, the European Union (EU), consisting of 28 member countries, is targeting to reduce by 50% the number of road fatalities between 2010 and 2020.[9,10] With the adoption of these new road safety strategies and the EU's target to drastically reduce road deaths, the evolution of road safety has taken a giant leap forward. This evolution has turned into a revolution.

Although the road safety strategies adopted by the Netherlands, Sweden, Australia and New Zealand have much in common, they vary in subtle ways, according to each country's vision, goals and ambitions. While it is unnecessary to review all four strategies, it will be of great value to our overall understanding of road safety to examine the thinking and philosophy behind Sweden's Vision Zero and Australia's Safe Systems strategies. Our review of these strategies will be through a number of statements made by those responsible for the conception and implementation of these revolutionary approaches to road safety. The quotations are light reading and although some may appear repetitive, each has subtle and significant differences from the others.

9.2 Sweden's Vision Zero Approach to Road Safety

The following quotations, taken from various articles on Sweden's Vision Zero approach to road safety, allow us to understand the philosophy and objectives of this remarkable and revolutionary road safety strategy:

- *"Vision Zero was adopted by Sweden in 1997 and has the long term goal of eliminating death and serious injury from the road transport system. Under this approach, it is unacceptable to trade off human life and health for other benefits of the transport system (e.g. mobility)."*[2]

- *"The Vision Zero is the Swedish approach to road safety thinking. It can be summarized in one sentence: No loss of life is acceptable. The Vision Zero approach...is based upon the simple fact that we are human and make mistakes. The road system needs to keep us moving. But it must also be designed to protect us at every turn."*[11]

- *"Human limitations are an important basis upon which to design the road transport system. This must be done through taking into account biological tolerance against external violence—in other words what the human body can stand. In this regard, there are scientifically established limit values based on the design of modern vehicles and roads:*
  - *Most people survive if they are hit by a car travelling at 30 km/h.*
  - *Most people are killed if they are hit by a car travelling at 50 km/h.*
  - *A safe car protects occupants at speeds of up to 65–70 km/h in a head-on collision and at speeds up to 45–50 km/h in a side impact collision, assuming of course that everyone is wearing a seat belt."*[12]

- *"We know that road traffic is a deadly and daily threat...Some might argue this is the price we have to pay for mobility and freedom. We think not. There can be no moral justification for the death of one single person. You should be able to move freely—and feel safe at the same time. This is what the Vision Zero is all about."*[5]

- *"Vision Zero is both an attitude to life and a strategy for designing a safe road transport system. It establishes that the loss of human life in traffic is unacceptable."*[13]

- *"The Vision Zero starts with a statement: we are human and we make mistakes. Our bodies are subject to biomechanical tolerance limits and simply not designed to travel at high-speed. Yet we do so anyway. An effective road safety system must always take human fallibility into account."*[14]

- *"In every situation a person might fail—the road system should not. This is the core principle of the Vision Zero."*[14]

- *"Road safety in the spirit of Vision Zero means that roads, streets and vehicles must be much more adapted to human capacity and tolerance. The responsibility for safety is shared between those who design and those who use the road transport system."[13]*

- *"Vision Zero emphasizes that the road transport system is an entity in which the different components such as roads, vehicles and road users must interact in order to ensure safety."[6]*

- *"Vision Zero alters the view on responsibility. Those who design the road transport system bear the ultimate responsibility for safety: road managers, vehicle manufacturers, road transport carriers, politicians, public employees, legislative authorities and the police. It is the responsibility of the individual person to abide by laws and regulations. Prior to this, practically all the responsibility had been put on the individual road user."[6]*

- *"System designers primarily include road managers, the automotive industry, the police, politicians and legislative bodies. These are the ones responsible for providing a system that can deal with the mistakes that road users will undoubtedly be making. However, there are also many other players who have a responsibility for road safety: transport carriers, health services, the judicial system, schools and road safety organizations..."[7]*

- *"The road transport system is not adapted to the fact that people sometimes make mistakes. There is no perfect human being. In road traffic it is all too often a case of simple mistakes being punished by death."[6]*

- *"The work conducted on road safety in compliance with Vision Zero is based on doing everything to prevent road deaths or serious traffic injuries. While effort is being made to prevent accidents, the road transport system must be designed from the realization that people do make mistakes and that traffic accidents can therefore not be avoided completely. Vision Zero can accept that accidents occur, but not that they result in serious human injury."[6]*

- *"An accident that results in serious human injury means that the components in the road transport system were not functioning well together. Vision Zero emphasizes the fact that all elements in the system are inter-related and affect one another."[12]*

- *"Since we can never escape the fact that human beings are not infallible, the road transport system must be designed so that any mistakes will not cause serious or fatal injury. This approach means shifting a major share of the safety responsibility from road users to those who design the road transport system."[12]*

- *"People's demands on being able to use the road transport system without putting their life and health at risk is a key driving force for achieving Vision Zero."[7]*

- *"It is not acceptable that any human being should be killed or injured due to fellow road-users' lack of consideration or lack of will to follow traffic regulations or due to questionable decisions from our decision-makers."[15]*

When Sweden embarked upon its new road safety strategy, it established goals for reducing deaths and serious injuries by specific dates.[10] It also committed to monitoring these goals to ensure progress was "both challenging and realistic."[16] By establishing both specific goals and a monitoring program, Sweden is able to identify and address any weaknesses with its new road safety strategy in a timely manner.

9.3 Australia's Safe System Approach to Road Safety

For our purposes, the following quotations summarize well the attitude and philosophy of those responsible for Australia's Safe System approach to road safety.

- *"The Safe System approach advocates for a safe road system, better adapted to the physical tolerance of its users. The Safe System was officially* endorsed by the Australian Transport Council in 2004 and adopted by all Australian state and territory road authorities...It has guided the development of subsequent National Road Safety Action Plans and underpinned the development of the National Road Safety Strategy for 2011 to 2020. The setting of speed limits is now based on this approach so that avoiding death and serious injuries, becomes a priority."[2]

- "Australia's Safe System approach shares principles in common with well known national strategies such as Sweden's Vision Zero and the Netherlands' Sustainable Safety approaches."[2]

- "The Safe System approach represents a significant shift in thinking about road safety."[2]

- "The Safe System will deliver reductions in deaths and severity of injuries by coordinating the management of all the components of the transport system that impact on safety."[2]

- "While the Safe System approach to road safety recognizes the need for responsible road user behaviour, it also accepts that human error is inevitable. It therefore aims to create a road transport system that makes allowance for errors and minimizes the consequences—in particular, the risk of death or serious injury. By taking a total view of the combined factors involved in road safety, the Safe System approach encourages a better understanding of the interaction between the key elements of the road system: road users, roads and roadsides, vehicles and travel speeds."[2]

- "The safe system aims to have alert and compliant road users and has three core components:
  - Safe roads and roadsides—a transport system designed to make a collision survivable through a combination of design and maintenance of roads and roadsides.
  - Safe vehicles—the design of vehicles and their safety equipment to include protective systems including electronic stability control, air cushions, etc.

   o *Safe speeds—the speed limit should reflect the road safety risk to the road users.*

   These three core components operate in an environment where road users are encouraged to be alert to risk and compliant with the rules of the system.

   Through a combination of these components, the Safe System approach aims to design and build a transport system that will protect road users and reduce the number of deaths and serious injuries."[17]

- *"Achieving a Safe System of road travel is based on an understanding that the human body is vulnerable and unlikely to survive an uncushioned impact at a speed of more than 30 km/h. Even relatively low speeds can kill or seriously injure unless the vehicle and the road and roadside environment take account of the physical vulnerability of all road users. The main objective of the Safe System is to ensure that in the event of a crash, the impact forces released are within the boundaries of human tolerance and that no fatalities should occur and serious injuries are reduced."*[17]

- *"The chances of surviving a crash decrease rapidly above certain impact speeds, depending on the nature of the collision."*[17]

- *"Of the elements in the Safe System approach, speed management is critical in limiting the impact energy of crashes and underpins almost every consideration involved in the development of new and existing safety initiatives."*[18]

- *"The Safe System approach maintains that travel speeds as well as roads, roadsides and vehicles should be designed and managed to reduce the risk of crashes and prevent serious injury or death to people in the event of a crash. This includes setting speed limits and road rules according to the safety of the road and roadside and ensuring road user awareness and compliance through signage, driver education campaigns and enforcement."*[18]

- *"Our role as individuals is critical in achieving the common goal of reducing deaths and injuries on our roads which is impossible unless we share our responsibility as road users with vehicle designers, road authorities and the road system itself.*"[19]

These quotations show us the thinking and philosophy behind Australia's Safe System approach to road safety. We see that both Australia's and Sweden's road safety strategies reject the long standing, widely accepted attitude that death and serious injury are an inevitable part of our road transportation system. They also reject the long standing attitude that road safety is primarily a road user responsibility. In these new road safety strategies, the responsibility for road safety is largely placed on system designers who become responsible for providing safe roads and roadsides, safe vehicles and safe speeds. The responsibility of road users is to remain alert and to comply with the rules of the system.

Clearly, a revolution is taking place in the Netherlands, Sweden, Australia and New Zealand, with the adoption of these new road safety strategies. The EU's goal to reduce road deaths by 50% by 2020 adds intensity to the battle against the death and destruction on the roads. There is, however, more to this revolution, this evolution in road safety, and that has to do with the improved design and construction of automobiles.

9.4 Volvo's Vision 2020

Volvo, a Swedish car manufacturing company, has embarked upon one of its most ambitious undertakings, "Volvo Vision 2020." Paralleling Sweden's Vision Zero road safety strategy, Volvo states:

"Our vision is to design cars that should not crash. In the shorter perspective the aim is that by 2020 no-one should be killed or seriously injured in a new Volvo."[20]

After over 100 years of death and destruction on the world's roads, it is almost unimaginable that an automobile manufacturer now has the vision to produce, within a short period of time, vehicles in which no one should be killed or seriously injured. In time, this manufacturer intends to produce cars that will not even crash! Such developments indeed offer hope for a better world. For parents and grandparents, this new world cannot come soon enough. The evolution of road safety is in full stride.

9.5 Driverless Cars

Only a few years ago, the concept of driverless cars was something we associated with science fiction movies. However, advances in technology and human ingenuity mean that driverless cars, and trucks, are becoming a reality. Google has, perhaps, received most of the attention for developing driverless cars, but many car manufacturers are also at various stages of producing such vehicles. The following brief statement in an article by the Eno Center for Transportation, in Washington DC, summarizes the status of the development of driverless cars in early 2013:

> *"As of April 2013, Google's Self-driving cars have driven over 435,000 miles on California public roads, and numerous manufactures—including Audi, BMW, Cadillac, Ford, GM, Mercedes-Benz, Nissan, Toyota, Volkswagen and Volvo—have begun testing driverless systems."*[21]

Thus the evolution of highway safety takes another leap forward. Although it remains to be seen to what extent driverless vehicles will eventually be used, it gives us hope for a more promising world for our children and grandchildren, and for the generations to follow.

9.6 Chapter Summery: The Road Safety Revolution

The revolutionary approaches to road safety in the Netherlands, Sweden, Australia, New Zealand and the EU, as well as the efforts to develop safer cars and driverless cars, are the result of visionaries who refuse to accept the extent of the death and destruction on the world's roads. These visionaries believe the carnage occurring on the world's roads is unacceptable and unnecessary, and that it can be drastically reduced. This, they believe, can be achieved by shifting the responsibilities for road safety and by developing safer roads, safer roadsides, safer vehicles, and by enforcing safer speeds.

Whereas road safety has traditionally been considered to be the responsibility of road users, in these new road safety strategies the responsibility for road safety is placed largely with the system designers, including those responsible for roads and roadsides, and those responsible for motor-vehicle-related matters. The responsibility for road safety also extends to law enforcement agencies—including the police, courts and legislative bodies—to transport carriers, health services, schools, road safety organizations and politicians. The primary responsibilities of road users, under these new road safety strategies are to remain alert and to comply with the rules of the system.

TEN

Conclusions and Recommendations

10.0 Conclusions: Staying Safe on Our Roads

We have completed our extensive review and analysis of the major components of our complex road systems. Our primary objective was to develop an understanding of the many hazards that exist on our roadways so that we, as individuals, understand how to reduce, to the greatest extent possible, the risks of being involved in a traffic collision. Our mission has been not so much to change the world, but rather to understand the world that exists, so we can make the best decisions for our safety and for the safety of our children and grandchildren.

We can summarize our conclusions as follows:

1. Based on the statistics presented in Chapter 1, the extent of collisions, injuries and deaths occurring annually on the roads in Canada, the U.S. and worldwide is horrifying. The costs associated with these events are staggering. From the information we have gathered throughout this book, we must agree with the World Health Organization that the extent of the deaths and injuries occurring on our roads is unacceptable and avoidable.[1]

2. The information in Chapter 3 and also section 8.2 of Chapter 8 identifies that the speeds at which we commonly travel on our

roads are of immense significance to our safety. All speeds, even those within the posted speed limits, are potentially hazardous. Exceeding the posted speed limits and driving too fast for conditions are especially hazardous.

3. Speed is fundamental to the impacts that occur in collisions. The greater our speed, the greater the impact will be in a collision.

4. Our fragile human bodies have a very limited ability to withstand the impacts that occur in collisions. The cushioning offered by seat belts, air bags and helmets helps to reduce the damages to our bodies resulting from impacts.

5. There are numerous features of our road systems that make them inherently hazardous to road users. This applies to our city streets, highways and freeways, intersections, shoulders, bicycle lanes, motor vehicles, roadside hazards, and includes the possibility of improperly maintained roads. The hazardous features of our road systems are amongst the many underlying causes of the collisions, injuries and deaths occurring on our roads.

6. Our review and analysis, in Chapter 6, of winter maintenance practices showed the numerous hazards that could arise in winter months, due to adverse road and weather conditions and the possibility of improperly maintained roads.

7. We saw that there is a very small margin for error on our streets, highways and freeways, due to the speeds at which we commonly travel, the widths of motor vehicles, especially transport trucks, and the limited widths of traffic lanes. This small margin for error is fundamental to our safety and to the extent of collisions, injuries and deaths occurring on our roads. With this small margin for error there is very little time and very little space to correct for any error made by any road user.

8. We saw in Chapter 7 that human behaviour and adverse road and weather conditions are the most frequently reported contributing factors of injury and fatal collisions.

9. In Chapters 7 and 8, we saw that the causes of the collisions, injuries and deaths on our roads are the result of four major problems:

    a. The numerous, inherently hazardous features of our streets, highways and motor vehicles.

    b. Human Behaviour

    c. Adverse road and weather conditions.

    d. The speeds at which we commonly travel.

10. As individuals, we have little or no ability to change the hazardous features of our streets, highways and motor vehicles. Our best defense against these problems is to understand the hazards that exist on the roads and to conduct ourselves accordingly.

11. As individuals, we have a great deal of control over our own behaviour on the roads. In this regard, it is of critical importance that each of us understands those behaviours that frequently contribute to collisions and to then ensure we refrain from such behaviours ourselves.

12. It is critical to our safety to understand the hazards that exist during adverse road and weather conditions. With the variable conditions that exist in adverse conditions, we must always drive more slowly than what may be a maximum safe speed. To drive at what we consider to be the maximum safe speed during adverse conditions is to risk driving too fast for conditions.

13. The road safety strategies recently adopted by the Netherlands, Sweden, Australia and New Zealand are a result of visionaries refusing to accept the extent of the death and destruction on the roads. The implementation of these new road safety strategies, combined with the design of cars that will not crash, and the design of driverless cars, holds great promise for coming generations. These fundamental and revolutionary shifts in attitude towards road safety should be further incentive to people living in Canada and the U.S. to adopt better and safer ways to travel on the roads.

14. Those responsible for road safety and road safety education in Canada and the U.S. need to do far more to disclose to the public the inherently hazardous features of our roadways. This includes identifying the hazardous features of our city streets, highways and freeways, intersections, shoulders, bicycle lanes,

motor vehicles, roadside hazards and the possibility for improperly maintained roads. More needs to be done to inform the public, and our youth, of the small margin for error that exists on our roads, due to the combined effects of the speeds at which we commonly travel, the widths of motor vehicles and the limited widths of traffic lanes. The public needs to understand that, at the speeds we commonly travel, there is a very small amount of time and distance to correct for any errors, made by anyone. Finally, more also needs to be done to educate the public on the numerous hazards inherent to adverse road and weather conditions and of the extent to which collisions, injuries and deaths occur during adverse conditions. People cannot defend themselves against hazards they do not properly understand.

10.1 Recommendations: Staying Safe on Our Roads

As we have learned, our roadways are complex. Statistics leave no doubt that this complexity results in terrible numbers of collisions, injuries and deaths, which threaten all road users. The leadership of the Netherlands, Sweden, Australia and New Zealand has demonstrated there is much that can and should be done to improve road safety.

As we have also learned, staying safe on our roads is a challenge for all road users, of all ages. Staying safe on our roads demands that road users understand the numerous hazards that exist, understand the need to be cautious at all times and understand the need to abide by the laws, rules and regulations governing the proper and safe use of the roadways. This applies to all road users, regardless of where they live or the road safety strategy of their particular country.

Based upon the complexities of our roadways, the numerous hazards that exist, and the desperate need to improve road safety, it is therefore recommended that a well-designed road safety educational program be included in every school curriculum. The information in this book should be a central part of such a program, aimed at people in their teens. Other parts of a road safety educational program would necessarily start with children in kindergarten and continue through to proper driver instruction and training.

Road Safety Educational Program

It is recommended that the following subjects—all of which we reviewed in this book—form a part of a road safety educational program, directed to people in their teens:

1. **Statistics on the collisions, injuries and deaths occurring on the roads in Canada, the U.S. and worldwide.**

These statistics enable road users to understand the risks involved with using our streets, highways and motor vehicles. By understanding the risks, those using the roads in any capacity are able to understand the need for caution and/or change.

2. **Statistics on the costs associated with road collisions, injuries and deaths.**

Everyone—the general public, politicians and the people responsible for road safety education—needs to be aware of the staggering costs associated with the carnage on our streets and highways. In Canada and the U.S. alone, it is recognized that this carnage costs in the order of 1 trillion dollars per year, which should easily justify the costs of introducing a well-designed road safety educational program into our schools.

3. **The significance of speed in terms of the impacts to our bodies, the distances we travel per second, and the height we would need to fall to reach the speeds at which we travel on our roadways.**

Everyone needs to understand the limitations of our bodies to withstand the impacts that occur in collisions. Further, people need to develop a concept of speed, not only in terms of kilometers or miles per hour, but also in terms of the meters or feet that vehicles travel every second. To tie the concepts of impact and speed together, it is useful to understand the distances we would need to fall in order to reach the speeds we travel on our streets and highways.

4. The hazards associated with the design and operation of our streets and highways.

The geometric design aspects of our streets and highways are critically important to road safety. Understanding these matters is therefore essential for all road users. All of the topics addressed in Chapter 4 are fundamental to gaining a proper understanding of road safety, including: speed limits, sight distance and stopping sight distance, brake reaction distance and braking distance, kinetic energy, traffic control devices, widths of traffic lanes, highway shoulders, rumble strips and roadside hazards.

5. The hazards associated with the dimensions and weights of various classifications of motor vehicles.

Understanding the hazards relating to the widths, heights, lengths, weights and number of axles of motor vehicles, especially transport trucks (Chapter 5) is fundamental to gaining a proper understanding of the hazards on our roads.

6. The hazards associated with adverse road and weather conditions and with highway winter maintenance practices.

The hazards associated with winter driving and with highway winter maintenance practices are amongst the most complex and dangerous aspects of our streets and highways. These topics (addressed in Chapter 6) rarely receive the attention they deserve, but are critically important to understanding how to stay as safe as possible on the roadways, in winter conditions.

7. The contributing factors of collisions, as identified in police reports on injury and fatal collisions.

Reviewing statistics on the extent to which human behaviour and environmental conditions are contributing factors of collisions is of fundamental importance to understanding road safety (Chapter 7).

Knowing the statistics on these matters allows us to better understand the numerous hazards on our roads. It also allows us to attempt to avoid making the errors people commonly make on the roads.

8. The underlying causes of collisions, injuries and deaths on our roadways.

- Understanding the hazards that exist due to the inherent features of our city streets, highways and freeways, intersections, shoulders, bicycle lanes, and motor vehicles is fundamentally important to road safety. In addition, road users need to be aware of the many roadside hazards that exist. Knowing these helps us to determine how we might reduce our risks while on the roadways.

- All road users must understand the significance of speed to road safety. This includes the numerous hazards that exist when driving within the posted speed limits as well as the increased hazards that are created when exceeding the speed limits and when driving too fast for conditions.

- It is also fundamentally important for road users to understand the hazards associated with adverse road and weather conditions. In particular, road users need to be aware of how quickly and frequently driving conditions can change during adverse conditions. Motorists must also be aware that roads, especially in winter months, may not be properly maintained. In addition, all road users need to understand that, especially in adverse conditions, motorists are often driving too fast to be able to properly control their vehicles.

- The many other underlying causes of collisions, injuries and deaths identified in Chapter 8 must also be addressed, including: hydroplaning, abuse of alcohol and drugs, following too closely, pedestrian error/confusion, driver inexperience, the elderly, herd mentality, lack of education, lack of self-discipline, poor time management, use of electronic devices, pets in vehicles, motorcycles, use of seat belts and helmets, and television commercials.

9. **The small margin for error that exists on our streets and highways and the small amount of time available to correct for any errors made by anyone.**

There is a very small margin for error on our streets and highways, due to the speeds we commonly travel, the dimensions of motor vehicles and the limited widths of our traffic lanes. This small margin for error allows for a small amount of time and distance to correct for any errors made by anyone. The small margin for error and the limited time and distance available to correct for errors are serious and fundamental problems on our roads. These problems are accentuated by the numerous, inherently hazardous features of our roads, by the hazards arising during adverse road and weather conditions and by the problems arising from human behaviour. Understanding these issues is basic to staying safe on our roads.

10. **The basis for the new road safety strategies adopted by the Netherlands, Sweden, Australia, New Zealand and the European Union.**

Everyone should be aware of the basis for the revolutionary road safety strategies adopted by the Netherlands, Sweden, Australia, and New Zealand (Chapter 9). These countries have rejected the common belief in Canada and the U.S. that the extent of serious injuries and deaths on our roads is the necessary price we must pay for our standard of living and for our mobile lifestyle. The thinking behind these new road safety strategies, combined with the need to develop safer cars, safer roadsides, safer speeds and even driverless cars, is further evidence of the extent of the problems with road safety in Canada and the U.S. A well-designed road safety educational program is essential for our youth to gain a proper understanding of the hazards on our roads and should, therefore, be included in every school curriculum.

10.2 Final Comments: Staying Safe on Our Roads

This concludes our discussions on road safety. Readers should now have a good understanding of the numerous hazards that exist on our roads, many of which are inherent to the design, operation and maintenance of our streets, highways and motor vehicles. Additional hazards arise during adverse road and weather conditions and others result from human behaviour. Speed is a fundamentally important aspect of road safety and plays a major role in the collisions, injuries and deaths on our roads. By understanding the hazards on our roads, and by using our roads wisely and in a low-risk manner, we can greatly reduce our risks of being involved in a traffic collision.

The initiatives to develop new road safety strategies in countries such as the Netherlands, Sweden, Australia and New Zealand, hold great promise for the safety of all road users in the years ahead. Canada and the U.S. will, we hope, adopt road safety strategies similar to those recently adopted in these other countries. However, regardless of a country's road safety strategy or the development of safer roads, safer roadsides, safer speeds, safer vehicles—possibly even driverless cars and trucks—it will remain essential for road users, for their safety, to have a proper understanding of the hazards that exist on our roads.

The complexities of the numerous hazards on our roads and the extent of the collisions, injuries and deaths occurring, demand that all road users be properly educated on matters relating to road safety. Staying safe on our roads and road safety education are inseparable.

REFERENCES

Introduction

1. Peden, M., R. Scurfield, D. Sleet, D. Mohan, A. Hyder, E. Jarawan, and C. Mathers, eds. "World report on road traffic injury prevention." World Health Organization, Geneva, 2004. Chap. 1, p. 3. Adapted by the author with permission. Accessed August 24, 2012. http://whqlibdoc.who.int/publications/2004/9241562609.pdf

2. The Swedish Government and Swedish Industry. "Freedom to move-No more acceptance." Vision Zero Initiative. Traffic Safety by Sweden. Accessed September 1, 2014. http://www.visionzeroinitiative.com/en/Concept/Freedom-to-move/

3. Roads and Traffic Authority of New South Wales. "Speeding—Did you know? 'Safe System'—the key to managing road safety." Fact Sheet 6 of 6. NSW Centre for Road Safety, NSW Government Transport Roads & Traffic Authority. Property of Transport for NSW, p.1. Accessed October 14, 2014. www.rms.nsw.gov.au/saferroadsnsw/safe-system.pdf

4. National Road Safety Committee; Ministry of Transport. "2020 Safer Journeys, New Zealand's Road Safety Strategy 2010-2020." New Zealand Government, p. 3. Accessed October 31, 2014. www.saferjourneys.govt.nz/assets/Uploads/SaferJourneyStrategy.pdf

5. Trafikverket Swedish Transport Administration. "Analytic report Review of interim Targets and Indicators for Road Safety in 2010–2020." The Swedish Transport Administration. June 2012, Publication Number 2012:162, p.5. ISBN: 978-91-7467-365-4. Accessed October 27, 2014. 2012_162_review_of_interim_targets_and_indicators_for_road_safety_in_2010_2020.pdf

6. The Swedish Government and Swedish Industry. "The Vision Zero." Vision Zero Initiative. Traffic Safety by Sweden. Accessed September 1, 2014. http://www.visionzeroinitiative.com/en/Concept/

Chapter 1: Statistics Tell an Alarming Story

1. Transport Canada. "Canadian Motor Vehicle Traffic Collision Statistics 2013." Her Majesty the Queen in Right of Canada, represented by the Minister of Transport, 2015. Transport Canada. Collected in cooperation with the Canadian Council of Motor Transport Administrators, p. 3. ISBN: 1701-6223. Accessed October 5, 2015. http://www.tc.gc.ca/media/documents/roadsafety/cmvtcs2013_eng.pdf

2. Statistics Canada. "Population by year, by province and territory." Government of Canada. Statistics Canada, CANSIM, table 051-0001. Accessed November 2, 2014. http://www.statcan.gc.ca/tables-tableaux/sum-som/l01/cst01/demo02a-eng.htm

3. National Defence, Canada (DND). "National Defence and the Canadian Forces:

Fallen Canadians." National Defence, Canada. 2011, pp. 1–31. Accessed November 20, 2012. http://www.forces.gc.ca/site/news-nouvelles/fallen-disparus/index-eng.asp

4. Transport Canada. "Road and Motor Vehicle Safety." Government of Canada. Transport Canada, p. 1. Accessed August 25, 2012. http://www.tc.gc.ca/eng/road-safety/menu.htm

5. U.S. Department of Transportation, National Highway Traffic Safety Administration (NHTSA). "Traffic Safety Facts 2013." (Report No. DOT HS 812 139). NHTSA National Center for Statistics and Analysis. Washington, DC. A Compilation of Motor Vehicle Crash Data from the Fatality Analysis Reporting System and the General Estimates System, p. 2. Accessed October 5, 2015. http://www-nrd.nhtsa.dot.gov/Pubs/812139.pdf

6. "Faces of the Fallen." The Washington Post. 1996–2012 Accessed August 25, 2012. http://apps.washingtonpost.com/national/fallen/

7. U.S. Department of Transportation, National Highway Traffic Safety Administration (NHTSA). "Traffic Safety Facts 2013." (Report No. DOT HS 812 139). NHTSA National Center for Statistics and Analysis. Washington, DC. A Compilation of Motor Vehicle Crash data from the Fatality Analysis Reporting System and the General Estimates System. Table 2, pp. 18–19. Accessed October 5, 2015. http://www-nrd.nhtsa.dot.gov/Pubs/812139.pdf

8. National Commission on Terrorist Attacks Upon the United States. "The 9/11 Commission Report Final Report of the National Commission on Terrorist Attacks Upon the United States." Executive Summary, pp. 1–2. Accessed February 2, 2013. http://govinfo.library.unt.edu/911/report/911Report_Exec.pdf

9. From "AASHTO Strategic Highway Safety Plan—A Comprehensive Plan to Substantially Reduce Vehicle-Related Fatalities and Injuries on the Nation's Highways," 2005, by the American Association of State Highway and Transportation Officials, Washington, DC. Introduction, p. 1. Used by permission. Accessed October 10, 2012. http://safety.transportation.org/doc/Safety-StrategicHighwaySafetyPlan.pdf

10. Peden, M., R. Scurfield, D. Sleet, D. Mohan, A. Hyder, E. Jarawan, and C. Mathers, eds. "World report on road traffic injury prevention." World Health Organization, Geneva, 2004. Accessed August 24, 2012. http://whqlibdoc.who.int/publications/2004/9241562609.pdf

11. World Health Organization. "Global Status Report on Road Safety: Time for Action." World Health Organization, Geneva, 2009. Accessed August 24, 2012. http://whqlibdoc.who.int/publications/2009/9789241563840_eng.pdf

12. World Health Organization. "Global Status Report on Road Safety: Time for Action." World Health Organization, Geneva, 2009. Chap. 3, p. 14. Adapted by

the author with permission. Accessed August 24, 2012. http://whqlibdoc.who.int/publications/2009/9789241563840_eng.pdf

13. Peden, M., R. Scurfield, D. Sleet, D. Mohan, A. Hyder, E. Jarawan, and C. Mathers, eds. "World report on road traffic injury prevention." World Health Organization, Geneva, 2004. Chap. 1, p. 11. Adapted by the author with permission. Accessed August 24, 2012. http://whqlibdoc.who.int/publications/2004/9241562609.pdf

14. Chan, Dr. M., World Health Organization. "Global Status Report on Road Safety: Time for Action." World Health Organization, Geneva, 2009. Preface, p. iv. Adapted by the author with permission. Accessed August 24, 2012. http://whqlibdoc.who.int/publications/2009/9789241563840_eng.pdf

15. World Health Organization. "Global Status Report on Road Safety: Time for Action." World Health Organization, Geneva, 2009. Chap. 4, p. 38. Adapted by the author with permission. Accessed August 24, 2012. http://whqlibdoc.who.int/publications/2009/9789241563840_eng.pdf

16. World Health Organization. Executive Summary, p. ix. Adapted by the author with permission.

17. Vodden, K., Dr. D. Smith, F. Eaton, and D. Mayhew. "Analysis and Estimation of the Social Cost of Motor Vehicle Collisions in Ontario Final Report." Transport Canada August 2007. N0779. TP 14800F. Accessed August 26, 2012. http://www.tc.gc.ca/media/documents/roadsafety/TP14800E.pdf

18. Transport Canada. "Analysis and Estimation of the Social Cost of Motor Vehicle Collisions in Ontario (2007 Report)." Government of Canada. Transport Canada. August 2007 TP14800 E, p. 1. Accessed August 26, 2012. http://www.tc.gc.ca/eng/roadsafety/tp-tp14800-menu-159.htm

19. Vodden, K., Dr. D. Smith, F. Eaton, and D. Mayhew. "Analysis and Estimation of the Social Cost of Motor Vehicle Collisions in Ontario Final Report." Transport Canada August 2007 N0779. TP 14800F. Executive Summary, p. ii. Accessed August 26, 2012. http://www.tc.gc.ca/media/documents/roadsafety/TP14800E.pdf

20. Vodden, K., Dr. D. Smith, F. Eaton, and D. Mayhew. Executive Summary, p. i.

21. Blincoe, L., T. Miller, E. Zaloshnja, and B. Lawrence. "The Economic and Societal Impact of Motor Vehicle Crashes, 2010." (Report No. DOT HS 812 013, May 2014). Washington, DC. National Highway Traffic Safety Administration. Technical Report Documentation, p. i. Accessed November 3, 2014. http://www-nrd.nhtsa.dot.gov/pubs/812013.pdf

22. World Health Organization. "Global Status Report on Road Safety: Time for Action." World Health Organization, Geneva, 2009. Chap. 1, p. 2. Adapted by the author with permission. Accessed August 24, 2012. http://whqlibdoc.who.int/publications/2009/9789241563840_eng.pdf

Chapter 2: The Use of Our Roads

1. Peden, M., R. Scurfield, D. Sleet, D. Mohan, A. Hyder, E. Jarawan, and C. Mathers, eds. "World report on road traffic injury prevention." World Health Organization, Geneva, 2004. Chap. 1, p. 3. Adapted by the author with permission. Accessed August 24, 2012. http://whqlibdoc.who.int/publications/2004/9241562609.pdf

2. Peden, M., R. Scurfield, D. Sleet, D. Mohan, A. Hyder, E. Jarawan, and C. Mathers, eds. Chap. 1, p. 7. Adapted by the author with permission.

3. National Highway Traffic Safety Administration (NHTSA). "Traffic Safety Facts 2010." (Report No. DOT HS 811 659). NHTSA National Center for Statistics and Analysis. Washington, DC. A Compilation of Motor Vehicle Crash Data from the Fatality Analysis Reporting System and the General Estimates System. Glossary, p. 209. Accessed October 28, 2012. http://www-nrd.nhtsa.dot.gov/Pubs/811659.pdf

4. Transport Canada. "Canadian Motor Vehicle Traffic Collision Statistics 2013." Her Majesty the Queen in Right of Canada, represented by the Minister of Transport, 2015. Transport Canada. Collected in cooperation with the Canadian Council of Motor Transport Administrators. ISBN: 1701-6223. Accessed October 5, 2015. http://www.tc.gc.ca/media/documents/roadsafety/cmvtcs2013_eng.pdf

5. Peden, M., R. Scurfield, D. Sleet, D. Mohan, A. Hyder, E. Jarawan, and C. Mathers, eds. "World report on road traffic injury prevention." World Health Organization, Geneva, 2004. Introduction, p. xix. Adapted by the author with permission. Accessed August 24, 2012. http://whqlibdoc.who.int/publications/2004/9241562609.pdf

Chapter 3: Speed and Impacts in Collisions

1. Vagverket Swedish Road Administration. "Safe Traffic - Vision Zero on the move." Vagverket, Swedish Road Administration, Sweden. Order No 88325, 2nd Edition, March 2006, p. 6. Accessed October 15, 2014. 88325_safe_traffic_vision_zero_on_the_move.pdf

2. Roads and Traffic Authority of New South Wales. "Speeding—Did you know? 'Safe System'—the key to managing road safety." Fact Sheet 6 of 6. NSW Centre for Road Safety, NSW Government Transport Roads & Traffic Authority. Property of Transport for NSW, p. 2. Accessed October 14, 2014. www.rms.nsw.gov.au/saferroadsnsw/safe-system.pdf

3. From PHYSICS THE EASY WAY by Robert L. Lehrman. Copyright © 1998, 1990, 1984 by Barron's Educational Series, Inc. Reprinted by arrangement with Barron's Educational Series, Inc., p. 31.

4. From PHYSICS THE EASY WAY, Section 2.8, p. 33.

Chapter 4: Road Design and Operation

1. Peden, M., R. Scurfield, D. Sleet, D. Mohan, A. Hyder, E. Jarawan, and C. Mathers, eds. "World report on road traffic injury prevention." World Health Organization, Geneva, 2004. Chap. 1, p. 3. Adapted by the author with permission. Accessed August 24, 2012. http://whqlibdoc.who.int/publications/2004/9241562609.pdf

2. Illinois Department of Transportation, Division of Highways, Bureau of Local Roads and Streets. "Highway Jurisdiction Guidelines for Highway and Street Systems." State of Illinois (4/2006). Chap. 1, p.1. Accessed August 19, 2012. http://www.dot.state.il.us/blr/JTGuide.pdf

3. Padova, Allison. "Federal Participation in Highway Construction and Policy in Canada." Library of Parliament. Ottawa, Ontario. PRB 05-69E. 20 February 2006, p. 2. Accessed August 19, 2012. http://www.parl.gc.ca/Content/LOP/Research-Publications/prb0569-e.pdf

4. Transport Canada. "Highways." Transport Canada. Canada. Accessed January 2, 2011. http://www.tc.gc.ca/eng/policy/acg-acgd-menu-highways-2141.htm

5. Gilchrist, C.W. "Roads and Highways." The Canadian Encyclopedia. Historica-Dominion, 2012. Jurisdiction, p. 3. Accessed August 18, 2012. http://www.the-canadianencyclopedia.com /articles/roads-and-highways

6. U.S. Department of Transportation, Federal Highway Administration (FHWA). "Highway Traffic Noise." (Report No. FHWA-HEP-06-020, April 2006). U.S. Department of Transportation, Federal Highway Administration, Washington, DC. The Highway System, p. 2. Accessed August 18, 2012. http://www.fhwa.dot.gov/environment/noise/regulations_and_guidance/probresp.cfm

7. California Department of Transportation. "Highway Design Manual." 2012 State of California. Caltrans Highway Design Manual, p. 60–5. May 7, 2012. Accessed August 18, 2012. http://www.dot.ca.gov/hq/oppd/hdm/pdf/english/chp0060.pdf

8. Delaware Department of Transportation. "DelDOT Road Design Manual." State of Delaware. July 2004. Section 3.1, p. 3-1. Accessed September 10, 2012. http://www.deldot.gov/information/pubs_forms/manuals/road_design/pdf/revisions042209/03_design_standards.pdf

9. Transportation Association of Canada (TAC). "Geometric Design Guide for Canadian Roads." Transportation Association of Canada, 1999, Ottawa, Canada.

10. American Association of State Highway and Transportation Officials (AASHTO). "A Policy on Geometric Design of Highways and Streets, 6th Edition," 2011. American Association of State Highway and Transportation Officials, Washington, DC.

11. Transportation Association of Canada (TAC). "Bookstore Geometric design for Canadian roads (1999)." Transportation Association of Canada, Ottawa, Canada. Accessed November 28, 2012. https://vws3.primus.ca/dev.tac-atc.ca/english/bookstore/products.cfm?catid=9&subcatid=18&prodid=54

12. From AASHTO Bookstore. "A Policy on Geometric Design of Highways and Streets,

6th Edition." Bookstore Advertisement by the American Association of State Highway and Transportation Officials, Washington, DC. Used by permission. Accessed September 9, 2012. http://bookstore.transportation.org/item_details.aspx?id=1917

13. British Columbia Ministry of Transportation. "BC Supplement to TAC Geometric Design Guide 2007 Edition." 2011, Province of British Columbia. Ministry of Transportation. ISBN: 978-0-7726-5800-5. Preface, June 2007, p. i. Accessed Sept 11, 2012. http://www.th.gov.bc.ca/publications/eng_publications/geomet/TAC/TAC_2007Supplement/2007BC_Supplement_to_TAC_Rev1.pdf

14. California Department of Transportation. "Highway Design Manual." 2012 State of California. Caltrans Highway Design Manual, p. 80–7. May 7, 2012. Accessed August 18, 2012. http://www.dot.ca.gov/hq/oppd/hdm/pdf/english/chp0060.pdf

15. City of Vancouver. "Construction standards." 2012 City of Vancouver, p. 1. Accessed December 1, 2012. http://vancouver.ca/streets-transportation/construction-standards.aspx

16. Province of British Columbia. *Motor Vehicle Act*. Queen's Printer, Victoria, British Columbia, Canada. Updated October 2010. Chap. 318, Section 146 (1), p. 121.

17. Province of British Columbia. *Motor Vehicle Act*. Chapter 318, Schools and playgrounds, Section 147, p. 122.

18. California Department of Motor Vehicles. "V C Section 22350 Basic Speed Law." 2011 State of California. California Vehicle Code section 22350. Accessed September 11, 2012. http://www.dmv.ca.gov/pubs/vctop/d11/vc22350.htm

19. California Department of Motor Vehicles. "V C Section 22352 Prima Facie Speed Limits." 2011 State of California. California Vehicle Code sections 22352(a)(1) (A)-(C). Accessed September 11, 2012. http://www.dmv.ca.gov/pubs/vctop/d11/vc22352.htm

20. California Department of Motor Vehicles. "California Driver Handbook." © California Department of Motor Vehicles 2012, p. 30. All rights reserved. Accessed September 12, 2012. http://apps.dmv.ca.gov/pubs/dl600.pdf

21. Parker, M., Huey-Yi Sung, and L. Dereniewski: Wade-Trim. "Review and Analysis of Posted Speed Limits and Speed Limit Setting Practices in British Columbia." Final Report Spring 2003. British Columbia Ministry of Transportation, Victoria. Project Number ZZZ2530.01T. Accessed August 19, 2012. http://www.th.gov.bc.ca/publications/eng_publications/speed_review/Speed_Review_Report.pdf

22. Parker, M., Huey-Yi Sung, and L. Dereniewski. Executive Summary, p. viii.

23. Parker, M., Huey-Yi Sung, and L. Dereniewski. Table 2, p. 6.

24. Parker, M., Huey-Yi Sung, and L. Dereniewski. Executive Summary, p. v.

25. Transportation Association of Canada (TAC). "Canadian Guidelines for Establishing Posted Speed Limits." 2009 by Transportation Association of Canada. Ottawa. December 2009. ISBN 978-1-55187-280-3.

26. TAC. Section 5.1-5.2, p. 8.

27. TAC. Section 1.2, p. 2.

28. TAC. Section 4.0, p. 7.

29. TAC. Section 6.7, p. 16.

30. Province of British Columbia. *Motor Vehicle Act.* Queen's Printer, Victoria, British Columbia, Canada. Updated October 2010. Chap. 318, Section 146 (3), p. 121.

31. U.S. Department of Transportation, Federal Highway Administration (FHWA). "Manual of Uniform Traffic Control Devices 2009 Edition." U.S. Department of Transportation, Federal Highway Administration, Washington, DC. Section 1A.13, paragraph 238, p. 22. Accessed September 12, 2012. http://mutcd.fhwa.dot.gov/pdfs/2009r1r2/mutcd2009r1r2edition.pdf

32. FHWA. Section 2B.13, paragraph 01, p. 56.

33. From "A Policy on Geometric Design of Highways and Streets, 6th Edition," 2011, by the American Association of State Highway and Transportation Officials, Washington, DC. Section 3.2.2, p. 3-2. Used by permission.

34. New York State. "Highway Design Manual." 1999-2012 New York State Department of Transportation. Chapter 5-Basic Design. Revision 62, April 13, 2011. Section 5.7.2.1, p. 5-50. Accessed September 13, 2012. http://www.dot.ny.gov/divisions/engineering/design/dqab/hdm/hdm-repository/chapt_5_final.pdf

35. Transportation Association of Canada (TAC). "Geometric Design Guide for Canadian Roads." Transportation Association of Canada, 1999. Ottawa, Canada. Section 1.2.2.2, p. 1.2.2.1.

36. From "A Policy on Geometric Design of Highways and Streets, 6th Edition," 2011, by the American Association of State Highway and Transportation Officials, Washington, DC. Section 3.2.3, p. 3-6. Used by permission.

37. From "A Policy on Geometric Design of Highways and Streets, 6th Edition." Table 3-1, p. 3-4. Used by permission.

38. Transportation Association of Canada (TAC). "Geometric Design Guide for Canadian Roads." Transportation Association of Canada, 1999. Ottawa, Canada. Table 1.2.5.3, p. 1.2.5.4.

39. TAC. Section 1.2.5.2, p. 1.2.5.2.

40. From *PHYSICS THE EASY WAY* by Robert L. Lehrman. Copyright © 1998, 1990, 1984 by Barron's Educational Series, Inc. Reprinted by arrangement with Barron's Educational Series, Inc., p. 122.

41. U.S. Department of Transportation, Federal Highway Administration (FHWA). "Manual of Uniform Traffic Control Devices 2009 Edition." U.S. Department of Transportation, Federal Highway Administration, Washington, DC. Accessed September 12, 2012. http://mutcd.fhwa.dot.gov/pdfs/2009r1r2/mutcd2009r1r2edition.pdf

42. U.S. Department of Transportation, Federal Highway Administration (FHWA).

"Frequently Asked Questions-General Questions on the MUTCD." Federal Highway Administration. Q #2, p. 2. Accessed March 30, 2012. http://mutcd.fhwa.dot.gov/knowledge/faqs/faq_general.htm

43. Transportation Association of Canada (TAC). "Pooled Fund Projects Manual of Uniform Traffic Control Devices for Canada Update Scoping Study." Transportation Association of Canada, Ottawa, Canada. Accessed February 18, 2012. http://www.tac-atc.ca/english/projects/trafficcontrol.cfm

44. Transportation Association of Canada (TAC). "Geometric Design Guide for Canadian Roads." Transportation Association of Canada, 1999. Ottawa, Canada. Section 2.2.3, p. 2.2.3.1.

45. TAC. Section 2.2.2, p. 2.2.2.1.

46. TAC. Table 2.2.2.1 and Table 2.2.2.3, pp. 2.2.2.1 and 2.2.2.2.

47. From "A Policy on Geometric Design of Highways and Streets, 6th Edition," 2011, by the American Association of State Highway and Transportation Officials, Washington, DC. Section 4.3, p. 4-7. Used by permission.

48. Transportation Association of Canada (TAC). "Geometric Design Guide for Canadian Roads." Transportation Association of Canada, 1999. Ottawa, Canada. Section 2.2.4.2, pp. 2.2.4.1 and 2.2.4.2.

49. From "A Policy on Geometric Design of Highways and Streets, 6th Edition," 2011, by the American Association of State Highway and Transportation Officials, Washington, DC. Section 4.4.2, p. 4-10. Used by permission.

50. From "A Policy on Geometric Design of Highways and Streets, 6th Edition." Section 4.4.2, p. 4-11. Used by permission.

51. From "A Policy on Geometric Design of Highways and Streets, 6th Edition." Section 4.4.6, p. 4-14. Used by permission.

52. From "A Policy on Geometric Design of Highways and Streets, 6th Edition." Section 7.2.3, p. 7-4. Used by permission.

53. Transportation Association of Canada (TAC). "Geometric Design Guide for Canadian Roads." Transportation Association of Canada, 1999. Ottawa, Canada. Section 3.4.2, page 3.4.2.1.

54. TAC. Figure 3.4.2.1, p. 3.4.2.2.

Chapter 5: Motor Vehicles

1. Dada, E. and M. Furuya, Bunt & Associates. "Parking Dimensions." First published by the Canadian Parking Association in *The Parker*, Q2, 2010. Accessed November 24, 2012. http://canadianparking.ca/files/ParkingDimensions_eng.pdf

2. Dada, E. and M. Furuya, Bunt & Associates. Design Vehicle, p. 2.

3. Dada, E. and M. Furuya, Bunt & Associates. Table 2, p. 2.

4. Transport Canada. "Data reporting." Government of Canada. Transport Canada, p. 1.

Accessed January 26, 2013. http://www.tc.gc.ca/eng/programs/environment-fcp-reporting-661.htm

5.   Ford Motor Company. "Taurus Specifications." 2012 Ford Motor Company. 2013 Ford Taurus. 3.5L V6 Base Curb weight (lbs.). Approved for use. Accessed September 20, 2012. http://www.ford.com/cars/taurus/specifications/exterior/

6.   Ford Motor Company. "Explorer Specifications." 2012 Ford Motor Company. 2013 Ford Explorer. Estimated Base Curb Weight (lbs.). Approved for use. Accessed September 20, 2012. http://www.ford.com/suvs/explorer/specifications/exterior/

7.   Ford Motor Company. "F-150 Specifications." 2012 Ford Motor Company. 2013 Ford F-150. Minimum Vehicle Base Curb Weight (lbs.) 4x4. Approved for use. Accessed November 28, 2012. http://www.ford.com/trucks/f150/specifications/

8.   Ford Motor Company. "F-150 Specifications." 2012 Ford Motor Company. 2013 Ford F-150. Regular Cab Exterior Dimensions, p. 1. Approved for use. Accessed November 11, 2012. http://www.ford.com/trucks/f150/specifications/exterior/

9.   Council of Ministers and Deputy Ministers Responsible for Transportation and Highway Safety. "Harmonization of Transportation Policies and Regulations: Context, Progress and Initiatives in the Motor Carrier Sector." Report to the Council of the Federation, June 2008, p. 20. Accessed September 25, 2012. http://www.comt.ca/english/coff-report.pdf

10.   NAFTA Land Transportation Standards Subcommittee-Working Group 2. "Harmonization of Vehicle Weight and Dimension Regulations Within the NAFTA Partnership." Report to the Land Transportation Standards Subcommittee, October 1997, p. 7. Accessed September 25, 2012. http://www.comt.ca/english/programs/trucking/NAFTA%20Side%20by%20Sde%20Oct2097.pdf

11.   Schulman, Joseph F. "Heavy Truck Weight and Dimension Limits in Canada" 2003. The Railway Association of Canada. Introduction, p. 5. Accessed September 25, 2012. http://www.highwaysafetyroundtable.ca/member/documents/RAC%20Heavy%20Truck%2003.pdf

12.   Task Force on Vehicle Weights and Dimensions Policy. Council of Ministers and Deputy Ministers Responsible for Transportation and Highway Safety. "Heavy Truck Weight and Dimension Limits for Interprovincial Operations in Canada." Resulting from the Federal-Provincial-Territorial Memorandum of Understanding on Interprovincial Weights and Dimensions. Summary Information, December 2011. Accessed September 25, 2012. http://www.comt.ca/english/programs/trucking/MOU%202011.pdf

13.   British Columbia Ministry of Transportation and Infrastructure. "Long Combination Vehicles Program Weights and Dimensions." British Columbia Ministry of Transportation and Infrastructure. Turnpike Doubles, p. 2. Accessed September 25, 2012. http://www.th.gov.bc.ca/cvse/LCV/weights_dimensions.htm

14.   Council of Ministers and Deputy Ministers Responsible for Transportation and

Highway Safety. "Harmonization of Transportation Policies and Regulations: Context, Progress and Initiatives in the Motor Carrier Sector." Report to the Council of the Federation, June 2008. Appendix A, Overall Height and Overall Width, p. 28. Accessed September 25, 2012. http://www.comt.ca/english/coff-report.pdf

15. U.S. Department of Transportation, Federal Highway Administration (FHWA). "Federal Size Regulations for Commercial Motor Vehicles." U.S. Department of Transportation, Federal Highway Administration, Washington, DC. October 2004. FHWA-HOP-04-022, EDL 14012. Width Requirements, p. 2. Accessed September 26, 2012. http://www.ops.fhwa.dot.gov/freight/publications/size_regs_final_rpt/index.htm

16. Task Force on Vehicle Weights and Dimensions Policy. Council of Ministers and Deputy Ministers Responsible for Transportation and Highway Safety. "Heavy Truck Weight and Dimension Limits for Interprovincial Operations in Canada." Resulting from the Federal-Provincial-Territorial Memorandum of Understanding on Interprovincial Weights and Dimensions. Summary Information, December 2011. Item 5, p. 8. Accessed September 25, 2012. http://www.comt.ca/english/programs/trucking/MOU%202011.pdf

17. U.S. Department of Transportation, Federal Highway Administration (FHWA). "Federal Size Regulations for Commercial Motor Vehicles." U.S. Department of Transportation, Federal Highway Administration, Washington, DC. October 2004. FHWA-HOP-04-022, EDL 14012. Figure 1, p. 2. Accessed September 26, 2012. http://www.ops.fhwa.dot.gov/freight/publications/size_regs_final_rpt/index.htm

18. California Department of Transportation. "Vehicle Widths." 2012 State of California. Section 35109, p. 2. Accessed September 26, 2012. http://www.dot.ca.gov/hq/traffops/trucks/trucksize/width.htm

19. Task Force on Vehicle Weights and Dimensions Policy. Council of Ministers and Deputy Ministers Responsible for Transportation and Highway Safety. "Heavy Truck Weight and Dimension Limits for Interprovincial Operations in Canada". Resulting from the Federal-Provincial-Territorial Memorandum of Understanding on Interprovincial Weights and Dimensions. Summary Information, December 2011. Category 5: Straight Truck, pp. 18–19. Accessed September 25, 2012. http://www.comt.ca/english/programs/trucking/MOU%202011.pdf

20. Task Force on Vehicle Weights and Dimensions Policy. Category 1: Tractor Semi-trailer, pp. 10–11.

21. Task Force on Vehicle Weights and Dimensions Policy. Category 3: B Train Double, pp. 14–15.

22. Province of British Columbia. *Commercial Transport Act, Commercial Transport Regulations*. Queen's Printer, Victoria, British Columbia, Canada. Vehicle width,

Section 7.06, p. 13. Accessed September 25, 2012. http://www.bclaws.ca/EPLibraries/bclaws_new/document/ID/freeside/30_78

23. Province of British Columbia. Vehicle height, Section 7.05, p. 13.

24. U.S. Department of Transportation, Federal Highway Administration (FHWA). "Federal Size Regulations for Commercial Motor Vehicles." U.S. Department of Transportation, Federal Highway Administration, Washington, DC. October 2004. FHWA-HOP-04-022, EDL 14012. Federal Size Regulations for Commercial Motor Vehicles (CMV's), p. 2. Accessed September 26, 2012. http://www.ops.fhwa.dot.gov/freight/publications/size_regs_final_rpt/index.htm

25. Transportation Association of Canada (TAC). "Geometric Design Guide for Canadian Roads." Transportation Association of Canada, 1999. Ottawa, Canada. Table 2.2.2.1 and 2.2.2.3, pp. 2.2.2.1 and 2.2.2.2.

26. From "A Policy on Geometric Design of Highways and Streets, 6th Edition," 2011, by the American Association of State Highway and Transportation Officials, Washington, DC. Section 4.3, p. 4-7. Used by permission.

27. New York City DOT. "Motorists Trucks & Commercial Vehicles." 2012 The City of New York. Cross Over Mirrors, p. 1. Accessed September 27, 2012. http://www.nyc.gov/html/dot/html/motorist/trucks.shtml

28. U.S. Department of Transport, National Highway Traffic Safety Administration (NHTSA). "5-Star Safety Ratings Frequently Asked Questions." NHTSA Washington DC. Q 1, p. 1. Accessed September 25, 2014. http://www.safercar.gov/Vehicle+Shoppers/5-Star+FAQ

29. Vagverket Swedish Road Administration. "Safe Traffic - Vision Zero on the move." Vagverket, Swedish Road Administration, Sweden. Order No 88325, 2nd Edition, MARCH 2006, p. 6. Accessed October 15, 2014. 88325_safe_traffic_vision_zero_on_the_move.pdf

30. Roads and Traffic Authority of New South Wales. "Speeding—Did you know? 'Safe System'—the key to managing road safety." Fact Sheet 6 of 6. NSW Centre for Road Safety, NSW Government Transport Roads & Traffic Authority. Property of Transport for NSW, p. 2. Accessed October 14, 2014. www.rms.nsw.gov.au/saferroadsnsw/safe-system.pdf

Chapter 6: Hazards of Winter Driving

1. National Geographic. *Atlas of The World.* National Geographic Society, Washington, D.C. 1966. Enlarged Second Edition, p. 54.

2. British Columbia Ministry of Transportation and Highways. "Frontier to Freeway–A short illustrated history of the roads in British Columbia." 2011, Province of British Columbia, p. 33. Accessed October 4, 2012. http://www.th.gov.bc.ca/publications/frontiertofreeway/frontiertofreeway.pdf

3. British Columbia Ministry of Transportation and Infrastructure. "Highway Maintenance Agreements." 2011, Province of British Columbia, p. 1. Accessed January 17, 2013. http://www.th.gov.bc.ca/bchighways/contracts/maintenance/hwy_maintenance_contracts.htm

4. British Columbia Ministry of Transportation and Infrastructure. "Value of Maintenance Agreements at Time of Signing." 2011, Province of British Columbia. Highway Maintenance Agreements. Accessed January 17, 2013. http://www.th.gov.bc.ca/bchighways/contracts/maintenance/ValueAtSigning.pdf

5. British Columbia Minister of Transportation. "Maintenance Agreement." 2011, Province of British Columbia. Maintenance Agreement BC Bid Version-Oct 19 05. Definitions, (tt) "Maintenance Services," p. 7. Accessed October 6, 2012. http://www.th.gov.bc.ca/bchighways/contracts/maintenance/Maintenance_Agreements/Maintenance_Agreement_Boilerplate_Oct05.pdf

6. British Columbia Minister of Transportation. Section 12.2, p. 33.

7. British Columbia Ministry of Transportation. "Schedule "21" Maintenance Specifications." 2011, Province of British Columbia. 2003-2004 Highway Maintenance Contracts Maintenance Specifications February 2003. Chap. 9, p. 4. Accessed October 6, 2012. http://www.th.gov.bc.ca/BCHighways/contracts/maintenance/Schedule_21_Maintenance_Specifications.pdf

8. British Columbia Ministry of Transportation. Chap. 3-300, Section 3.1.1 a) i), p. 3.

9. British Columbia Ministry of Transportation. Chap. 3-300, Section 3.1.1 c), p. 4.

10. British Columbia Ministry of Transportation. Chap. 3-300, Section 3.1.1 e), p. 4.

11. British Columbia Ministry of Transportation. Chap. 3-320, Section 3.1.1 a) (vi), p. 3.

12. British Columbia Ministry of Transportation. Chap. 3-310, Section 1, p. 1.

13. British Columbia Ministry of Transportation. Chap. 3-310, Section 3.1.1.c), p. 3.

14. British Columbia Ministry of Transportation. Chap. 3-310, Section 3.1.1.b), p. 3.

15. British Columbia Ministry of Transportation. Chap. 3-310, Section 3.1.1.b) (i), p. 3.

16. British Columbia Ministry of Transportation. Chap. 3-310, Section 3.1.1.b) (iv), p. 3.

17. British Columbia Ministry of Transportation. Chap. 3-310, Section 3.1.1.b (ii) and (iii), p. 3.

18. British Columbia Ministry of Transportation. Chap. 4-380, Section 3.1r), p. 2.

19. British Columbia Ministry of Transportation. Chap. 3-340, Section 3.1c, p. 2.

20. British Columbia Ministry of Transportation and Infrastructure. "Boundary Maps." 2011, Province of British Columbia. Detailed Service Area Boundary Maps. Accessed January 17, 2013. http://www.th.gov.bc.ca/bchighways/contracts/maintenance/hwy_maint_boundary_maps.htm

21. Parker, M., Huey-Yi Sung, and L. Dereniewski, Wade-Trim. "Review and Analysis of Posted Speed Limits and Speed Limit Setting Practices in British Columbia." Final Report Spring 2003. British Columbia Ministry of Transportation, Victoria. Project Number ZZZ2530.01T. Executive Summary, p. viii. Accessed August

19, 2012. http://www.th.gov.bc.ca/publications/eng_publications/speed_review/Speed_Review_Report.pdf

Chapter 7: Contributing Factors of Collisions

1. Insurance Corporation of British Columbia (ICBC). "Traffic Collision Statistics - Police-attended Injury and Fatal Collisions - British Columbia 2007." British Columbia Motor Vehicle Branch -1994. Accessed December 15, 2011. http://www.icbc.com/road-safety/safety-research/traffic-coll-stats-2007.pdf
2. ICBC. Introduction. This publication, p. vii.
3. ICBC. BC 2007 collision statistics at a glance, Section 1, p. 1. Reprinted from the 2007 Traffic Collision Statistics with permission from ICBC.
4. ICBC. Procedure for reporting contributing factors, Section 3, p. 11.
5. ICBC. Table 3.06, p. 16. Reprinted from the 2007 Traffic Collision Statistics with permission from ICBC.
6. ICBC. Tables 3.02/3.03/3.04/3.05, pp. 13–15.
7. ICBC. Section 3. Contributing factors summary, p. 11.
8. ICBC. Tables 3.02 and 3.03, p. 13. Reprinted from the 2007 Traffic Collision Statistics with permission from ICBC.
9. ICBC. Table 3.04, p. 14. Reprinted from the 2007 Traffic Collision Statistics with permission from ICBC.
10. ICBC. Table 3.05, p. 15. Reprinted from the 2007 Traffic Collision Statistics with permission from ICBC.

Chapter 8: Underlying Causes of Collisions

1. Transportation Association of Canada (TAC). "Geometric Design Guide for Canadian Roads." Transportation Association of Canada, 1999. Ottawa, Canada. Table 2.2.2.1 and Table 2.2.2.3, pp. 2.2.2.1 and 2.2.2.2.
2. From "A Policy on Geometric Design of Highways and Streets, 6th Edition," 2011, by the American Association of State Highway and Transportation Officials, Washington, DC. Section 4.3, p. 4-7. Used by permission.
3. Dada, E. and M. Furuya; Bunt & Associates. "Parking Dimensions." First published by the Canadian Parking Association in The Parker, Q2, 2010. Table 2, p. 2. Accessed November 24, 2012. http://canadianparking.ca/files/ParkingDimensions_eng.pdf
4. Council of Ministers and Deputy Ministers Responsible for Transportation and Highway Safety. "Harmonization of Transportation Policies and Regulations: Context, Progress and Initiatives in the Motor Carrier Sector." Report to the Council of the Federation, June 2008. Appendix A, Overall Width, p. 28. Accessed September 25, 2012. http://www.comt.ca/english/coff-report.pdf

5.   Task Force on Vehicle Weights and Dimensions Policy. Council of Ministers and Deputy Ministers Responsible for Transportation and Highway Safety. "Heavy Truck Weight and Dimension Limits for Interprovincial Operations in Canada". Resulting from the Federal-Provincial-Territorial Memorandum of Understanding on Interprovincial Weights and Dimensions. Summary Information. December 2011. Item 5, p. 8. Accessed September 25, 2012. http://www.comt.ca/english/programs/trucking/MOU%202011.pdf

6.   From "A Policy on Geometric Design of Highways and Streets, 6th Edition," 2011, by the American Association of State Highway and Transportation Officials, Washington, DC. Section 3.2.2, p. 3-2. Used by permission.

7.   U.S. Department of Transportation, National Highway Traffic Safety Administration (NHTSA). "Crash Factors in Intersection-Related Crashes: An On-Scene Perspective." (Report No. DOT HS 811 366, September 2010). NHTSA's National Center for Statistics and Analysis, Washington, DC. Based on FARS and GES data. Introduction, p. 1. Accessed December 3, 2012. http://www-nrd.nhtsa.dot.gov/Pubs/811366.pdf

8.   Transportation Association of Canada (TAC). "Canadian Guidelines for Establishing Posted Speed Limits." 2009 by Transportation Association of Canada, Ottawa. December 2009. ISBN 978-1-55187-280-3. Section 4.0, p. 7.

9.   TAC. Section 6.7, p. 16.

10.   Province of British Columbia. *Motor Vehicle Act.* Queen's Printer, Victoria, British Columbia, Canada. Updated October 2010. Chap. 318, Section 146 (3), p. 121.

11.   Transportation Association of Canada (TAC). "Geometric Design Guide for Canadian Roads." Transportation Association of Canada, 1999. Ottawa, Canada. Section 1.2.5, p. 1.2.5.1.

12.   Transportation Association of Canada (TAC). Section 1.2.5.2, p. 1.2.5.2.

13.   From *PHYSICS THE EASY WAY* by Robert L. Lehrman. Copyright © 1998, 1990, 1984 by Barron's Educational Series, Inc. Reprinted by arrangement with Barron's Educational Series, Inc. Section 5.4, p. 122.

14.   From "A Policy on Geometric Design of Highways and Streets, 6th Edition," 2011, by the American Association of State Highway and Transportation Officials, Washington, DC. Table 3-1, p. 3-4. Used by permission.

15.   Insurance Corporation of British Columbia (ICBC). "Traffic Collision Statistics - Police-attended Injury and Fatal Collisions - British Columbia 2007." British Columbia Motor Vehicle Branch -1994. Table 3.06, p. 16. Accessed December 15, 2011. http://www.icbc.com/road-safety/safety-research/traffic-coll-stats-2007.pdf

16.   Parker, M., Huey-Yi Sung, and L. Dereniewski: Wade-Trim. "Review and Analysis of Posted Speed Limits and Speed Limit Setting Practices in British Columbia." Final Report Spring 2003. British Columbia Ministry of Transportation, Victoria. Project Number ZZZ2530.01T. Executive Summary, p. viii. Accessed August

19, 2012. http://www.th.gov.bc.ca/publications/eng_publications/speed_review/Speed_Review_Report.pdf

17. From "A Policy on Geometric Design of Highways and Streets, 6th Edition," 2011, by the American Association of State Highway and Transportation Officials, Washington, DC. Section 4.2.4, p. 4–7. Used by permission.

18. Insurance Corporation of British Columbia (ICBC). "Traffic Collision Statistics - Police-attended Injury and Fatal Collisions - British Columbia 2007." British Columbia Motor Vehicle Branch -1994. Table 3.07, p. 17. Accessed December 15, 2011. http://www.icbc.com/road-safety/safety-research/traffic-coll-stats-2007.pdf

19. Traffic Injury Research Foundation of Canada. "Alcohol-Crash Problem in Canada: 2010." Canadian Council of Motor Transport Administrators and the Minister of Public Works and Government Services, represented by the Minister of Transport, 2013. Ottawa. Section 3.1, p. 14. Accessed September 27, 2014. http://www.ccmta.ca/images/publications/pdf/alcohol_crash10_e.pdf

20. Transport Canada. "Smashed: A Sober Look at Drinking and Driving." Government of Canada. Transport Canada. TP1535E, revised 2009, p. 3. Accessed August 11, 2012. http://www.tc.gc.ca/eng/roadsafety/safedrivers-impaireddriving-smashed-index-580.htm

21. U.S. Department of Transportation, National Highway Traffic Safety Administration (NHTSA). "Traffic Safety Facts 2010 Data Overview." (Report No. DOT HS 811 630, June 2012). NHTSA's National Center for Statistics and Analysis. Washington, DC. Alcohol, p. 4. Accessed October 28, 2012. http://www-nrd.nhtsa.dot.gov/Pubs/811630.pdf

22. World Health Organization. "Global status report on alcohol and health." World Health Organization 2011, Switzerland. Introduction, p. xi. Adapted by the author with permission. Accessed October 28, 2012. http://www.who.int/entity/substance_abuse/publications/global_alcohol_report/msbgsruprofiles.pdf_

23. World Health Organization. Section 2.3.1, p. 35.

24. World Health Organization. Section 2.3, p. 34.

25. Transport Canada. "Smashed: A Sober Look at Drinking and Driving." Government of Canada. Transport Canada. TP1535E, revised 2009, p. 14. Accessed August 11, 2012. http://www.tc.gc.ca/eng/roadsafety/safedrivers-impaireddriving-smashed-index-580.htm

26. Ontario Ministry of Transportation. "The Official MTO Driver's Handbook." © Queen's Printer for Ontario, 2010. ISBN 978-1-4249-4041-7. The Road User Safety Division of the Ministry of Transportation of Ontario, pp. 35–36.

27. Transport Canada. "Canadian Motor Vehicle Traffic Collision Statistics: 2009." Government of Canada. Transport Canada. Collected in co-operation with the Canadian Council of Motor Transport Administrators. TP 3322 Cat. T45-

3/2009 2011, p. 7. Accessed August 24, 2012. http://www.tc.gc.ca/eng/roadsafety/tp-tp3322-2009-1173.htm

28. U.S. Department of Transportation, National Highway Traffic Safety Administration (NHTSA). "Traffic Safety Facts 2010 Data Overview." (Report No. DOT HS 811 630 June 2012). NHTSA's National Center for Statistics and Analysis. Washington, DC. Pedestrians, p. 11. Accessed October 28, 2012. http://www-nrd.nhtsa.dot.gov/Pubs/811630.pdf

29. Insurance Corporation of British Columbia (ICBC). "Traffic Collision Statistics - Police-attended Injury and Fatal Collisions - British Columbia 2007." British Columbia Motor Vehicle Branch -1994. Section 13, p. 103. Accessed December 15, 2011. http://www.icbc.com/road-safety/safety-research/traffic-coll-stats-2007.pdf

30. U.S. Department of Transportation, National Highway Traffic Safety Administration (NHTSA). "Traffic Safety Facts 2010 Data Overview." (Report No. DOT HS 811 630 June 2012). NHTSA's National Center for Statistics and Analysis. Washington, DC. Occupant Protection, p. 3. Accessed October 28, 2012. http://www-nrd.nhtsa.dot.gov/Pubs/811630.pdf

31. NHTSA. Occupant Protection, p. 4.

32. NHTSA. Motorcycles, p. 8.

33. U.S. Department of Transportation, National Highway Traffic Safety Administration (NHTSA). "Traffic Safety Facts 2010 Data Bicyclists and Other Cyclists." (Report No. DOT HS 811, 624 June 2012). NHTSA's National Center for Statistics and Analysis. Washington, DC. Important Safety Reminders, p. 2. Accessed October 28, 2012. http://www-nrd.nhtsa.dot.gov/Pubs/811624.pdf

Chapter 9: The Road Safety Revolution

1. World Health Organization. "Global Status Report on Road Safety: Time for Action." World Health Organization, Geneva, 2009. Executive Summary, p. ix. Accessed August 24, 2012. http://whqlibdoc.who.int/publications/2009/9789241563840_eng.pdf

2. Roads and Traffic Authority of New South Wales. "Speeding—Did you know? 'Safe System'—the key to managing road safety." Fact Sheet 6 of 6. NSW Centre for Road Safety, NSW Government Transport Roads & Traffic Authority. Property of Transport for NSW, p. 1. Accessed October 14, 2014. www.rms.nsw.gov.au/saferroadsnsw/safe-system.pdf

3. New Zealand Government, Ministry of Transport, National Road Safety Committee. "2020 Safer Journeys, New Zealand's Road Safety Strategy 2010–2020." Ministry of Transport, p. 3 Accessed October 31, 2014. www.saferjourneys.govt.nz/assets/Uploads/SaferJourneyStrategy.pdf

4. Peden, M., R. Scurfield, D. Sleet, D. Mohan, A. Hyder, E. Jarawan, and C. Mathers, eds. "World report on road traffic injury prevention." World Health Organiza-

tion, Geneva, 2004. Chap. 1, p. 3. Accessed August 24, 2012. http://whqlibdoc. who.int/publications/2004/9241562609.pdf

5. The Swedish Government and Swedish Industry. "Freedom to move—No more acceptance." Vision Zero Initiative. Traffic Safety by Sweden. Accessed September 1, 2014. http://www.visionzeroinitiative.com/en/Concept/Freedom-to-move/

6. Vagverket Swedish Road Administration. "Safe Traffic - Vision Zero on the move." Vagverket, Swedish Road Administration, Sweden. Order No 88325, 2nd Edition, March 2006, p. 5. Accessed October 15, 2014. 88325_safe_traffic_vision_zero_ on_the_move.pdf

7. Vagverket Swedish Road Administration, p. 7.

8. Nader, R. "Updated Unsafe at Any Speed." 1972. Grossman Publishers, New York, p. 233.

9. European Union. "EU member countries." © European Union, 1995-2014, p. 1. Accessed October 23, 2014. http://europa.eu/about-eu/countires/member-coun- tries/index_en.htm

10. Trafikverket Swedish Transport Administration. "Analytic report Review of Interim Targets and Indicators for Road Safety in 2010-2020." The Swedish Transport Administration. June 2012, Publication Number 2012:162, p. 5. ISBN: 978-91-7467-365-4. Accessed October 27, 2014. 2012_162_review_of_interim_ targets_and_indicators_for_road_safety_in_2010_2020.pdf

11. The Swedish Government and Swedish Industry. "The Vision Zero." Vision Zero Initiative. Traffic Safety by Sweden. Accessed September 1, 2014. http://www. visionzeroinitiative.com/en/Concept/

12. Vagverket Swedish Road Administration. "Safe Traffic - Vision Zero on the move." Vagverket, Swedish Road Administration, Sweden. Order No 88325, 2nd Edition, March 2006. P. 6. Accessed October 15, 2014. 88325_safe_traffic_vision_ zero_on_the_move.pdf

13. Vagverket Swedish Road Administration, p. 2.

14. The Swedish Government and Swedish Industry. "The Human Factor." Vision Zero Initiative. Traffic Safety by Sweden. Accessed September 1, 2014. http:// www.visionzeroinitiative.com/en/Concept/Freedom-to-move/

15. Donlemar, Ernst. "Swedish Road Safety and The Traffic Safe Society." Ernst Don- lemar. 2003-12-15, p 3. Accessed October 15, 2014 http://www.swedishroadsafety. se/document/pdf/webb/swedish-road-safety-and-traffic-safe-society.pdf

16. Trafikverket Swedish Transport Administration. "Analytic report Review of interim Targets and Indicators for Road Safety in 2010–2020." The Swedish Transport Administration. June 2012, Publication Number 2012:162, p. 4. ISBN: 978-91-7467-365-4. Accessed October 27, 2014. 2012_162_review_of_interim_ targets_and_indicators_for_road_safety_in_2010_2020.pdf

17. Roads and Traffic Authority of New South Wales. "Speeding—Did you know? 'Safe System'—the key to managing road safety." Fact Sheet 6 of 6. NSW Centre

for Road Safety, NSW Government Transport Roads & Traffic Authority. Property of Transport for NSW, p. 2. Accessed October 14, 2014. www.rms.nsw.gov.au/saferroadsnsw/safe-system.pdf

18.	Roads and Traffic Authority of New South Wales. P. 3.

19.	Roads and Traffic Authority of New South Wales. P. 4.

20.	Eugensson, Anders. "Towards Zero Fatalities-Volvo Vision 2020 and Swedish Vision Zero." Volvo Car Corporation, p. 2. Accessed September 1, 2014 Anders_euggeson_1.pdf

21.	Reprinted, with permission of the Eno Center for Transportation, Washington, DC, from "Preparing a Nation for Autonomous Vehicles: Opportunities, Barriers and Policy Recommendations", page 2. Copyright 2013 Eno Center for Transportation. Accessed October 22, 2014. AV-paper.pdf

Chapter 10: Conclusions and Recommendations

1.	Peden, M., R. Scurfield, D. Sleet, D. Mohan, A. Hyder, E. Jarawan, and C. Mathers, eds. "World report on road traffic injury prevention." World Health Organization, Geneva, 2004. Chap. 1, p. 3. Adapted by the author with permission. Accessed August 24, 2012. http://whqlibdoc.who.int/publications/2004/9241562609.pdf

Made in the USA
Las Vegas, NV
29 May 2023